Entertaining the Doughboys

Entertaining the Doughboys
Two Accounts of American Concert Parties 'Over There' During the First World War

Entertaining the American Army
James W. Evans & Gardner L. Harding

Trouping for the Troops
Margaret Mayo

Entertaining the Doughboys
Two Accounts of American Concert Parties
'Over There' During the First World War
Entertaining the American Army
by James W. Evans & Gardner L. Harding
Trouping for the Troops
by Margaret Mayo

FIRST EDITION

First published under the titles
Entertaining the American Army
Trouping for the Troops

Leonaur is an imprint of Oakpast Ltd
Copyright in this form © 2018 Oakpast Ltd

ISBN: 978-1-78282-752-8 (hardcover)
ISBN: 978-1-78282-753-5 (softcover)

http://www.leonaur.com

Publisher's Notes

The views expressed in this book are not necessarily those of the publisher.

Contents

Entertaining the American Army   7
Trouping for the Troops   259

Entertaining the American Army

Contents

Foreword	13
Preface	15
The Performers Enter	17
The Men Behind the Scenes	21
The Advance Guard in France	25
The Pioneer Company	32
The Troupers in Action	36
The Ames-Sothern Reconnaissance	49
The Stage Called to Arms	55
A Message From France	65
The American Stage Answers	73
A Stock Company Under Fire	80
A Regular American Girl	87
The Over There Theatre League Enters	94
A Bombardment of Songs and Fun	100
Strenuous Days for the Troupers	112
Keeping Step With the Doughboys	120
Pushing Up To the Front	130
Knights and Ladies	143

Two Makers of Entertainment History	152
Spreading Joy Along the Line	162
Soldier Shows After the Armistice	171
Broadway Successes on the Big Circuit	185
Famous Casinos in a New Role	189
Entertainment in Camps at Home	198
Singing Their Way to Victory	204
Enlisting Eminent Lecturers	216
"Movies Tonight!"	224
Curtain	235
Appendix	238

Respectfully Dedicated
To
All Those Who Served as Entertainers
With
The American Army

Foreword

No doubt every book published should have a dedication to the public, for by them it will be read and by them judged, but in presenting this particular history in narrative form, one must realise that while it may bring much interest to the general reading public, it belongs by its very title to those women and men who wisely saw the writing on the wall and indifferently turned their backs upon their everyday life with its creature comforts, never counting the cost nor exaggerating the danger, but gladly joining the great crusade.

History repeats itself! But in this present book there is no repetition—for, search as we may through the annals of past wars, we can find no precedent for a work of this nature. In very fact, when the opportunity came and the idea grew into a resolve, those who believed in the gospel of recreation realised that by the creation of just this particular type of amusement, an anachronism was being inaugurated. But by the very nature of its novelty it found a hearty response in the minds of the men in the camps in this country and overseas, and by its inherent opportunity for service it commended itself to the women and men who had no other chance of showing how solidly they stood behind the representatives of their country.

From its very moment of inception it carried with it the support of two men, without whose whole-hearted assistance it must have failed—Mr. William Sloane, Chairman of the War Work Council of the Young Men's Christian Association, and Dr. John R. Mott, its General Secretary. Through its early stormy days, when the sceptical and the timid hesitated at the very innovation of the proposition, they stood absolutely convinced of the power of entertainment, and by the very authority of their cogency carried with them the more doubtful and hesitating.

Where shall we turn for an adventure more novel than that undertaken by those valiant people who crossed the seas that they might bring maybe the last smile to those "going over the top," that they might be perhaps the first "real American" girl the doughboy had seen since he sailed from the land of Home?

Into the theatre or the cow-barn, to the tent or station platform, they brought the gospel of laughter, and even while the shells burst over their heads or whizzed by like rent cloth, the song of sentiment soared like a wave of comfort to tired and homesick men.

No sympathy need be extended to those who went—only to those who did not see the opportunity to get out of themselves and learn the joy of losing, that others might be the gainers, the joy of relinquishing a real money-making position and going out to meet whatever came, so that when the roll call is answered they will not be ashamed to answer to their names.

No record, however complete, could tell all the individual sacrifices that were made, or the story of the soldiers' appreciation, but this volume is offered as a lasting tribute to those who went, that their contribution may be recorded and their offering chronicled.

That the Young Men's Christian Association was privileged to be the instrument through which this presentation was made it feels duly grateful, for the recollection of this service will last when others may be forgotten.

To each and every man and woman who did his and her part in this work and received an honourable discharge, this book carries a greeting from those whose privilege it was to be the instrument through which this service was consummated. The work was an inspiration and the service rendered adds the only comment necessary.

Thomas S. McLane.

Preface

The greatest books of the war have not yet been written. While we now have contemporary records of incalculable value, upon which many future judgments will be based, the permanent histories of the conflict are yet to come. The General Staffs of all the governments are now preparing their military records. The diplomatists have only just begun to write their memoirs. The time has not arrived when standard works, weighed in the scales of historical perspective and scientific research, can begin to give the final judgment of the world struggle.

It is with this understanding that we ask the privilege of submitting to contemporary records a phase of America's participation in the World War which might otherwise be overlooked. The purpose of this volume is to sketch some of the adventures and experiences of what we may term "our American troubadours," professional, semi-professional, and amateur, who followed our army through the war; to show what the entertainers, the American stage and lyceum, did in the World War; how they undertook one of the most important missions in the struggle; how, like true soldiers, they did their duty to the end.

While it is conceded that this was one of the most effective arms of the army, and it is generally understood that the American stage and lyceum performed a great service, the magnitude of it is little known by the public. It is realised that the American stage was one of the powerful forces behind all the Liberty Loans, Red Cross drives, and United War Work campaigns; that it was directly instrumental in raising hundreds of millions of dollars; that it recruited the entertainers from every available source, including actors, lyceum entertainers, lecturers, singers, musicians, song leaders, motion picture stars and operators, vaudeville performers, soldier shows, stock companies—all merging in this achievement, which required the organisation of play bureaus, costume and scenic factories, transportation offices, and the leasing of many of the most famous theatres in Europe; that it enrolled in its operations at home and abroad more than 35,000 men and women.

We trust that the experiences and anecdotes related will give a new insight into the hearts and characters of our soldiers. Names are named, not so much to honour individuals, as to illustrate situations. The problem has been to select. There are almost endless records of mirth and misery, romance and tragedy, such as the bards of other days used in ballad and epic. This volume is submitted, therefore, as a tribute not only to the entertainers, but to the American Army—one more contribution to the records of America's fight for humanity in the World War.

The readers of this book are particularly indebted to Miss Neysa McMein, Miss Anita Parkhurst, and Miss Ethel Rundquist, entertainers all, who have brought the very life of overseas service into these pages through the illustrations they have contributed.

Chapter 1

The Performers Enter

They have their exits and their entrances;
And one man in his time plays many parts,
                              As You Like It.

It is June, 1917. An aristocratic old mansion at 31 Avenue Montaigne, Paris, is the scene of the beginning. This former palace, with its mass of gilding mirrors, and satin upholstery, is transformed suddenly from its stately elegance into the headquarters of our troubadours; a movement through which those in America are to touch hands with their sons along the battle fronts of France. It is here that the pioneers start the plans for the stupendous achievement. Six months later, we find the old palace unable longer to hold the rapidly expanding forces, and in December, 1917, all the splendour is left behind for a commodious French office building at 12 Rue d'Aguesseau.

Let us climb to the fifth floor. It is reached by a winding marble stairway, or a personally conducted French lift holding four people. The building is unfinished and unheated and the plaster is oozing moisture. Mail sacks block the hall and all the nearby office entrances, since next door is the post office and mailing room.

Parties of Americans, just arriving from "home" or coming in from the front, sweep along the hallway, hopping over mail sacks and struggling with the knob of the door leading to the two rooms known as the "Entertainment Department" on this fifth floor. The office is horribly crowded and grows worse week by week as the Americans are coming on every ship, climbing the long staircase, tripping over their hand-baggage, seeking information regarding their destinations, demanding to be sent right out to the front line, and finally waving goodbye as they disappear with their red permits and start off on their individual missions.

So great did the office and other activities become that it was found necessary to move again to larger quarters and take over a house on 10 Rue de Elysée—a street running from Faubourg St. Honoré down to the Champs Elysée, along the west side of the president's palace. The Entertainment Department was housed on the third floor and given overflow rooms: over the stables in the courtyard, the driveway leading through the house in regular French fashion. And the department filled these quarters and "cried for more."

What scenes there were through all the hours of the day and late into the night—rehearsals, tuning instruments, trying out songs, costuming, playwriting, all going on at the same time with the regular office routine of booking and routing. You met doughboys, medieval ladies, knights in armour, and French widows, hurrying to rehearsals, up and down the carved and *frescoed* marble stairway. Out on the Rue de l'Elysée big army trucks were drawn up to the curb, loading and unloading musical instruments, and the sidewalks were covered with bass drums, banjos, trombones, and violins.

This, then, is the story of how the American stage and lyceum sent out an army of volunteers which finally numbered more than 35,000. It tells how they furnished entertainment in cantonment and training camp, in cities and towns, in shipyards and ports of embarkation for more than 4,000,000 men who at one time and another passed through the great war organisation of the American Army; how they followed the A. E. F. through the campaigns and out to the battlefields; and how they fought and won continuous battles against a common enemy—gassed, bombed, and under fire in the greatest crusade in the world's history.

Let us line up our forces for review: The first line is composed of the 1,064 who were sent from America overseas to France and the 300 recruited from the French; the second line consists of the recruits whom they trained in the American Army in France, 4,000 soldier-actors, who in turn coached 11,000 more from their own ranks for soldier shows; the third line comprises the 200 trained song leaders with their forces augmented by 1,000 recruits; the fourth line brings the 1,500 enrolled in the motion picture service; the fifth line presents the 200 lecturers augmented by 500 more recruits and volunteers; the sixth line includes the costumers, theatre managers, general staff, and transportation service, over 300 more—the field strength now exceeds 20,000. Behind this are the reserve entertainers in America, working in the home camps or in the War Fund drives, numbering 15,000, bringing the fighting strength to 35,000.

In estimating the full service of the profession in the foregoing forces, it is necessary to mention the American theatre owners who opened their houses for war service in whatever capacity needed; the actors working from all the stages in the loans; the managers delivering personal appeals, and purchasing bonds in the millions; the solicitors working in the aisles of the theatres. More than 25,000 theatres (motion picture and legitimate) throughout America became the central points for all the organised efforts.

It is impossible to estimate the huge funds raised in the theatres. Such favourites as Mary Pickford, Douglas Fairbanks, Charlie Chaplin, and William S. Hart alone raised more than $17,200,000 on their tours through the country. It is further safe to state that there probably was not a professional or semi-professional entertainer in America who did not give his services either among the soldiers in their camps or at benefit performances during the war. They became one of the most powerful arms of the government and "did their bit" in the true tradition of the profession. It is to the war experiences of the troupers 1,064 strong who went to France, and their augmented forces, that this volume must largely confine itself, with occasional reference to those who served at home. To put through this tremendous task there was organised the biggest entertainment enterprise in the history of amusements:

It gave 109,794 separate performances to the soldiers, with an approximate attendance overseas of 87,000,000 and more than 40,000,000 at home.

It gave overseas 157,000 movie shows aggregating over 8,000,000 feet, or more than 1,500 miles, of film. The aggregate attendance at these movie shows alone (between April, 1918, and July, 1919) was over 94,000,000 at 5,261 different places. It is estimated that in the United States and overseas the gross attendance at motion picture shows reached 210,000,000.

It gave performances by stock companies and performances by soldier shows throughout the area of the American Army.

It organised four great "play factories" which were centres for rehearsals and costume equipment. It improvised plays and vaudeville acts.

It provided overseas alone 23,000 costumes and accessories, 18,000 musical instruments, and 450,000 pieces of sheet music.

It took over and ran in the leave areas and important cities behind the fighting line the largest circuit of theatres, casinos, and amusement halls ever administered under one management.

The adventures of these modern troubadours, if each could be persuaded to relate his own experiences, would give a deep insight into the most human side of the war. There would be tales aboard ship, nights on submarined seas, the first hours ashore at the base ports, the journeys into the bleeding heart of France, the last march on the road to battle.

From trench to stevedore camp, from the leave areas to the great supply centres, in dugouts, ruined *châteaux*, cathedrals, barns, village squares, and trucks backed against barns, these couriers of cheerfulness and sanity and courage, the troubadours of our time, sang the American Army on to victory, the splendid consummation of its mission across the sea.

Throughout the whole range of the profession, from the Shakespearian actor to the burlesque comedian, from the classical singer to the juggler, the ventriloquist, and the chalkologist, no one could set a limit to their enthusiasm or their devotion. One little jazz soubrette, whose lightning dance steps brought her to complete exhaustion after a single performance in America, coming across a trainload of forlorn, show-hungry soldiers, gave this amazing dance eighteen times at different sections of the train, and then exclaimed, "All right, go on with the war!"

But let us now observe how this crusade was put into operation and become acquainted with the forces behind it.

CHAPTER 2

The Men Behind the Scenes

Turn him to any cause of policy,
The Gordian knot of it he will unloose,
Familiar as his garter
                King Henry V.

The cast of characters in this dramatic invasion is so great that if given in the method of the profession it would include, directly or indirectly, every celebrated name on the American stage. It will be necessary, therefore, to select the characters as they appear and watch them in action, that we may judge the work of many from the experiences of a few.

It will be well, however, to stop a moment behind the scenes and meet some of those who planned, developed, and kept this continuous campaign of entertainment in operation throughout the war. Here in America we find the forces of the Red Triangle, under the direction of the National War Work Council, as the motive power behind the whole achievement, with Mr. William Sloane, an able and progressive administrator, as its chairman. We meet Thomas S. McLane, as Chairman of the Overseas Entertainment Bureau, in "command" of the recruiting and movement of the entertainment army across the seas to France; we meet James Forbes, the dramatist, with his able lieutenant, John Briscoe, in command of the forces of the Over There Theatre League.

Those in France, we find engaged in the constantly expanding headquarters described in the preceding chapter. Here is the "Director General" of all the operations of the A. E. F.-YMCA, Edward C. Carter, who entered the war in India at its outbreak in 1914, followed the British-Indian armies into the campaigns in Mesopotamia, came to the seat of operations in London, and, upon America's entrance into the war, went to Paris, extending full cooperation in any and every capacity in which the organisation which he represented might be able to serve.

We have looked into the crowded headquarters of the Entertainment Department, from which we found the operations of the Troupers being directed. Here, in command during the big campaigns were a progressive business man from the Middle West, Charles Steele; Walter H. Johnson, Jr.; and one of the most lovable personalities in the whole army, A. M. Beatty, a man who probably knows more actors intimately than any man who went to France. With all these men and many more we shall be face to face in the coming chapters.

The First Division arrived in France in June, 1917, and settled in its training areas around Gondrecourt by the middle of July. By the end of October the other divisions of America's first contingent began to arrive. Within a few days of each other, early in November, the Second, Twenty-Sixth, and Forty-Second Divisions landed in France, and went into training quarters. The Forty-First Division arrived at the end of the year, and by January, 1918, there were something over 190,000 American soldiers in France, of whom about two thirds were combat troops.

The Second Division, including the Marines, went into quarters around Bourmont; the Twenty-Sixth, the Yankee Division, composed of the National Guard units from the New England States, spread out around Neufchateau; while the Forty-Second, the Rainbow Division, made up of National Guardsmen from all over the country, moved into the Rolampont Area between Chaumont and Langres. These were pioneers of the commonwealth of fighting Americans from whom the world expected so much. They settled in an area something less than fifty miles in diameter around the newly founded General Headquarters at Chaumont, occupying in all over one hundred and fifty villages and towns, strung out for the most part along the lines of communication, but concentrated here and there in centres outnumbering the neighbouring French villages five and even ten to one.

Hard work and indomitable cheerfulness carried the Americans a long way through the almost unrelieved monotony of their routine in this environment. The courtesy and hospitality of the French inhabitants aided enormously in staving off homesickness and keeping up the spirits of the troops. But the American soldier is the most social human being in the whole world—and he soon began to realise, amid the dreary rain and mud of the fall and winter, how completely he was cut off from home. The mails had failed. The leave system was still undeveloped. Leisure time after work became a thing rather to dread than to enjoy.

Our action begins here. The American soldier felt free to express his real feelings—he wanted to hear American voices, American jokes, American laughter, and American songs, to see American girls, American movies, American shows. In September and October, Chief Secretary Carter had cabled to New York urging that an organisation be set up immediately to fill the demands of the soldiers for entertainment. Every army in the War had been forced to meet this same situation.

Already "back home" in America the profession was beginning to take up the call. Hundreds of volunteers were performing among the American camps and the ranks soon swelled into thousands. Before the first demands from overseas were heard, in September, 1917, Dr. Paul Pierson had brought a long experience in managing Chautauquas to the task of covering the home camps with entertainment troupes and had established, under Mr. William Sloane, a central booking office in New York.

The problem now arose of finding the right man for the important task of sending an army of entertainers overseas on a scale sufficient to cope with the vast need of the rapidly expanding army in France.

One day early in October, 1917, there came into Mr. Sloane's office a man on his way to Washington to volunteer for war work. On Mr. Sloane's desk lay a cablegram from Paris, reiterating the extreme need of entertainment for the men in France, which he handed to the caller, and thus Thomas McLane became director of what was soon to be the greatest entertainment enterprise in the world's history. The following twenty months wrote a new tradition into the history of America's entertainment.

Mr. McLane first organised a successful campaign for "that spare ukulele on the top shelf." He searched the country, in other words, for new and second-hand instruments, sheet music, plays, and sketches. This was but one of his jobs. He then organised a "drive" to reach every professional and amateur in America, to impress them with the need on the other side of every eligible entertainer. And the volunteers responded by the thousands—by letters, by telegrams, and in person—all the way from eminent actors down to stage-struck girls and the elevator boy who wanted to play Hamlet.

From four to six every afternoon he "received" hopeful talent. For months a quiet New York home resounded to the clatter of jazz-dancing feet, the wheeze of saxophones, the chirping of lady singers, the gusto of male quartets, the patter of monologists in all dialects and known forms of speech—all to save the soldier from a career of crime. There were times when life for Mr. McLane was one long round of tragediennes telling him wrathfully that "The Hun Is at the Gate," large ladies in white singing "Goodbye Summer" (in January); and breezy soubrettes always leaving for the "Darktown Strutters' Ball."

Mr. McLane looked for three main qualifications: First, the ability to entertain; second, a watertight list of recommendations; and third, personality as tested by his own instinct. Using these standards, he travelled out to Chicago and Pittsburgh. Later, Francis Rogers, when he came back in the spring of 1918 from a six-months' tour of entertainment "over there," consented to trying out candidates in his own home.

All this, however, was only the beginning of the McLane campaigns. His was the foresight which endorsed and forwarded the plan to send dramatic coaches to France, as well as actors and entertainers. Thomas Wood Stevens, a professor of dramatic technique at the Carnegie Institute of Technology, and Joseph Linden Smith, a well-known pageant director, were the principal protagonists of this idea. After months of firsthand experience in France, Stevens, in cooperation with Dean Bossange of the Carnegie Institute of Technology, organised at Pittsburgh a short course in the technique of play directing which required but three weeks, and graduated a group of trained people, who, when they went over to France, stepped into action at once as trained personnel ready at hand to put on soldier shows. This was how the soldier show got its real chance for professional finish and expert leadership. A second course was all ready to open at the Carnegie Institute to prepare another group of directors when the Armistice cut across its plans.

As this story unfolds, the service of this man back in America bulks larger. For many weeks he was the link between the Army in France and the entertainment world. The results are known. The accomplishment is the more impressive when it is understood that Mr. McLane was neither a member of the profession, nor a welfare worker, but an American business man volunteer, who was searching for some form of service to the soldiers when he was swept into the task by Mr. Sloane.

CHAPTER 3

The Advance Guard in France

*I would applaud thee to the very echo
That should applaud again.*
                    Macbeth.

The experiences of the first American troubadours in France began with the arrival of the American troop—some four months before the crusade "back home" was organised. In truth, they even preceded the arrival of Pershing in France.

The man to whom the honour should probably go of being! the first American entertainer to go "overseas" after America's declaration of war is Jack Barker. This pioneer arrived in Bordeaux on May 16, 1917, six weeks before the arrival of General Pershing and the first American contingent. Barker was a young college man just graduated from North-western University. He was sent to England, where he sang his way into the hearts of the Britishers and got up shows, not only for the Americans coming through on their way to France, but also for many British camps. His gift of holding an audience and of conducting a sing-song made him invaluable.

After more than two months in England he went over to France to cover the American camp circuit at a time when entertainers were "worth a regiment." With his "one man shows" and his popular sing-songs he covered the camps at Brest, Issoudun, Gondrecourt, Neufchateau, and elsewhere through the American sector. He was taken ill and lay for a time in Neuilly Hospital, returning home to enlist early in 1918.

The first American to go directly to the American Army in France, was Gerry Reynolds. He sailed from New York on July 29, 1917. (Barker was then in England.) Reynolds had been music director at a

E. C. Carter

Lt.-Col. R. M. Lyon

Major J. O. Donovan

Warren Dunham Foster

New York high school, a church organist, and an entertainment coach. He went to France as the first musical and dramatic director. He was at once assigned to the First Division at Gondrecourt. He tried continually to get into the army as a volunteer and was rejected, but his spirit was irrepressible—he could sing, tell stories, and give rollicking imitations.

Gerry Reynolds spent twenty-six months in France when he had planned to spend two; he went up with the First Division in August, 1917, the first full-time entertainer in the field; he opened up the amusement enterprises in Paris in October and put on its feet the splendid organisation for entertaining men on leave there, which later grew to such huge and capably managed proportions; he went to Aix-les-Bains as Entertainment Director in February, 1918, and wrote, rehearsed, and staged shows in a single day, led the local orchestra, took a chance as *impromptu impresario* of a real grand opera company, and handled the collective temperaments of the Comédie Française Company, the finest players in France, as well as innumerable stellar French vaudeville attractions. He ran the Aix Casino, the social centre of one of the most notable watering places in Europe, with dances, parties, and shows put on nightly to the delight of the soldiers on leave; he helped to organise entertainment circuits in the Riviera; he spent two months at Brest, of muddy misery; he reopened the Festhalle in Coblenz with a show that finished its last rehearsal five minutes before the curtain went up; he put on the show *Let's Go* and clothed his soldier chorus with amazing gowns which he had secured from the leading costumers of Paris.

The first male entertainer to appear among the fighting troops was a "song and piano" artist—C. E. Clifford Walker. He came over at the end of September, 1917, and stayed about three months. Walker was with the First Division when they went into the line. He had a piano on which he "vamped" as he told his various stories and gave his divers imitations, but as they neared the firing line he was forced to leave his piano behind, and at the front he simply let his legs hang over a stage and told stories to the boys.

Along the lines at this time was a magician, Maletsky. He was one of those marvellous one-man-shows, the rest of his company being made up of rabbits. He had to return to Paris every now and then to stock up on rabbits, as those he had with him grew amazingly and soon got too large to fit into silk hats. Maletsky could not speak a word of English and as he would say, "*Eh, Monsieur, voila!*" or "*Alors,*

General Y.M.C.A. Headquarters, Paris

un, deux, trois, vous voyez?" the men took great delight in mimicking him and in counting in unison. Fortunately, besides being a prince of prestidigitators he had a great sense of humour, so, after all, he spoke the American language in his own way.

The first woman entertainer to appear with the A. E. F. was a grand opera *contralto*—Mme. Cobbina Johnson, wife of Owen Johnson, the novelist. This charming artist came up from Monte Carlo, where she had been singing with great distinction in the opera after successful tours through France and Italy. She volunteered to go with the First Division toward the end of September, 1917.

They wanted somebody to go out to the Mallet Reserve at Soissons for Christmas. It was in the French Zone and at that time there was great difficulty in getting the passes. They had planned to have her go with Nicholas Sokoloff, a fine violinist and conductor, and spend Christmas with the boys. Mme. Johnson was told that these boys did not have anybody to help them out on Christmas.

"I will go if you will get me my passes," she exclaimed.

"We can't."

"All right, I'll get them for myself."

She went to the French Embassy, got the passes, and spent Christmas with the Mallet Reserve. She lost her voice and could not speak for two months; then she went down to Aix in the summer of 1918. Mme. Johnson made a great hit because of her versatility and willingness. She would sing at any time, under any conditions, whether with a band, a piano, or alongside a canteen counter.

No account of this period will be complete without recording the superlative good luck of the American Army in having at their disposal the services of Mrs. August Belmont who, as Eleanor Robson, will always be remembered as one of the most gifted and beloved actresses of the American stage. Mrs. Belmont went over in special work with the American Red Cross in the fall of 1917, and found time to make several trips around the American camps. Before she returned home in March, 1918, she gave selections from all her great successes. Mrs. Belmont took an active interest in the work from the start, and it was she who suggested to Mr. Carter the happy choice of Mr. Winthrop Ames as the man best qualified to become the chief recruiting officer for the American stage. No measure can be placed on the value of this single suggestion.

Another of the pioneers with the First Division at this time was Miss Anna Hughes, a Philadelphia girl. She went over to France with the "American Fund for French Wounded" and filled a very important niche as a delightful personality, who not only gave songs for the boys, without number and without price, but who could raise more volume of song from the men in a given space of time than anyone else in reach. She literally was the first to set the army to singing its way to victory.

It was in these modest beginnings in France that the stage was being set for this greatest entertainment enterprise in history, the little beginning of a big achievement—and right here let us record the fact that it began as a lecture bureau.

Arthur H. Gleason, an American who had served as a private in the French Army, and written the volume *Golden Lads* as an account of his war experience, was now in England. At Mr. Carter's invitation, he came to France and joined Emmet O'Neil in the Publicity Department. It was Mr. Gleason's idea that much could be gained by an interchange of speakers, familiar with both nationalities, between the American and French Armies, and on his own initiative he went ahead on this idea. Its original purpose was to send lecturers into both armies—and these lecturers did take an important part as the vast enterprise developed.

Dr. John G. Coulter, of Chicago, was appointed on September 15, 1917, as sole head of the Bureau of Lectures and Entertainments. Dr. Coulter had just finished six months' service with the French Army as a captain in the American Ambulance Corps. With two young ambulance drivers as his assistants, he found himself installed in the little office on the Avenue Montaigne, with facilities for entertaining the American Army—consisting of ten men and women who had been serving in the field as lecturers and half a dozen entertainers who had been sent over by the New York office. This was the nucleus of a great idea. Dr. Coulter expanded it with all the means at his disposal. He engaged French concert and music hall artists, whenever his funds would stand it, and sent repeated calls for help to America.

Before the First Division arrived in France, the organisation was asked by the French Government for a group of men to state the causes of the War clearly to some of the flagging units of the French Army, in the Foyers du Soldat established at the divisional bases. These lecturers first brought to the French Army the promise of the immense American assistance that was to come. Later they reported to the French the first arrival of the American troops. When the First Division sent a raiment to march through Paris on July 4, 1917, these secretaries with the French Army in the field shared in the wonderful demonstration of gratefulness and relief with which the French greeted this symbolic act of their great ally. There was no such pressing need at that time for stimulating the American Army, but some of the same group of lecturers performed a splendid service in putting before American soldiers in the field, at the very beginning of their operations, the basic issues of the war.

At this time, also, the first prominent American entertainers began to arrive in France. The story of these pioneers will be told as this powerful human drama develops—it is one of the many intensely interesting scenes to come.

CHAPTER 4

The Pioneer Company

So we'll live and pray, and sing, and tell old tales, and laugh.
King Lear.

It was the twenty-fifth day of October, 1917, that the first "company" to leave America sailed for France. This pioneer "company" consisted of Francis Rogers, a prominent baritone of New York; Mrs. Francis Rogers (Cornelia Barnes), a well known and talented elocutionist; and Roger Lyons, an accompanist, and it set sail on an historic voyage—a tour that was to make history—for the Rogers were not only to be the first company to travel through the battle areas tackling the hardships of transport and staging under the most primitive conditions, but they were to bring home with them the first message of the great hunger with which the American doughboys were waiting for "real American shows."

The Rogers were recruited by Mr. Sloane, in response to the urgent call from France for entertainers, and set sail shortly after Mr. McLane took control. It was a stroke of wisdom and excellent judgment during a critical time. The Rogers were truly patriotic, and immediately upon America's entrance into the war had volunteered their services. They had been appearing in the army camps in this country before the boys "went over" and were anxious to get into the conflict. Rogers set aside his professional work to give his entire services, in company with his wife, to the American Army.

And so they sailed on one of the early troop ships—their adventures would alone fill a volume. They began to entertain on the ship until it passed into the submarine zones, Mr. Rogers singing many of his own songs, and Mrs. Rogers in her monologues impersonating quaint characters with a joyous humour that soon made the boys forget their dangers.

The first letter "home" from Mr. Rogers described the experiences of these American pioneers:

> In the first eight days ashore we gave ten concerts, eight in the American camps and two on the side in the French hospitals. The responsiveness of our boys is really pathetic. They all say that they measure the passage of time by the arrival of letters from home. They all want to hear the latest songs and anything fresh from home. Their taste in music is frankly Broadway. The boys want songs with chorus and ragtime. Their favourites are: 'When the Red Dawn Is Shining,' 'Sunshine of Your Smile,' 'I May Be Gone for a Long, Long Time,' 'Oh, Johnnie, Oh,' 'Goodbye Broadway, Hello France,' 'Tipperary,' 'Carry Me Back to Old Virginny,' 'I Want to Be in Dixie,' 'Keep the Home Fires Burning,' 'Indiana,' 'Joan of Arc,' 'Where Do We Go from Here?' 'Huckleberry Finn,' 'Over There,' 'A Long, Long Trail,' 'Pack Up Your Troubles,' 'Poor Butterfly.'
>
> All mother songs the boys are crazy about—no matter how sentimental they are. They love such solos as: 'I Hear You Calling Me,' 'Mother o'Mine,' 'Mother Machree,' 'Irish Love Song,' 'Little Grey Home in the West,' 'Perfect Day,' 'Absent,' 'That Little Mother o'Mine,' 'An Irishman's Dream.'
>
> Nellie has found a great liking for the poems of R. W. Service among the boys—especially *Rhymes of a Red Cross Man*. She has had great success, too, with her poem, *Now That My Boy Has Gone to France*.

After persistent demands and many difficulties, the Rogers were granted permits to tour first in the Bordeaux Area, but went as soon as they could make the connection—that is, late in November—up to the First Army Area around Gondrecourt, where 30,000 Americans were getting ready for action. They were one of the first entertainment groups ever to play in the big artillery camp at Valdahon. There were Americans serving on the front line even then. Mr. and Mrs. Rogers put on their "show" under real war conditions in cities and camps under bombing fire within German artillery range. They went to Rheims, covering a long line of British front up toward Bapaume in that breathless period just following the Cambrai offensive, when the British revealed for the first time in the war the redoubtable tank.

In those days Americans were still doing all they could to help entertain the French in the Foyers du Soldat, especially along the Champagne front, where a perilous morale still persisted from the unhappy days of that summer. The Rogers pitched in nobly. Mr. Rogers translated his songs and Mrs. Rogers her stories and monologues into French, and you might have beheld the unique sight of huts filled with French soldiers actually laughing at American jokes translated into French, but with their American origin showing through every chink of the translation.

The tense and most dramatic moments came, however, after the performance. The Rogers were real folks. Mrs. Rogers, a charming, home-loving woman, loved every mother's son of them. So after each performance they went out and shook hands all around and wanted to know if there was anything, anything at all, they could do for the boys—and they never failed to find a heartfelt response. What they did will never be known. Only the boys can tell. They probably relieved more lonesomeness to the square inch than any other people on the circuit during that winter.

"When they gave you cigarettes or a bar of chocolate in the days when stocks of these articles were just beginning to get through the transportation jam, it was like getting a personal gift from folks in your own home town," say the soldiers, who do not forget. Sometimes they ate with the men; sometimes they took boys back to their own hotel to give them a taste of real home preserves and an hour of real U. S. A. talk. No one knows how much this meant to men who were just shaking down to war, three thousand miles from home. Again Mr. Rogers sent word back to America:

> The response of the boys is wonderful. We are 'carrying on' under the greatest difficulties—there has been only one clear, dry day since we landed in France. In the region where we have been the ground is always covered with mud. When it rains, the mud is inches deep; when the heavens cease to weep, the mud is just the same.
> My wife and I did our best to keep going, but she gave out on one night and I on the next. We are now in Paris recovering our voices. We hope to resume work next week. It is a wonderful work and we love it. Our boys need and deserve everything anybody can do to cheer, encourage, and support them.

And on they went, these pioneer American messengers, carrying happiness to the ports and the S. O. S., arriving at Brest just in time for the big Christmas celebration organised by Gerald Reynolds and Karl Gate. For this celebration "friends" back in America had sent a load of gifts for the boys. Mr. Rogers wrote:

> The 'Y' is doing a beautiful work. My greatest admiration goes to Mr. Garter, Miss Ely, and Miss McCook, who never seem to lose their tempers under the most untoward circumstances, and to the brave women canteen workers and secretaries who exist in cold, damp, fireless rooms and are subject to any kind of hardships and who do their work with good cheer and courage. It is splendid.

By this time the Rogers had lost their identity as a single party and were giving joint shows with most of the other early pioneers on the circuit. They toured the British front, for instance, with the Dushkin party which had been organised in France. It was one of those wonderful violin, singing, instrumental combinations, which did magnificent work in every sort of environment. The personnel of the Dushkin party consisted of Samuel Dushkin, the famous American violinist, Mlle. Mona Gondre of the Theatre Odeon in Paris, Jean Verd, accompanist, and Pablo Casals, one of the world's great cellists. The Dushkin party not only toured all over the front and stayed with the American troops through their hardest campaign periods, but stuck to the game until way along in May, 1919, one of the longest periods of service, if not actually the longest, achieved by any concert troupe in France.

The last message from Mr. Rogers at the front reads:

> We have now given more than 100 concerts and are planning to go home in about a fortnight. We ought to be in New York by April 15th. After that date we shall be entirely at the service of the YMCA for concerts, advice, or any old thing. We have had a wonderful experience and are sorry it is nearly over. But we are going to work harder than ever in our American camps at home.

Mr. and Mrs. Rogers finished their service in France by providing the *pièce de résistance* of the concerts which greeted the first regular leave of the First Division at Aix-les-Bains in the spring of 1918. On their return home they sang in camps near New York City and assisted in war work and Liberty Loan drives. As the first concert people to respond to the call, theirs is a splendid and enviable record.

CHAPTER 5

The Troupers in Action

*Screw your courage to the sticking-place
And we'll not fail."*
    Macbeth.

The problems which were developing in the American Army at home and abroad in the fall of 1917 called for indent action. General Pershing, with the whole American nation behind him, was accomplishing the '"impossible"—the creation of a huge fighting machine behind the lines in France. Mr. Carter in Paris foresaw the burdens and responsibilities that were to be placed upon his organisation with the continual arrival of troops. His cables warned "the folks back home" of the increasing needs. The pioneers on the field were proving the incalculable value of sustaining the spirits of the soldiers at the fighting pitch with which they had embarked on their great adventure. In America, the same farsightedness was actuating Mr. Sloane and Mr. McLane—the latter now in full control of the task of recruiting and sending over the volunteers.

The problems were without precedent—never in the history of warfare had such an undertaking been attempted. Whether a hundred or a thousand recruits would be needed, or for what period they should enlist, was entirely unknown. There was no way to judge what type of entertainers would be most acceptable to the soldiers. The factors of the human equation on which everything was to depend were still unknown. Then there were the problems of present contracts, of passports and war regulations, of recruiting exclusively above the draft age, of transportation—innumerable difficulties that must be met and overcome when the recruits went into service.

Mr. McLane's first move was to get in touch with the responsible agencies where entertainers, such as Mr. and Mrs. Francis Rogers, could be secured. This initiative resulted in the survey of the entire field of concert singers, church organists who could play a wide range of popular music, Chautauqua readers, and gifted amateurs and volunteers of all kinds. His second move was to secure thousands of musical instruments— guitars, banjos, *mandolins*—whatever might be sent to the doughboys to help them create their own "spirit." His third move was to secure hundreds of thousands of copies of popular songs to start the Army singing its way to victory.

The public quickly responded to Mr. McLane's campaigns. Thousands of letters began to flood his office. The cooperation of the big music publishers proved a very valuable asset. Mr. Walter Damrosch, from the platform of Carnegie Hall, made an eloquent appeal for the movement. Mrs. John Philip Sousa appealed for band instruments, and the result was literally carloads of gifts. When Mr. McLane sent out his nation-wide call for everybody to take down "that old ukulele" from the top shelf and send it to the boys "over there," the public threatened to bury him under mounds of instruments.

The first regularly organised unit to be sent to France was forced to sail on three ships. First went the famous Liberty Quartet with an accompanist and its organiser, who later became director of the whole entertainment bureau in Paris—Walter H. Johnson, Jr. This pioneer unit sailed on the *Rochambeau* on November 30, 1917. It included Mr. Johnson, two church choir singers—Miss Beulah Dodge, *contralto*, and Miss Kate Horisberg, *soprano*—and Albert Wiederhold, who had been bass soloist for some time at Dr. Parkhurst's church in New York. On the second ship, the *Niagara*, on December 16th, went William Janauschek, an organist from Englewood, N. J., who later became Elsie Janis's accompanist extraordinary in her record-breaking tour of the armies. On the third ship, *La Touraine*, sailing December 28th, was John Steel, one of the bright lights of Broadway, who also had been a church choir singer.

The Liberty Quartet was a splendid organisation. Collectively, it was an aggregation of stars endowed with a fine esprit de corps; individually, the members of the unit all made magnificent records and displayed unconquerable spirit and unswerving loyalty to the cause they went abroad to serve. From the beginning they encountered many difficulties which were inseparable from the conditions of the time, but they stuck through everything with a perseverance and pluck which set a high standard for those to follow.

The initial difficulty—a typical instance of the unforeseen circumstances which created continual obstacles—was met on the pier on the very day of sailing. Mr. Johnson says:

> We got down to the dock of the French Line and everybody thought they would all meet there. When we got there we found Bill Janauschek, the accompanist, and we said, 'Hello, Bill,' but he said, 'I can't go.' Word had come from Washington at the last moment cancelling his passport until further investigation.

Thus the strong hand of the government's necessary precaution was interposed, as many times afterward, to make assurance doubly sure of the hundred *per cent* American quality of the men and women who were going over to join the fighting forces. Mr. Janauschek's detention was a purely technical matter and this loyal American sailed on December 16th on the next French liner, the *Niagara*, to join his comrades in France.

Meanwhile, the quartet, minus accompanist and tenor (for Mr. Steel was not able to sail until December 28th), sang all the way over on board the *Rochambeau*, and on their arrival in Paris December 10th spent no time waiting for the missing members of their little group, but went out to sing in the camps around Paris, with Mlle. Colet, a Franco-American girl, as their accompanist. their programs ranged over a wide field, all the way from opera numbers and religious selections to the beautiful old Negro melodies. They also had a goodly sheaf of humorous and comedy songs, for in this dreary winter every laugh was as good as a letter from home.

And at the end of every show they saw to it that the boys had a good sing-song of their own. "It was then," Mr. Wiederhold modestly says, "we had some real music." Anyhow, each evening a thousand or more happy soldiers went away from the show feeling that life was worth living and that a million loving thoughts from America were still on their trail in muddy, dreary France. Then they started for Chaumont and the training areas round Neufchateau and Gondrecourt. On Christmas Day, they commenced a long tour through the hospitals along the whole American line of communication. The prodigality with which they gave themselves to the work is shown by the fact that on Christmas Day they gave fourteen different programs.

Meanwhile, Mr. Johnson was having his first taste of service in the Twenty-Sixth Division. Mr. Carter sent him immediately on his arrival to the little town of Pompierre, to learn at first hand, as a hut secretary, the life of the soldier under war conditions. He stayed there till February 1, 1918. No better training for the man who was eventually to supply such splendid and practical initiative at entertainment headquarters could be imagined.

Entertainment facilities during this period were primitive, indeed. Mr. Johnson tells this story of the Christmas show at Pompierre:

> I will tell you an experience at my own hut at Christmas. I had been there a few days. We had any quantity of cigarettes, big tin boxes of five hundred each. So we took the tin boxes and bent them out to make reflectors for footlights, and used candles. All the lights we had in that hut of ours were three lamps; the chimneys of two were broken and we had no oil, but we used candles, with these tin boxes as footlights, and we built a stage out of wooden crates that cigarettes came in and things like that. I will never forget the show we got up. The average French peasant in such a little town had about two suits of clothes, the one he had on and worked in and his Sunday clothes.
>
> The Sunday clothes might be fifteen years old, but they were his Sunday clothes and they were neat, not particularly stylish, but serviceable and clean. We put on a show at Christmas, entitled *School Days*; the idea was a school in which there could be any quantity of horse play that appealed to the masses and was automatic. It really took little rehearsing and it was automatic. But we had to have a certain amount of costumes and in feeble French I went around the village and tried to get clothes from the French. We got a few women's dresses and a few pairs of civilian trousers and out of courtesy to the French people who had loaned their other suits of clothes we asked them in to see the show. We borrowed desks from the schoolhouses. I think they were the desks that Napoleon Bonaparte studied over; the old schoolteacher must have been seventy-five easily.
>
> I don't think we had ever had a dress rehearsal. The first time they had those clothes on was the real thing, and every conceivable prank that you can imagine might be pulled off in a schoolroom—only rather intensified—was pulled off at that show. Not throwing cream puffs but paste or anything like that, and the kicking of seats out from under one another, all of which I am telling because of the effect it had on those Sunday

clothes of the French populace who were in the back of the house and were just raving mad at seeing their clothes, their only other suits, going to rack and ruin. The crowd of doughboys thought it was a wonderful joke and the sorer the French got the better the show was. It took a considerable number of *francs* to make up to the French. They never really did get over it.

Every day of Mr. Johnson's six weeks at Pompierre was not so eventful as this, but the job was training of the kind that gains real value when the need comes. Mr. Johnson remembers with particular affection, as does everybody who worked overseas, the quality of his soldier assistants.

On the first of February, 1918, there came a brief telegram from Mr. Carter:

> Report to Paris to C. M. Steele.

Although Mr. Steele, before he went to Paris to become Director of the Entertainment Department, had had an experience as hut secretary similar to Johnson's in a little town not twenty miles from Pompierre during this very time, this was the first Johnson had ever heard of the man with whom he was to accomplish such far-reaching results in the entertainment initiative overseas. Johnson had been selected as Assistant Director, so he was informed when he arrived in Paris. But Steele was "out on the road" accompanying Messrs. Ames and Sothern on their tour through the camps, so Johnson's first job was not to report to his chief, but "to chase and catch him." He caught him at Tours.

Mr. Steele was extremely glad to see his young assistant, for the trip he was then taking with the Ames-Sothern party around the American area revealed to all how much there was to be done before even a fair beginning could be made in entertaining the fast-growing American Army. They returned to Paris about the 15th of February and then began that long connection which lasted, with the exception of a six weeks' trip to America which Mr. Steele took between late July and early September, until the end of December, 1918. Then Mr. Johnson carried on the campaign in sole control until May 8, 1919.

Charles M. Steele had arrived in France in December, 1917, and gone out with the First Division to become hut secretary at the little town of Baudigncourt. He won a considerable reputation in the early days as the man who had put on more good shows than anybody else in the First Division, a record that culminated in the Christmas celebration at Baudigncourt, which Mr. Steele presented to six enthusiastic audiences of doughboys. He describes it in this modest fashion:

> From the time that I first went out to take over the hut at Baudigncourt, I saw that one of the big things was to have entertainments, and so, having had a little experience in getting up shows in Detroit at the Board of Commerce, I started to do it. It wasn't hard because one of the first things the gang said to me was, 'Why don't we have a show?' So we had some very crude entertainments, sort of rough and tumble, wild-west kind, and that developed a certain amount of dramatic talent or what we were pleased to call our Dramatic Club in the battalion.
>
> When Christmas came we put on a show which we called *The Soldier's Dream* and because the hut was not big enough to hold the whole battalion we gave the show by companies. We gave the show four times Christmas Eve with the distribution of presents, and then Christmas afternoon we gave a part of the show for the children of the village and Christmas morning we had an athletic meeting—so that made a program of six entertainments within twenty-four hours."

Meanwhile, in all this period of beginnings, especially from January 1, 1918, to the crisis of the great German drive which began on March 21st, the Liberty Quartet continued to be the most active of the entertainment units in the field. Mr. John Steel and Mr. Janauschek joined the quartet soon after Christmas and for two months they went on a grand tour which covered the areas of the five American divisions and swung down on the S. O. S. and leave area circuits as far as Aix-les-Bains on the east and Brest and the other deep-sea ports on the west.

At Brest, the quartet was the first entertainment group to board the American transports then coming in great numbers to the shores of France. They sang on the old *Prometheus*, the big repair ship which became famous as the "mother ship" of the American Navy; they gave a show on the *Seattle*, the American cruiser which brought Secretary Daniels to France. At Issoudun, they gave one of the first shows to the American Air Force in a hangar which the boys had converted into a stage. Miss Dodge says:

> They had put lovely white crash on the floor, and on either side of the stage were machines owned by the boys themselves,

which they called their private boxes. The mud out there was simply dreadful, and we with our muddy feet felt just criminal going on their lovely white flooring.

Miss Dodge tells another anecdote:

> One day at Issoudun, we went into a hut after mess with the officers to get warm, and saw three young lieutenants shaving at the far end. We started to back out at once, but one of the young men, who afterward proved to be Quentin Roosevelt, waved his razor and called out, 'Oh, come right in! This is just a little of the home touch, you know.'
> (*Eagles Rampant Rising* containing *The Way of the Eagle* by Charles J. Biddle and Quentin Roosevelt *A Sketch With Letters* is also published by Leonaur.)

After the Brest performances the quartet split up and went out separately, for by that time entertainers had come to be so much in demand that everybody as far as possible had to be a little quartet all by himself. Mr. Wiederhold paired up with the inimitable Mary Rochester, who not only played the piano beautifully, but was one of the earliest of the singers who discovered in themselves a fine ability to get the boys to sing, which made all of their performances memorable. Miss Rochester, by the way, who had been a music student in New York and an ambitious beginner in church and concert work, was one of the real musical discoveries of the war. She arrived in France on February 24, 1918, and her brief account of some of her early experiences reveals a loyal and intrepid soldier admirably worthy of her splendid opportunity.

> My earliest experiences were with the First Division in the Toul area. At this time the men hadn't seen an American girl for months and when I entered the large camouflaged tent where hundreds of men were waiting wide-eyed for their first glimpse of an American girl, their eager, concentrated stare embarrassed me very much, but I soon came to realise what it all meant—that I stood for someone of their American women at home. The one thing that impressed them more than any other was that I could speak English. 'She talks English, she's an honest-to-God American girl,' they would cry. I used to wear my gas mask in *alerte* position when I played accompaniments, but only once was I ordered to put it on. One night the shelling was so

JAZZ AND JAZZERINOS

loud I stopped playing and asked whether they were going or coming, which amused the boys very much.

'I shall never forget the way the boys would file past me, pumping my hand up and down, some of them too timid to look in my face, but squeezing my hand so hard I always had to remember to take my ring off. One man stuttered so when he talked I could hardly understand him. When I asked him why he stuttered, he replied he was so embarrassed meeting a girl. They were just like children out there, it was too pathetic.

One night an officer took me out to his battery. He telephoned his men to be prepared, that he was bringing an important visitor to call. They, of course, thought it was no less than a general himself, and were all standing at attention when we arrived. It was late at night and it seemed to me we had walked through miles of mud to get there. They stood at attention all the while, but the smiles on the boys' faces, especially when I sang for them in their dugouts, was worth the long ride out and my wet muddy feet. Only a few nights after that, all these boys were killed when their battery was blown up, and the house where I had dined was wrecked.

Miss Beulah Dodge, the quartet *contralto*, after the trip to Brest was assigned with Jean Nestoresen, the violinist to the royal court of Roumania. She says:

> We toured together for six months, a most successful concert tour. We were all over in the lines and were in several bombardments and night raids in camps near the front, giving several interrupted concerts during the great drives of a year ago in which our Americans figured so prominently up in the region of Châlons. We were stationed in Mailly and gave concerts all around. For instance, we went up into the Vosges woods, where the men were so delighted to have anything at all, and simply mobbed us with appreciation. The men were almost stumped by the fact that an American woman had really come up there to entertain them.
>
> These trips were not all mere mud and frolic, as the front was simply poisonous, then as always, with tonsillitis and other deadly throat and bronchial rides. Miss Dodge got back to Aix, after her tour with M. Nestoresen, and found that she had lost her beautiful voice and nothing could bring it back again save an interminable rest. So this

gallant little soldier, to whom the loss of her voice meant nothing less than her whole vocational and artistic future, put her own troubles behind her and pitched in to canteen work in the Aix Leave Area. For more than eight months she worked there loyally and unselfishly. Her voice came back, but she sang for the men too soon and lost it again. In those days it did not seem to matter much, when the very men to whom you were singing had faced death cheerfully and were going back in a few days for another bout, that a singer should lose a little thing like her voice. The real artistic spirit was to offer one's best, but if ever any non-combatant deserved a wound stripe, it was Beulah Dodge.

Such sacrifices were legion; the pity of it is that many of the entertainers, early and late, who suffered the most in voice or physical impairment or in falling behind in that hard competitive struggle which goes on so remorselessly even in the world of art—the pity of it is that most of those who suffered did not tell. Another girl who lost her voice came back to the leave areas and became one of the best dramatic coaches in France. Others kept on with the cheering reflection that, after all, if the boys did not mind the cracked pianos they seemed so fond of, they couldn't object very much to cracked voices, especially if they could join in the choruses and give the singer a rest.

Another party which belongs unforgettably to this period is the "Five Hearon Sisters," a quintet of dainty English girls who had won deserved recognition in American vaudeville and who were lovingly referred to by the boys as the Sardine Ladies. They were Winifred, Anna, and Charlotte Hearon, Clara Gray, and Eunice Prosser.

These five girls hold one of the long-distance entertainment records of the war. They sailed February 17, 1918, immediately after finishing a long circuit on the American Chautauqua. They played to twelve different combat divisions, including all the veterans, the First, Second, Third, Fourth, Seventh, Twenty-Sixth, Twenty-Eighth, Forty-Second, Seventy-Ninth, Eighty-Fifth, Eighty-Ninth, and Ninety-Second; they made a circuit of all the base hospitals, and played for four months in most of the large cities where the American Army of Occupation in Germany was stationed, finally coming home and "calling it a war" late in March, 1919.

Five girls appearing on the stage at the same time were bound to be a success in the prevailing psychology of the A. E. F. But the popularity of the Sardine girls was founded on enduring qualities. They seemed to turn up wherever the fight was the thickest and the need for diversion and relaxation of overstrained nerves was the greatest. When the Twenty-Sixth Division took over its first hard sector from the French on the Marne in May, 1918, the Hearon Sisters played every unit in the division, and in the weeks just before July 15th, when the morale of the Allied Armies was probably at its lowest ebb, they played every single unit of this crucially situated American division. General Edwards, the idolized commander of the Twenty-Sixth, saw that the girls made the circuit as complete as possible by sending them about in one of his own staff cars. Many of the men of the Yankee Division got their last real message from home from the plucky and laugh-compelling show put on by this courageous quintet. They were on hand at Château-Thierry, this time helping in dressing the wounded, and giving impromptu entertainments at the first aid stations all along that historic line.

In half a score of places the girls played a good part of their show under fire. In Essey, for instance, where they were playing to a *ballon* squadron, a German shell fell close to the car in which they were leaving the performance, only missing them by a miracle; while at Bouillonville, where they played in a gun pit one and a half kilometres behind the lines, they were in the midst of a very lively artillery duel for the greater part of their stay in town. In this town, which had only recently been captured from the Germans, they gave a show at a Red Cross hut which had formerly been a German moving picture theatre.

Half an hour after their departure and the dispersal of the audience of over five hundred men, a German airplane came over and industriously machine gunned the town. The next day an officer counted over fifty bullet holes in the roof of the theatre. The Hearon Sisters were on deck during the St. Mihiel drive, and carried up supplies to the advance units just before the offensive opened. They were then stationed with the First Division, and just on the day it went into the line they entertained the Sixteenth and Eighteenth Regiments of that division all day.

On Dominion Day, July 1, 1918, the Hearon Sisters were the central attraction of the great Canadian celebration, and made that patriotic festival as memorable for the Canadian soldiers as Elsie Janis made the Fourth of July eventful for the American doughboys in Paris. They found time also to put in a week's intensive entertaining among the British Tommies.

That they came out of all these tireless months of travelling and trudging was miraculous. Charlotte Hearon was severely injured while riding on a truck near Verdun, but she soon came back fit for action again, and never even asked for a wound stripe. Certainly the Hearon Sisters lived up to Winthrop Ames's amply justified claim that entertainment was as practical and vital an everyday necessity in the American Army as overcoats and entrenching tools, or any other of the indispensable auxiliaries to a victory.

CHAPTER 6

The Ames-Sothern Reconnaissance

*Strange things I have in head, that will to hand;
Which must be acted ere they can be scanned.*
                                            Macbeth.

Great events were now brewing in both France and America. There was a premonition throughout the American Army that things were doing, when early in January, 1918, Mr. Steele had arrived in Paris to take over the entertainment service, and was joined later in the month by Mr. Johnson as his assistant. Mr. Steele had arrived just in time to link up with the first emissaries of the American stage two of its most distinguished representatives—a great producer and a great actor—Messrs. Winthrop Ames and E. H. Sothern, who arrived in France late in the month to survey the whole entertainment field and to report to the theatrical profession in America what the American Army expected of them.

The Ames-Sothern mission is notable in dramatic history. It originated, like most of the important movements, at the New York end, from the initiative of Mr. McLane. A cablegram was received one day bearing simply the cryptic message:

Belmont suggests Ames.

McLane decided that it meant in plain English that Mrs. August Belmont, who was then in France, suggested Winthrop Ames as the ideal man to survey the entertainment problem in France, and to get what was wanted from the American stage to cover that field. He communicated this suggestion to Mr. Ames, who protested that he was a "high brow," but finally said, "I will go if Ed Sothern will." The result was that Messrs. Ames and Sothern decided to go.

Throughout the American lines these emissaries of the American stage gave shows and watched shows, looked over huts and got out among the men, conferred with General Pershing in Chaumont and with the "Y" head in Paris, and finally evolved a thorough working plan, which they drafted in the form of a report as to what the American theatrical profession could do—and what they were determined to see that it would do—to bring relaxation and happiness, and to help hold up the spirits of the American Army in France. Theorists had been expounding for a long time before the spring of 1918 just what kind of entertainment the American Army in France wanted.

Students in crowd psychology, military authorities, and newspaper writers had proposed various solutions, from stock companies to programs exclusively devoted to clog dances and pretty girls. The splendid entertainers who had already been sent over to France were beginning to report back some real experience. But it was from the report of Messrs. Sothern and Ames that the astonishingly simple solution was finally and decisively learned. This was that the same show that was good at home was good over there, and that when the really good shows came to camp, the S.R.O. sign went up outside of huts just as it did in a crowded theatre on the Great White Way.

Mr. Sothern tested this out for himself before huge audiences of cheering soldiers. His repertoire in France was what is generally known in the profession as "classical heavy," specializing on the immortal passages with which he has thrilled a generation of American audiences. It ranged from Petruchio's boisterous Elizabethan advice about handling women in *The Taming of the Shrew* to Francois Villon's romantic love-making in *If I Were King*. He recited the great poems of the War, *In Flanders Fields*, *Verdun*, *The Hun Is at the Gate*, *The Landlord's Daughter*, and the stirring war songs of Alan Seeger and Paul Scott Mowrer. Besides this, Mr. Sothern discovered in himself an altogether new talent—he told stories.

Standing on the dark and shaky stages of the little huts, Mr. Sothern found in these rows and rows of sturdy, brave, attentive faces the greatest audiences of his lifetime. Instead of polite handclapping, he was greeted with cheers, pounding, stamping of feet, and real American yells. His programs were always followed by friendly handshakes, long comradely talks, and an exchange of war yarns for the latest stories from home, hours which made Mr. Sothern, in a way neither he nor his audiences can ever forget, a real member of the A. E. F.

Sometimes the effect of the performance was greatly heightened by the unexpected thrills which were always lurking about at the front. One night Mr. Sothern was doing a recitation from "Hamlet," in a town where the German airmen often put over a different kind of entertainment. The actor had just got to that impressive point, following the murder of Polonius, where the queen says, "O, what a rash and bloody deed is this," when a soldier stuck his head in the half lighted room and yelled, "Air raid, lights out."

Out went the lights and the audience sat perfectly still in the dark except for the ominous murmur that arises from several hundred men in a state of considerable tension. Then a sharp voice rang out in the colonel's well known tones, "Attention! Turn on one light on the stage. We have air raids every night, but we don't have Mr. Sothern. Mr. Sothern, would you mind going on with your readings?" So Mr. Sothern continued, "O, what a rash and bloody deed is this,"—"I'll tell the world," sang out a doughboy's voice from the dark. The spontaneous laugh which followed broke the tension and the show went on. This is probably the only time that this solemn speech from *Hamlet* ever "got a laugh"—and deserved it.

On another occasion, Mr. Sothern's automobile passed through an intensive homemade barrage coming from an American ammunition dump which had just been hit, and which was going off in all directions. His car continued, however, and finally landed him in an old *château*. Climbing up to the second floor, he found a large room filled with doughboys and officers, waiting for him in the midst of this weird scene. Two candles on the mantelpiece gave the only illumination. All the windows were boarded up. The audience sat on camp stools and boxes, or lay about the floor. Such was the setting in which he recited Alan Seeger's poems, nor could that heroic soldier poet himself have wished a better one.

At another time, Sothern found himself. in the cellar of a ruined house, before two hundred men with their steel helmets and gas masks, and only one sputtering candle for illumination. Here he decided that recitations on Verdun and heroism were out of order and that the only thing to do with these men was to talk to them. Sitting down in the midst of the bunch, he told stories about Kankakee and Cincinnati and Broadway, and the folks back home in that country about which every boy had agreed that there was only one real slogan—"*See America First*."

The gallant little party went everywhere. Mr. Ames made the arrangements and saw and studied everything from the S.O.S. to the front. In Bordeaux Mr. Sothern put on four shows, including a special performance for the Negro stevedores which was perhaps the most enthusiastically applauded show of the whole trip. Everywhere they found doughboys who had been scene shifters, actors, property men, advance agents, and other acquaintances in the brotherhood of the stage. They dined with General Pershing and received from him a cordial and personal approbation of their foster child, the Over There Theatre League.

Mr. Steele made practically the whole trip with them, and his enthusiastic and tactful collaboration laid the foundation for the harmonious relations which prevailed in the months that followed between the entertainers and the directing heads of the "Y."

Mr. Ames spoke to the men on many occasions, and caught at first hand the splendid spirit of the audiences he was going back to supply with the best talent of the American stage. Doughboys who met the party on their tour around France remember them with humorous affection, for the distinguished travellers were encountering for the first time the wreck that the war had made of the French railway service. Hot water bags, thermos bottles, cushions, and other signs of a desperate attempt to be comfortable protruded at various angles from their baggage.

Later in the year Mr. Sothern gave in England one other set of impromptu performances which deserved special mention. This was in August, 1918, when American wounded, following the generous invitation of the British authorities, had already begun to arrive in British hospitals. Mr. Sothern on this occasion made a special tour of Great Britain, giving not only Shakespearian readings but real performances wherever possible, in company with Miss Mary Anderson, the famous and beloved Shakespearian actress, and Ben Greet, leader of the Ben Greet Shakespearian Players. The party played under all sorts of circumstances, from a "real" show at the Eagle Hut in London to an improvised string of scenes which was put on at the big hospital near Evesham.

This last show was one of the greatest examples of what an actor can do with nothing to work with. The play was *Macbeth*, and the stage was a kind of scaffolding across one end of a room. There was an erratic curtain but no footlights, no scenery, no properties. The company finally cut the property list down to five items, as follows: Two bloodstained daggers, a saucer of blood (or rather, two saucers in case one got spilled or lost), a bell, and the mechanism for producing "the dull ominous knocking at the gate." Sir John Hare, the famous English actor, whose daughter Miss Mollie Hare played one of the parts, volunteered to supply the knocking, and contrived for that function a croquet mallet swathed in a silk scarf. The only exit door was very considerably lowered by planking, and there was a precarious passage off the stage, ending in one plank through the door. As a result Mr. Sothern, engrossed with his lines, smartly banged his head against the door every time he entered the stage and every time he left. His most effective exit, however, was on the occasion when, as Macbeth, he escorted the weeping Lady Macbeth off the stage.

At this great moment Macbeth walked the plank one step too far to the left and disappeared amid some confusion, only to clamber back again and make a dignified exit, while the house maintained a sympathetic silence. The dark and creepy murder of Duncan had to be contrived in the broad sunshine, there being no footlights. The great scene where Macbeth is surprised by the knocking at the gate found Macbeth waiting on the stage in an agonised attitude, for there was no knocking. Sir John Hare was reading the manuscript and all signs failed to disturb him. Finally Lady Macbeth, from behind the scenes, stamped her foot three times, whereat Macbeth gave the required guilty start. Just then the mallet, not to be denied its part, protruded in full view of the audience, gave three solemn knocks, and was stealthily withdrawn.

The audience, according to Mr. Sothern, was the most chivalrous aggregation that ever listened to Shakespeare. Their chance to be magnanimous came when a messenger, who had carefully rehearsed the part of announcing the coming of the king, violently knocked his head on entering the stage, and then said in a strange voice, "The king comes here tonight." Lady Macbeth duly replied, "Thou'rt mad to say it." Whereupon the messenger rendered a perfectly good Shakespearian speech thus:

> So please you. it is true. One of our fellows told me about it, who could scarcely speak because he was dead.

Mr. Sothern admits that this performance was not far short of that classic situation of melodrama when the villain stands before the firing squad, but to the command "Fire" only a series of feeble clicks replies. Somebody has forgotten the cartridges. But the villain must die. "My God," suddenly cries the doomed man, "I have broken my neck," and so he falls dead.

The Sothern-Ames party returned to New York in the middle of April, 1918, with the material for a fruitful and inspiring message for the American stage, and with a vivid idea of the splendid democracy of service overseas. One of the ways in which the latter conception got home to them may be told in the following anecdote. One day Mr. Sothern, who had noticed for a long time that his chauffeur seemed exceptional, asked him what he did in the States.

"My name is Danforth," was the reply, "William H. Danforth. I'm from Missouri," and he named a nationally known cereal milling company.

"Maybe they will promote me," said Mr. Danforth, in answer to Mr. Sothern's inquiries as to why he did not ask for work more in his line, "but if they don't, I am going to stick to this job for the duration of the war."

"Well, that is the best recruiting story I ever heard," said Mr. Sothern, "I will use it on the actors." And he did.

CHAPTER 7

The Stage Called to Arms

*If it were done when 'tis done, then 'twere well
It were done quickly.*
                    Macbeth.

When Messrs. Ames and Sothern returned to America, the great German offensive of March 21, 1918, had already broken upon the Allied Armies. The terrible shadow of that spring impelled every American to seek the means readiest and nearest to him to back up the army. Amid this general spirit of self-sacrifice and deepening loyalty, Messrs. Ames and Sothern confidently prepared their appeal to the theatrical profession.

The arrival "home" of the Sothern-Ames mission, with its message to the American stage, and the scenes which followed form in themselves a drama of American spirit and American character. They returned to America with a definite purpose and plan by which through eighteen months of unstinted work the American stage was to serve the army.

Messrs. Sothern and Ames announced on their return home:

> The opportunity for the American stage and lyceum to do a great service in standing back of the men behind the guns— behind the American doughboys— is without parallel. The first step is to prepare the way, under the 'Y,' by erecting 'war theatres' or auditoriums throughout the war areas.
>
> It was proposed to grade all the halls in France to meet the needs; to concentrate on plans for a great chain of small, home-like, standardized theatres where 700 soldiers could easily be within sight and hearing of the stage; and then to recruit from the American stage and

lyceum every man and woman who could go "over there" to do his or her "bit."

Messrs. Sothern and Ames brought home a specimen itinerary on which American entertainers could spend ten weeks in France for the back areas, and a similar period for the front, so as to cover the maximum amount of territory. This report suggested a plan to supply trained dramatic coaches for the soldier shows, which were even then breaking out everywhere.

It also communicated the vivid impression of its authors of the great need for plays of all kinds in manuscript and synopsis form, for grease paint, false moustaches, rouge, and the hundred other props and accessories of the make-believe world, required for minstrel shows and costume nights; to relieve, if only for an occasional evening, the strain and tension of war.

On the night of April 6, 1918, at the Metropolitan Club, Mr. McLane gave a dinner to the Sothern-Ames mission, which was in the nature of a preliminary conference. Among the guests were Daniel Frohman, the great producer, E. F. Albee, head of the B. F. Keith enterprises and dean of vaudeville, George W. Perkins, General T. Coleman Du Pont, C. W. McAlpin, John Sherman Hoyt, Harold I. Pratt, and William Sloane, Chairman of the National War Work Council. In the midst of this group, Mr. Sothern told his story with an eloquence and a conviction which swept all before him. Mr. Ames followed his colleague's vivid portrayal of the need "over there," with an account of the inspiring suggestions which they had devised to begin the work.

The next step was to mobilise the managers. Mr. Ames gave a dinner at Sherry's, the old Fifth Avenue rendezvous which passed with the War, to every prominent manager who could be reached on short notice. George M. Cohan came, and Marc Klaw, Abraham Erlanger, Lee Shubert, Daniel Frohman, E. F. Albee, and many others. Mrs. August Belmont, who had just arrived from France, re-enforced Mr. Ames's appeal for prompt action, and the only question the meeting had to discuss was what to do and how soon to begin.

The American managers rose magnificently to the occasion. They guaranteed their full cooperation not only to release every actor who wanted to go to France, but to put their weight behind a great mass meeting of the theatrical profession which would be a stirring call to service for every actor in America. Before the dinner was finished, the Over There Theatre League was christened.

Original Proclamation

New York, April 17, 1918.

Mr. E. H. Sothern and Mr. Winthrop Ames have returned from a three months' tour through the American camps in France. They report that entertainment, and particularly entertainment sent from "home," is vital to the morale of our troops there. They bring a message from General Pershing emphasising the need.

The opportunity has come for our men and women of the stage to serve, in person, our soldiers abroad.

This opportunity for service is so important that we feel it should be put before the American Theatre as a whole.

Will you not attend a meeting at the Palace Theatre on Tuesday Morning, April 23rd, at eleven o'clock, to consider the situation?

Mr. Sothern and Mr. Ames will describe the conditions in France.

The need is urgent. We bespeak your presence.

    E. F. Albee
        (The B. F. Keith Circuit of Theatres)
    George M. Cohan
        (Abbot of "The Friars")
    Rachel Crothers
        (President "Stage Women's War Relief")
    Walter Damrosch
        (President "Musicians' Club")
    Charles B. Dillingham
        (Captain N. A.)
    Joseph Grismer
        (Shepherd of "The Lambs")
    Marc Klaw
        (Klaw and Erlanger)
    Willard Mack
        (President "National Vaudeville Artists")
    Lee Shubert
        (President "Shubert Theatrical Company")
    Augustus Thomas
        (President "American Dramatists and Composers")
    Francis Wilson
        (President "Actors' Equity Association")

You are mistaken, you who think the life of an entertainer was one of luxury and ease and floating about in a limousine. You see here a common occurrence—the sore-throated and wet-footed soprano, ruining her voice for the sake of her country, while the young gallant shields her with his marvelous find—yes, an umbrella—unheard of in the A.E.F., but miraculously produced by that astonishing and obliging wonder of humanity, a doughboy.

John Drew
      (President "The Players")
Daniel Frohman
      (President "Actors' Fund of America")

The scene now changes to the Palace Theatre, in the heart of America's dramatic world. "The actors are going to recruit for the War." This was the word along the Great White Way. Thousands of actors from every nation were fighting in the ranks of all the armies. Tens of thousands of professional musicians were in the trenches as common soldiers. The flower of the British stage, the artists of France, the actors and musicians of Italy were in the ranks.

At last the hour had struck for the American artists. It was eleven o'clock on the morning of April 23, 1918. The Palace Theatre was crowded with the greatest gathering of actors "before the footlights" in the history of the profession. More than 2,200 theatrical folk stormed the doors, filled every available seat, crowded the boxes, and even sat in the aisles. Mr. E. F. Albee, head of the Keith Circuit, was host of the occasion in the finest of his great chain of theatres. He raised his hand for order and named George M. Cohan chairman. Mr. Cohan, hero of a lifetime of patriotic hits, but never so much as on this occasion the leader of real patriotic public spirit among his profession, brought the audience sharply to the seriousness of the task in hand with a few trenchant words.

"General Pershing," he announced, "'has called upon the actor to line up with the rest of the manhood and womanhood of America, and now is the time to send him his answer.'"

"I say to General Pershing," exclaimed Cohan, "that whatever he wants from us we are ready to give him."

This was the keynote appeal; the audience broke into its first cheer. He read the following telegram:

> I learn with greatest interest of the work you are undertaking in collaboration with Mr. E. H. Sothern and Mr. Winthrop Ames. It has my most cordial approval and I wish you the best possible success. It is a big undertaking, but I have no doubt you will accomplish it.—Woodrow Wilson.

There was no doubt of the stand of the American actors in the World War. The response came from all parts of the house. They spoke from the audience, from boxes, and from the stage—but all spoke to a house imbued with an electric spirit of sympathetic enthusiasm.

A DIVERSIFIED PROGRAMME BY THE SOLDIERS

The dean of American dramatists, Augustus Thomas—the only American dramatist to have been honored with an election to the presidency of the American Institute of Arts and Letters—stood before the assembled actors.

> I came this early because I have to leave to take the train for Boston where I am doing some government work. I regret not being able to remain here and see the inspiriting sight that I know all who will be here will witness. The war has done a great deal to turn over old opinions. It has brought a great many changes in our social fabric, and is bringing a great one to the theatre and the status of the theatre. We of the theatre come into the field with our contribution as one of the most effective in the whole push behind the drive. We are not especially renowned as business men, and a lot of us make bad contracts. The world does not call upon us when it wants to revise its philosophy, but business and logic are not the only things in this life. The great thing is the spiritual effect and nothing is done at all where the emotions are not stirred. Now in that field of emotional stir, we do not take off our bonnet to anybody. That is our reason for being. That is the thing in which we specialise and we are going to go into this whole-heartedly, and the whole theatrical community is going into it.

Mr. Thomas, knowing full well the soul of the actor, then prophesied:

> I know when the proper time comes—and this meeting is called on for volunteers—that there will be a wonderful sight. I am reminded of the captain who had come to his company for volunteers. He was talking to his line of fine young fellows. He told them he wanted three, but that if one went through the work would be done. He did not disguise the danger. He said, 'Now I want the men who will volunteer to step out one pace.' As he thought of what they were going into, he momentarily crossed his hands over his eyes. 'Not one volunteer?' The whole line had stepped out one pace.

Mr. Sothern stepped to the edge of the stage. He has appeared for a quarter century before distinguished audiences, but never before a gathering of celebrities such as greeted him here.

> A very great distinction, as Mr. Thomas has just told you, has

been conferred upon our calling. It is very important that you should be aware in the beginning of the origin of this meeting. In the middle of December a message was conveyed by Mr. McLane of the Y.M.C.A. to Mr. Ames here in New York, from General Pershing. It appears that General Pershing, in consultation with Mr. E. C. Carter, General Secretary of the Y.M.C.A. in Paris, stated that it was very necessary to aid and uplift the spirits of the forces at the front by some formulated plan, preferably from the profession of entertainment from this country. Mr. Ames was appealed to, and he asked me if I would care to look over the ground. We had very little time to call a mass meeting of our fellows. We just got on board a steamer and we went. The object was to find out under what conditions entertainment could be given to the troops in France.

The master of the art of Shakespeare here related some of his experiences:

We went to the American front and to the British front, and we brought back, I believe, a very complete report of what the condition is and how we are able to serve. I need not tell you with what pride Mr. Ames and I went upon this mission. I felt that the calling of which we are very happy to be members, had been very distinctly honoured.
The necessity of entertainment at the front becomes very obvious when you land amongst the forces—when you perceive their life, the conditions under which they live, the monotony of their existence. The vehicle for this service is necessarily in the hands of the Y.M.C.A.. They have built at the front, as Mr. Ames will shortly explain to you, a great number of buildings which are called huts. In these buildings, which are the club, the general meeting place for prayer, for gatherings of all organisations, these performances will have to take place. The Y.M.C.A., therefore, becomes the inevitable place where these performances, we hope, will be held."
The situation of the American forces is more difficult than that of the French or the English. The Englishman can go home to England. He is content with what small entertainment is provided amongst his own fellows. The same conditions prevail amongst the French. They also can visit their homes occasionally. Our men will not come back to this country until the war

is over; it may last for two or three years, and then they may not come back to this country until eighteen months after the war is over.

Mr. Sothern dramatically presented some of the scenes which he had witnessed along the battle front.

We, who have travelled all over this country, and have been known to all the boys in the army more or less, know that the desire they have for some thread with their homes is very pathetic. You find them sitting in the huts looking at the women canteen workers with the greatest longing. They sit around dumb, with their eyes full of wonder and full of affection which they dare not express.

This anecdote is very familiar in the huts, and has occurred again and again. A boy, after watching one of the women canteen workers for days and days, will edge his way up to the counter where the 'Y' woman is serving. She will ask, 'Is there anything I can do for you?' The boy will look very sheepish and say, 'No, lady, I just wanted to hear you talk.'

When I was about to go on this mission with Mr. Ames, I confided my purpose to a friend. He immediately began to smile and said: 'This is the first time that I ever heard that fighting men found it necessary to carry about their company of comedians.' He had not been recalling his history, because there was a time when distinguished monarchs took their dancing girls and accompanying vaudeville teams on all their military expeditions.

And here the great classical actor paid an historic tribute to the vaudeville stage—to the man who can tell a story, to the girl who can sing the latest jazz music and "do a dance," to the fellow who can play the banjo, to the inimitable "all-evening-by-himself vaudevillian."

Those of us who have taken part merely in plays will have to learn a very important lesson from our brothers and sisters in vaudeville. When we get over, we shall find conditions of such a nature that we shall not be able to perform our plays. I am stating the facts of my own experience when I tell you that I was practically useless for entertainment. I went to investigate, but I was very eager to entertain and consequently I persuaded myself to recite, a thing I have never done before in my life. I am sure I did not do it very well. There was no stage. I got on tables and on counters and I stood amongst the soldiers and did what I could. I have been in the habit of being supported by a company. I have never been able, as the vaudeville artists so brilliantly do, to get up and entertain by myself. But you will be called upon to do it and if you are not able to do it now, the thing to do is to get to work and learn. I am very sure that those qualities that have enabled you to distinguish yourself in the theatre proper will enable you to do something worth while which is important.

When I arrived in France and contemplated what the Y.M.C.A. was doing, I was entirely overwhelmed, as were Mr. Ames and Mrs. Ames, who accompanied us. The function that the Y.M.C.A. fulfils in France is one of the most amazing and most difficult accomplishments that you can possibly imagine. That also Mr. Ames will explain to you. I merely wish to offer my own tribute to the activities which are carried on at the front by the Y.M.C.A. and to plead on behalf of the Y.M.C.A. that you will recognis in it the inevitable help, the great instrument with which you are favoured in fulfilling this service.

May I humbly plead with you to respond to the appeals that are going to be made to you? I should be very proud if any work of mine could induce you to such a response. If I can induce you to go over there and stay over there until all is over, over there, I shall be very happy to have contributed to the result.

And right here let us ring down the curtain—not that the curtain was rung down, for it was a continuous performance—but the ovation literally "stopped the show."

CHAPTER 8

A Message From France

Stand not upon the order of your going,
But go at once
        Macbeth.

As the curtain rises on what we may call the second spectacular scene in the national drama at the Palace Theatre on this April morning of 1918, we find Winthrop Ames occupying the centre of the stage. Home from the battle front, Mr. Ames told his experiences in France. With Mr. Sothern and Mr. McLane—"the power behind the throne"—he completed the triumvirate which became the "godfathers of the American stage" in the world conflict.

Nobody can say that our profession hasn't done its full share in this war. Actors have given their services and managers have given their theatres for benefit after benefit. Our work for the Liberty Loans has probably exceeded that of any other profession. I think one cause of our eagerness has been a secret feeling that in this world crisis entertainment had no vital place. The farmer, the manufacturer of munitions, and the shoemaker can each see the direct need of his work. But the artist—the painter, the actor, and the singer—somehow couldn't see any direct use for his personal service except as an advertiser of some other fellow's efforts. I think in our hearts we've felt a little out of it.

At this moment Mr. Ames delivered the message that he had brought home from General Pershing.

I've just come back from France, and I can tell you, as a fact beyond dispute, that entertainment is not a luxury to the modern man. Once deprive him of it, even for a little time, and he learns that it is a necessity as vital to him as sugar in his food. We actors make something that is as needful in this war as overcoats or shovels. And at last our opportunity has come to serve—not through some other fellow any longer, but in person—to fight side by side with our soldiers, to enter actively the service of America's Army in France.

Mr. Ames thus explained the situation as it confronted him in France:

> In France there are two organisations that are the right and left hands of the American Army, accredited by and working under its control—the Red Cross and the Y.M.C.A.. Both are semi-militarized, and the functions of each are assigned by military order. You will be practically in army service and subject to its discipline. Indeed, I have no doubt that if any of your performances over there should be bad enough to warrant it, the officers in command might order you out and have you shot at dawn.

Vividly he pictured the exigencies of war and its demands:

> You must wear the Y.M.C.A. uniform, not only because you belong to the entertainment organisation, but because you'd have as much chance of getting about the camps in civilian dress as a convict in stripes would have of strolling down Broadway. I think you will get very fond of that uniform, and may be pretty proud of it before you've worn it long," he exclaimed. "It is a badge of service to the soldier that he has grown to esteem and respect. When I got back to New York and passed our boys in the street I missed it when they didn't smile and say 'Hello,' as they almost always did when I was in uniform over there. And my wife particularly missed the half affectionate greeting 'Hello, "Y,"' which is their pet name for women in that service.

The speaker told how he found wearing that uniform abroad presidents of big manufacturing concerns, bankers, and college presidents, and all sorts of other men, many of whom had given up large incomes and big positions for the duration of the war.

> You will find them in the huts getting up at daybreak, making their own beds, and spending the day selling cigarettes, sweeping the floors, and moving heavy benches for your evening

performance. In one of the huts I met a woman canteen worker whom I had known in New York. The last time I saw her here, she gave me a lift in her limousine. There were two men on the box and she was wearing the finest sable coat I ever saw. In France, she was standing behind a counter, wearing a soiled uniform, and doling out letter paper. When she shook hands with me, her hands were chapped and red from days spent in washing chocolate cups. And she told me she had never been so happy in her life.

Many dramatic scenes to be expected in the life of a volunteer American, making the voyage to France to "do his bit" for the doughboy, were graphically presented by Mr. Ames and he predicted that his experience would soon become that of thousands of others.

> Before you sail you may have an opportunity to acquire a little of that patience under orders that is part of military life. For instance, maybe the very day you are ready to start the government may commandeer your berth (I say 'berth' advisedly and not 'stateroom') for some officer, and you'll be left to cool your heels till the next steamer. Well, there is nothing to do about that sort of thing but to bear it—and grin if you can. In any case, you'll be wise to acquire early, before you face the inevitable little discomforts and irritations of war service, the useful French habit of shrugging your shoulders and saying cheerfully, 'C'est la Guerre'—'Well, it's war!'
> But no trifling discomforts will count in face of the great experience that is coming to you—of learning what war really is at first hand. You'll begin to get some hint when you see your steamship—camouflaged perhaps to look like a cloud on the horizon; or when you find that all your fellow-passengers, without exception, are either officers or workers in some war service like yourself. The mere 'visitor' to Europe doesn't exist any more. You will feel it when your portholes are battened shut at night, and covered with tin lest any gleam of light escape, and you are forbidden to smoke on deck. And before you see the shores of France there will come out of the sky to meet and watch over you, an American airplane followed by an American destroyer flying Old Glory.
> And before you reach the dock you may gather some notion of what it means for an entire nation to be at war when, instead of

the smart French customs inspector of former days, a little file of middle-aged women clad in black climbs the rope ladder up your steamer's side to examine your baggage.

It was a thrilling story of adventure that Mr. Ames related—perhaps the clearest insight that has been given of the varied phases of hardship and self-sacrifice for the great cause.

> As the train takes you through France—for you will first go direct to Paris for instructions—you will see no men out of uniform, except those actually decrepit, and only women working in the fields. And everywhere there will be barracks and more barracks, and crawling freight trains laden with cannon and ammunition, and boxes and bales labelled from every part of the world. You'll pass encampments of English troops and Canadian troops, and troops from India and Senegal and Africa, and gangs of day labourers by the thousand brought from China.
> The whole stream seems somehow headed in one direction, crawling toward 'the line.' That thin line—only about 450 miles long, the distance from Washington to Boston, and never wider than a mile—that crack in the earth is the centre and focus of the whole world today. And toward that crack—that narrow crater of destruction—the whole world is flowing in two streams from opposite sides of the globe. And you are carried with the current, and are part of it.
> In Paris the Y.M.C.A. will take charge of you and tell you what area of camps you are to visit first. Most of the camps are not actually in the towns, but from two to seven miles outside. But the base town is where you will lodge—some of them are the most interesting historical towns in France—and go out by motor to the camps themselves for your performances. And when you've given performances in all the camps near that town, you'll go back to Paris and get a bath (hurrah!), and start for another base town. And so on!

The observations of Mr. Ames, with his keen analysis of character and his sense of humour, must here become a permanent part of war literature.

> You will be met at the station by your local boss, that is, the Y.M.C.A. secretary in charge of the district; and about nightfall he'll load you all into one open Ford motor car—so there

mustn't be more than six of you in the company at the very outside—and you'll start for the camp to give your performance.

All the scenery you'll be able to carry ought to be under your hat; and your costume, if you take one, must pack in a flat handbag; otherwise there won't be room in the Ford. But, oh! respect that humble Ford! It cost $1,000 in France, and had to be fought for at that! And the gasoline that feeds it can be had only by order from the army, and it's a penal offense to use a drop for pleasure riding.

On your way to the camp your car may be halted two or three times by a sentry—and his rifle is really loaded,

'Halt! Who goes there?'

'Y.M.C.A..'

'Pass Y.M.C.A..'

And finally you do pass the bounds; and inside you'll find a flat, treeless expanse of trodden mud, covered close with the barracks where the boys live. The camp looks like a newly built mining camp without the saloon. Imagine a big sleeping car, without wheels, built of matched boards, and you have a picture of a barrack. Inside it there is a centre aisle, and on either side of this aisle is a double row of bunks. This is the soldier's home!"

Our boys are the finest, healthiest, most upstanding set of young giants you ever saw. They are as keen as mustard to get to the front, and when they are at the front, they are as keen as mustard to get at the Boche, and we are going to have reason to be mighty proud of them.

It is to Mr. Ames also that our war records are indebted for a clear vision of the "soldier's home" in besieged and war-ridden France.

Some genius realised what this absence of any touch of home in the soldier's life might mean, and the Y.M.C.A. in France is the result. Wherever there is a camp, you'll find a Y.M.C.A. hut or house. It isn't decorative. It is made of matched boards, and it looks just like a larger barrack, or a shooting gallery at Coney Island without the paint. It might cost at the outside $3,000 to put up in America; in France it costs $15,000, because the lumber has to be smuggled out of Spain or Switzerland under the nose of German agents, and when the army can't spare the men to help put it up, or there are no German prisoners available, it sometimes has to be put up by French women. But it's there in every camp now with its Red Triangle over the door, and it is the soldier's home and club, and comer grocery store, and church—and it wants to be his theatre.

There is always a canteen (or counter) at one end, where they sell, at cost, the minor luxuries that Uncle Sam doesn't supply, such as cigarettes and hot chocolate and shaving brushes and biscuits. Along one side is a row of plain wooden tables, always crowded, where boys are writing back to you letters home. You may have noticed the Red Triangle on the corner of the letter paper. On the other side is another row of tables where they are playing checkers or cards. There is a little library of books. And here's where the old magazines go that you put a stamp on and drop into the post-box without address. There is probably a phonograph grinding out 'Mother Machree.' And at the end, opposite the canteen, is a little platform. This is your stage. Sometimes the hut hasn't even a platform, and they will put two tables together for a stage.

In some of the more important camps there are separate auditoriums—except that auditorium is altogether too grand a word, for they are just like the other huts, except that there are no tables or canteens and they are filled with closely packed benches. Sometimes the little stage has a drop curtain, oftener it hasn't. Once in a while the boys have painted a rudimentary back-drop. It almost always represents New York harbour with the Statue of Liberty. There may be a little gasoline engine coughing its life away outside, and so you may have the luxury of electric lights. Sometimes the light is kerosene lanterns, and once in a while candles. But even when there is light enough, it's hard to see because the place is so filled with smoke.

The fact that you are coming to play there will have been chalked up a week ahead on the bulletin board outside the hut, and the hut will be packed with boys to welcome you. They will be standing outside the windows as far as they can hear. If you are late they will wait.

And Mr. Ames told a story about getting to one hut where Mr. Sothern was announced to read. Their car broke down ("You may expect that, and it may be raining. too—but *'C'est la Guerre!'*") and they were an hour and a quarter late.

But the boys had waited all that time, whistling and singing in chorus to keep themselves amused. Not one left his place, because he knew that some one else would take it if he did. You see, it's not only entertainment you'll be bringing them, but entertainment from home—home that's 3,000 miles away. Over there in France everything about home has come to have a kind of golden halo. You know how it is yourself when you've been away for a long time. Every man from America seems to the doughboy a kind of messenger and representative from 'God's country,' and every American woman represents, not merely a woman, but his own mother or wife or sweetheart.

He related how when Sothern and he went up to the trenches they took Mrs. Ames as far as a woman was allowed to go. They left her in a canteen hidden away in a little wood, at nightfall. The shack was lighted by three candles. In it there were about two hundred boys who had come in to smoke because they couldn't light matches outside, or to get a cup of hot chocolate before they went out for their night's shift in the trenches, or to mend the broken barbed wire on "No Man's Lane." They had to mend that wire by feeling. They showed her their hands. She was the only woman within two miles.

When we came back I asked my wife how she felt among all those boys. And she said: 'If I had a daughter of sixteen, I'd leave here there alone. And if any man touched her with his finger, these boys would tear him into a thousand pieces.'
The place was within reach of gas shells, and she had been ordered to carry a gas mask. But the boys took it away from her. One of them held it near. 'I'll put it on you quicker than you can if there is need,' he said. 'But we just can't bear to see an American woman wearing a gas mask.' Is it any wonder that everyone who saw our men in France feels that there has come to them a new dignity?
They are just great, happy, wholesome, fine American boys. They haven't lost their sense of humour. For instance, one division has taken for its motto: '*See America First.*' They don't want you to lose your sense of humour, when you come to them. They want cheerfulness, and gaiety, and clean laughter, and good catchy music, and stirring recitations, and little swift plays—oh, anything that's good of its kind, and well done, and that is 'Made in America.' That's it—'Made in America.' You'll

never realise how much it will mean to those boys to have you come 3,000 miles to serve them—how much they need you—till you stand before your first audience and get their welcome. I envy you that feeling.

We of the theatre can personally help to speed the victory, because our men will fight better if we keep them happy and contented in their exile, and because in addition to entertainment we can bring the unspoken message that America is with them and behind them every day and every hour. The service we are asked to do is not a duty—it is a great privilege. And we owe a debt to the Y.M.C.A. in France, who have asked us to join with them in serving our soldiers there, and whose pioneer work has made our service possible.

Mr. Ames's simple narrative thrilled his auditors. He had brought to them a professional message from the war zone. He had pictured in the imaginative minds of the creative artists of his time the true vision of war. The doughboys were calling to them—waiting for them. Is it at all surprising that the adventure which followed on the scene in the Palace Theatre was to become one of the heritages of the American stage?

CHAPTER 9

The American Stage Answers

We are ready to try our fortunes, to the last man"
                                   King Henry IV.

If the S. S. *Leviathan* could have been made fast at the door of the Palace Theatre, it is safe to say that the audience would have gone on board en masse, prepared to sail for France at once, with the cordial consent of the managers, booking agents, producers, dramatists, and the whole theatrical world, leaving the American public to shift for its dramatic future as best it might.

And this despite Mr. Ames's warnings:

If a commander disapproves of your performance he can have you shot at sunrise.

All the scenery you can carry must be under your hat.

Your costumes must be carried in a handbag, and your company be squeezed into a Ford.

You will be dirty, bedraggled, tired, hungry, and homesick.

You will travel through a desolate country, in which the graces of civilisation have been suspended by war.

You will get utterly lost, from time to time, amid the planless confusion which is inevitable in a great war where every soldier is more important than you are

—but with the assurance of Mr. Sothern;

You will play before such audiences as you never believed existed on earth, and you will hear applause that will drown the air raids.

JOHN W. BEATTIE

JOSEPH LINDON SMITH

WILLIAM H. DUFF, 2ND

CARL J. BALLIETT

But when the American stage becomes imbued with a great idea, when it hears the call of country or humanity, it never fails to answer with heart and soul—as was demonstrated in every Liberty Loan drive, in every Red Cross and United War Fund campaign, in the response to the appeals of every relief organisation.

And so it was on this historic occasion in the Palace Theatre, as Sergeant Arthur Guy Empey pointed his aggressive finger at the audience and shouted:

> The biggest job in the war is to send the boys over the top with a smile. It is the men who go over the top with a song in their hearts who keep their wits about them and come back—and you've got to provide the songs.

Empey told of running a show 600 yards behind the lines with shells flying over so regularly that "the bass drummer would wait and let the shell make the noise for him while he rested." He told the actors they probably would be disappointed with Europe until they played their first engagement before the soldiers, then "no matter how rotten you are, you're going to get a wonderful hand."

Mrs. August Belmont inspired her hearers:

> The boys over there are giving their best, and they deserve yours; the service you can render, small as it may seem amid the great sacrifices that are being made, will come back to you in after years as the greatest experience of your lives.

Mr. McLane pledged the support of the National War Work Council.

No element of the profession was forgotten. Joseph Grismer, a Union veteran of the Civil War, pledged the full ranks of "The Lambs" and its thousand or more members.

Margaret Mayo promised to turn actress again for the occasion, though she admitted, even in George Cohan's presence, that a playwright was only a bad actor whom the managers would not hire.

Francis Wilson, who was called upon to respond for the Actors' Equity Association, made probably the happiest one-minute speech of the morning. He said:

> It was understood that a few of us would address you, and I was to be among the few. I want to call your attention to the change that is coming over our opinion of the Y.M.C.A.. We used to think of them as pink tea folks, but now we know that

SOLDIER AUDIENCE IN HUTS SHOWING PICTURE BOOTHS

they are a power of manhood. The 'Y' has made its discovery, too. It is learning how great an influence for good there is in the American stage. The members of the Actors' Equity Association will go.

With such an audience, won a thousand times over by these irresistible appeals, the response went far beyond control. Volunteers rose from all parts of the house before any call was made, and when Mr. Cohan finally asked all those who were "ready to go" to stand up, three fourths of the audience rose.

To the standing crowd, Mr. Cohan read telegram after telegram pledging the great names of the American stage for service overseas—Julia Marlowe, Maude Adams, Lillian Russell, John Drew, John Barrymore, William Collier, Frances Starr, Viola Allen, Marguerite Clark, Grace George, James T. Powers, Grant Mitchell, Jessie Busley, John Charles Thomas, Jane Cowl, Ruth Chatterton, Louise Dresser, Donald Brian, Walter Jones, Billie Burke, Otis Skinner, Kittie Edwards, Eugene O'Brien, Julia Sanderson, Joseph Cawthorne, David Bispham, Blanche Ring, Tom Wise, Marie Doro, James J. Corbett, Weber and Fields, Barry McCormack, Nora Bayes and Company, Amos Sutherland—and a long roll call of celebrities covering every branch of the profession.

Miss Amelia Bingham volunteered from a stage box, and Edith Wynne Mattison and Charles Rann Kennedy were announced as among the volunteers, as were Charles B. Dillingham, Joseph Riter, and Florenz Ziegfeld, Jr. The last three offered their services as producers. Organisations offering to organise companies to go overseas were the Players, Lambs, Friars, Green Room Club, Stage Women's War Relief, Actors' Equity Association, and the National Vaudeville Artists.

Elsie Janis cabled from London making a date with the whole audience in France. Willie Collier volunteered to "head a company, or carry a spear or gun or anything."

The tide of emotion reached its topmost crest when Secretary Henry Chesterfield, of the National Vaudeville Artists, announced that more than 9,000 members of that great organisation had signified their willingness to go at once. As the famous Tammany politician said, from then on "pantomime reigned."

Thus there emerged from this historic meeting, held on the birthday of Shakespeare, the Over There Theatre League, fully organised, officered, and ready for duty. Its officers were:

George M. Cohan, President (Abbot of "The Friars").

E. F. Albee, Vice-President (The B. F. Keith Circuit of Theatres).

Directors: Winthrop Ames; Rachel Crothers (President "Stage Women's War Relief"); Walter Damrosch (President "Musicians' Club"); Charles B. Dillingham (Captain N. A.); John Drew (President of "The Players"); Daniel Frohman (President "Actors' Fund of America"); Joseph R. Grismer (Shepherd of "The Lambs"); Marc Klaw (Klaw and Erlanger); Willard Mack (President "National Vaudeville Artists"); Lee Shubert (President "Shubert Theatrical Company"); E. H. Sothern; Augustus Thomas (President "American Dramatists and Composers"); Francis Wilson (President "Actors' Equity Association").

The following individual contract was drawn up:

America's
Over There Theatre League
and
Y.M.C.A. Contract

By my signature below, and because of the receipt by me of a uniform and living expenses from the YMCA, and a salary of $2.00 per day from America's Over There Theatre League, and because I shall be employed in a country at war, I hereby pledge myself to

1. Obey all Military Authorities in command,

2. Obey the Secretary of the Y.M.C.A. to whom I am directly responsible.

3. Remain in Entertainment Service abroad *not less* than three months, unless otherwise ordered.

4. Return to the United States at any time upon the request of the head of the Y.M.C.A. organisation in France or England.

5. Deliver to the Y.M.C.A., immediately after my return to America, the uniform furnished me by them.

Signed ....

Accepted by T. S. McLane

For the National War Work Council, Y.M.C.A..

Witnessed by ....

Accepted by Winthrop Ames

For America's Over There Theatre League.

In order to facilitate the handling of entertaining companies abroad, I further agree to recognise .... as the manager of the unit with which I am connected, and to conform to such arrangements in regard to travelling, etc., in France as he may make.

Signed....................

Received from the Y.M.C.A. and America's Over There Theatre League:

(1) $100 in French money, to be used for trip expenses, an expense account and any balance left over to be delivered to the Y.M.C.A., 12 Rue d'Aguesseau, Paris, France.

(2) $5.00 to be spent on taxi fares, etc., to steamer here.

(3) Order No.—, entitling me to America's Over There Theatre League's allowance.

(4) Service contract.

(5) The balance of my passport photographs.

The offices and headquarters of the Over There Theatre League were for nine months in the Little Theatre, the use of which was extended to the organisation gratuitously by Mr. Ames.

The list of volunteers for immediate service exceeded seven hundred personal applicants in two days and steadily went on growing; and the vigorous and unstinted enthusiasm of organisations representing more than 15,000 members placed the resources of the whole dramatic world at the feet of the American Army.

Chapter 10

A Stock Company Under Fire

*'Tis true that we are in great danger;
The greater therefore should our courage be.*
          King Henry V.

Before Messrs. Ames and Sothern sailed for home, they met the first American professional stock company which had come to France. This was the Craig Company, which had been sent over by Mr. McLane, on the initiative of Mr. and Mrs. John Craig themselves, the heads for many years of the famous Craig Players of Boston. The sacrifices and experiences of the Craigs would require a volume in themselves.

"I would not trade my experience for a million dollars," was the answer of Mr. Craig when questioned regarding his nine months' tour of the A. E. F.

John Craig and his gifted wife, Mary Young, co-leaders of Boston's time-honoured Castle Square Stock Company, decided as early as September, 1917, to put everything aside and go to France. They had given their two sons to the cause—both had volunteered in the service of the French Army without waiting for the call of their own country—and one was to make the supreme sacrifice. It is an heroic story of an American stage family that gave all they had to the call of humanity.

There are two very interesting phases of the Craig experiences: the first was their persistence in getting to France; the second, their fight to go to the front and play clear up to the trenches. The spirit which actuated them is such that it deserves a special place in this story.

The first play selected as the medium for overseas production—Margaret Mayo's rollicking farce, *Baby Mine*—had enjoyed a record run on Broadway some years before. It was a play which required the minimum of costumes and scenery— the chief items being three rubber babies and a portable telephone as the props, with citizens' clothes as the costumes. Also it was a play with inextinguishable humour of situation, the first and funniest of its type of farces.

Mr. Craig, Mary Young, his wife, and the capable players who supported the Craigs, Charles Darrah, Ivy Troutman, Robert Tabor, Theresa Dale, Rose Saltonstall, and Wilfred Young, sailed from New York February 3, 1918. Mr. Craig explained:

> The company had to be reduced to six, so that all the players and properties could be gotten into a Ford. We went from camp area to camp area by train and then by automobile over each area. These were sometimes forty miles in extent, but we had to make every centre in a day if possible. We carried draperies for scenery, and these were hung in a field, in the woods, or in a hall, as the case might be, wherever the soldiers congregated. Many a performance was given outdoors, and we always had an appreciative crowd. If we couldn't borrow an army cot, we would requisition a chair for the bed that is used in the play. We even put on *Baby Mine* in a dugout one night for a few officers, most of whom had to sit on the edge of the 'stage.'

Their first regular assignment was Aix-les-Bains. It was in March. The First Division was turned loose in that area, for their first real leave of the War. There the Craig Company went to give America's veteran fighting division the sight of the first real show they had seen in France. The town was placarded with posters—the unbelievable news that an honest-to-goodness American comedy in four acts, "not a movie," was being staged at the local casino by America's best known stock company.

When the players arrived, they found for the first time in their lives that the theatrical writer's ancient boast, "*The house was crowded to the rafters*," had really come true. The last square inch of floor space had been pre-empted. The nimble doughboys had climbed to the girders; they even decorated the short slanting joists that upheld the roof. The delighted yells and cheers of this irrepressible audience would have made any show a riot. But when the stage husband, who yearned in vain for a "che-ild" and found himself presented with one, then two, then three infants, who bobbed on and bobbed off the stage in a series of astonishing miracles—one finally being produced of altogether the wrong colour for its parentage—the doughboys howled and cheered until some of them nearly dropped off the rafters. This was a "regular show." And this was its usual reception.

As we follow the Craig players, as they go toward the front and play under *impromptu* conditions which differ at every performance, a series of pictures arises which show that the nimble wit and resourcefulness of the American actor had a share in helping the army to win the war.

There is the time, for instance, when the company is jogging along the road in its own "tin Lizzie." It meets an outfit of plodding doughboys on the march. Somebody recognizes them or sees the entertainment insignia on the uniform and there is a general yell of greeting. The column halts and one of the officers says: "These boys have been in France six months and haven't seen a real show yet. We don't know when we shall see you again. Can't you give us something?" Mr. Craig looks at the open field, with a little hill on one side, shaded by some trees, and then at the long line of upturned lively faces, and says: "Sure! We will give you a whole play right here and now." And so the news passes from rank to rank, the men give a whoop as the order is given to break ranks, and soon Mr. Craig is stepping forward and coolly announcing

> Our first scene is laid in a Chicago drawing-room, and you who know what a Chicago drawing-room looks like will feel perfectly at home—the rest can use their imagination.

The audience is ranged in a broad circle on the ground under the trees. At one side of the "stage," which is furnished with square boxes for chairs, with long boxes for sofas, and a tall box on end for a table, stand the local villagers who make a very good screen behind which the actors can disappear and make their modest changes. When the great bed scene comes on it is an army cot borrowed from a salvage wagon which takes the place of the Chicago brass bedstead, and a soap box serves as a cradle for the unhappy infants. As the excited heroine dashes across the stage and leaps on to the bed in order to be safely tucked up before her husband enters, the bed gives way with a crash; but after a little carpentry the scene goes on, funnier than before.

A volunteer is called for to enact the star part of an irate janitor in the last act. He is rehearsed in front of the whole audience, made perfect in his lines, and at the right moment rushes on to the stage and sometimes—it happened once or twice—he gets the lines right. But there is terrific applause as the play finishes. Then the ranks form up again. The army boots again take up their rhythmic tread as the boys go off over the hill with a laugh in their hearts. The company packs up its India rubber babies and its telephone and wends its way to the next camp.

There is the time, repeated over and over again, when the company is playing close up behind the firing line to a tense crowd of men who have only recently come out of action, or who may be going in the next morning. Gradually the tenseness relaxes and into their eyes comes the fresh, care-free look of men over whom a breath of air from home is visibly blowing. In the midst of the performance comes an order. All over the house men get up quietly and steal away. They are going to the front. The rest of the audience sits quiet, but the tenseness comes again. Then when the show is over, *tramp, tramp, tramp,* go the boots again up toward the lines, as the actors go, tired and spent, to their cold but well-earned beds.

Half a dozen times *Baby Mine* is interrupted by other kinds of infants of German extraction, which come from enemy aviators above. Actors and audiences are forced to seek shelter until the pests are driven off. From camp to camp the company travels in the indestructible "Lizzie," a war product which runs with many of its parts missing and apparently with all nourishment taken from it except water. They play in railroad stations, with trains coming and going, the audience leaving as their trains come in and being swelled by newcomers from other troop trains.

At one camp they are playing *Baby Mine* before the Sixth Marines of the immortal Second Division. The place is a barn and the illumination is candlelight. The only exit is through the closely packed Marines. On another occasion when there is absolutely no illumination, the resourceful soldiers, not to be beaten out of a show, all turn on their electric pocket torches and focus them on the actors' faces. This is the first time in the history of the stage that every actor has had not only one spot light to himself but hundreds of them.

They play in quarantine camps where spinal meningitis, diphtheria, and many other contagious cases are confined. At one place they have 2,500 contagious cases in the audience, yet they cheerfully take the risk and are a thousand times rewarded in giving limitless pleasure to men who have not seen a show since they have been in France. On another occasion they play before the Polish-American soldiers who are on their way to join the Polish Legion. They play to Negro stevedores and French soldiers. And they give a never-to-be-forgotten show before the Ninety-Ninth Aero Squadron—at the conclusion of which, as a special tribute, Mary Young is taken up and given a flight in a plane by one of the best known aviators in the British Army.

All through these months John Craig gives readings from Shakespeare—one-man shows. He specializes in *Twelfth Night* or *The Taming of the Shrew*, and writes some special new interpolations in Petruchio's famous part which the twentieth century doughboys understand and cheer frantically. Finally, he finds time to help the hard-pressed administration of Johnson and Steele in Paris, and is a useful liaison officer between his fellow entertainers and the "Y" directors, inaugurating the first outlines of the reception and assignment work, later so ably taken up and conducted by A. M. Beatty.

The Craig players covered the entire front and played in practically every American advance base of any size. Besides *Baby Mine*, the company occasionally gave *The Circus Girl*, a musical comedy which had been one of Mary Young's early successes. They also presented some one-act plays hastily adapted and condensed for use when only a very abbreviated show could be given. Then there were the pageants—*The Drawing of the Sword*, and *Joan of Arc*.

The Drawing of the Sword was written by Thomas Wood Stevens of the Carnegie Institute, Pittsburgh, the well-known play and pageant creator who was in France under the Entertainment Department. Another distinguished American dramatic writer, Frederick Cowley, assisted in the production, and the Craig players filled the principal parts and helped to coach. Two performances were given in the large yard or drill ground of Napoleon's old barracks at Camp Pontanazen near Brest, while a third was given in the big American "Y" Navy Hut at Brest, which was choked and crowded in the best war style.

The music was furnished by one of the best bands in the U. S. Navy, and soldiers, sailors, telephone girls, "Y" workers, British Tommies, and many others were liberally called upon to fill the parts. The pageant put in broad historical setting the Allies' cause in the war. It was a successful and stirring dramatic exploit. At any other time it would have been a national event; but in the War's profusion of splendid initiative, it was just one more Craig success.

The *Joan of Arc* pageant was based on one of Mr. Stevens's plays, which was awarded the gold medal of the Joan of Arc Society in America when it was first performed in Pittsburgh some years ago. Mr. Stevens never dreamed that it would one day be given in its own atmosphere at the birthplace of Joan of Arc. Not only did this happen, but the fitness of this splendid and moving spectacle was heightened by costumes designed by a member of the Institute de France. The play was staged in front of the cathedral in Domremy, enacting with striking fidelity the life of France's peasant girl saint in the place of her birth. (*Personal Recollections of Joan of Arc* by Mark Twain is also published by Leonaur.) To enact Joan of Arc, standing thus on this hallowed stage centuries old, and looking out on another army of her own countrymen and their allies, thousands strong, engaged in the greatest of all wars of liberty-that is a dream whose fulfilment might make any actress feel that she had not lived in vain. Miss Young's performance, though no theatrical critic or sophisticated audience was there to give it fame, was one of the greatest of her career, for she herself, like the stoic peasant mothers in the audience, had made the supreme sacrifice and had given her eldest son on the battlefield of liberty.

Here, too, on one occasion, comedy trod the boards, inseparable from romance and tragedy. Miss Young had made the criticism after a previous performance that the fire for Joan's martyrdom had been, for safety's sake, so limited that the result was not the moving spectacle it should have been. "Tom" Cushing enlisted the services of members of the Camouflage Corps. This was their opportunity and they made their preparations but did not rehearse their fire. The result was a success of a kind, but such a success that Joan was concealed so completely and apparently consumed so rapidly that she was unable to read her final lines.

After *Baby Mine* completed its tour, Mr. Craig was sent on an inspection trip of the Y.M.C.A. huts, scouting for all which might prove suitable for performances by other companies of players who would come later, and arranging for such changes in construction as were necessary for the adaptation of the huts to theatrical purposes. He said:

> On this trip I used to recite *The Taming of the Shrew* in the huts at night, taking all the parts. I usually followed this with a recitation of the poem, *Christ in Flanders*. One night I read it to a large assemblage that was waiting to go into the action that wiped out the St. Mihiel salient. After I had finished, the boys asked the 'Y' man, a noted Boston pastor, to pray. This he did while every head was bowed and knee bent. Immediately afterward the order came to move forward.

Miss Young did not accompany her husband back to America. She waited in Paris for their son, John Craig, Jr., who had been serving as a second lieutenant in artillery, commanding one of the French seventy-fives. Before Mr. Craig's return—after the Armistice—he and his wife went on a pilgrimage to their shrine. It was the journey to the grave of their other son, Harmon Craig, a former member of the French Volunteer Ambulance Field Service, who fell in action at Verdun and lies buried just back of France's impregnable fortress.

CHAPTER 11

A Regular American Girl

Make the doors upon a woman's wit and it will out at the casement; shut that and 'twill out at the key-hole; stop that, 'twill fly with the smoke out at the chimney.
As You Like It.

In the spring of 1918 began one of the most memorable individual adventures of the war. It is an exploit, the like of which has no parallel in theatrical history. The first scene is laid in most unromantic surroundings—and is one of the war's most thrilling prologues. It is in a big locomotive shed at the American railway repair shop at Nevers. Present: four thousand waiting doughboys. The boys are standing on the tracks. They are swarming up the sides of the shed, keyed up to great expectancy. Suddenly there is a shout. A big Baldwin locomotive puffs up one of the tracks. The men make way on either side, cheering madly, for there on the cowcatcher, her famous fluted skirt streaming in the breeze, her hand waving the usual breezy salute to everybody, is "the girl." Up to the very platform she proceeds, jumps nimbly off, turns a handspring, and shouts: "Boys, are we downhearted?" There comes a thunderous ear-splitting answer: "Hell, no!" It is Elsie Janis, who from this day becomes the "Sweetheart of the Army," in the most spectacular stage entrance in the annals of the theatre.

What this American girl was to accomplish in the armies in France; how she was to go along the battle areas to arouse the cheers of "my boys;" how she worked day and night for six months in camps, hospitals, leave areas, with fighting regiments, in dugouts, up to the very lines where it required the army to hold her back from going "over the top" is one of the war's classics. General Pershing echoed the opinion of every doughboy when he declared at his own dinner table to the for-once shy and abashed star:

> Elsie, when you first came to France they said you were more valuable than a whole regiment. Then somebody raised you to a division, but I want to tell you that if you can give our men this sort of happiness you are worth an army corps.

Elsie Janis came over to France on March 3, 1918, having been in England since October, 1917. An unexpected breaking of a French contract was the providential means of her beginning at once. Nobody is a better authority on how she happened to start out for the "Y" than Elsie herself. She tells the story in her breeziest style in her book, *The Big Show*:

> When I left home we had no arrangement with the Red Cross or Y.M.C.A.; we came ostensibly to fulfil contracts in Paris and London. But the Y.M.C.A. was right on the job that very next day after our arrival. They had a map of France with dots all over it where their circuit would take me if I would go. At first I was not too keen on being with the Y.M.C.A. It sounded rather like it might cramp my speed—and I asked them quite frankly if my friends could come to the shows whether they were Young Christians or not! They explained that they had only one idea, that was to make the boys happy. As we had the same idea, we agreed to start at once. That very afternoon they sent a pianist up, and we rehearsed. I must say that for a Christian Association they have some speed. It was arranged I would start on tour one week later, and in the meantime would practice on the soldiers in and around Paris.

Elsie's performance was simplicity itself. It consisted of a few songs, some stories, some imitations, a little dancing, another story, and "Goodnight." This could be repeated over and over again, and nobody ever seemed to get tired. Elsie sang French songs as well as English songs, and when her French songs failed she would translate English songs into French songs and *vice versa*, with amazing results. Her imitations depended upon the whim of the audience. She could do anything from Queen Mary of England to Chauncey Olcott. She claimed she could imitate anybody.

One night a boy called out from the ranks:
"How about Will Rogers?"
"Haven't got the rope."

"Yes, but here's one," said the boy, producing a nice long one.

Elsie was caught that time, but she took the rope, made a lasso and danced in it, like the famous Follies cowboy himself. Result, a riot.

Elsie's accompanist was William Janauschek who, as narrated in a preceding chapter, had gone over as pianist for the Liberty Quartet. Mrs. Janis, or "Mother Janis" to the doughboys, accompanied the party. She is a lovable, motherly woman who served her country as nobly as any soldier. The party at first struck into the Old First Division training region around Gondrecourt, Chaumont, and Neufchateau, where Elsie caught the inevitable cold that dogged the steps of all entertainers who faced that lung-searching spring weather. Elsie was laid up for ten days in Paris as a result, but was off again as soon as she was able even to whisper her stories or to sing in a hoarse and husky voice.

She swung around the entire circuit, spending three months of tireless zigzagging and volplaning over the war-torn roads of the American area, going into the heart of that Homeric region northwest of Toul which had already become known to the American public as the American front. She travelled in a General Staff car, with a constantly accumulating collection of silver stars from T. A. G.'s. T. A. G. means, in the Elsie vernacular, "Terribly Attractive Generals." She was one of the few entertainers who sought out and made a special trip among the American units which were tucked in along the British Front. When she finally had to depart in October, 1918, to fulfil a long-planned engagement to head the cast of *Hello, America* in London, she had come as near to playing to the whole American Army as any entertainer on the road at that stage of the war.

The experience of Elsie Janis with the American Army was unique. Owing to a combination of circumstances, in which Elsie's inability to contract herself for a six-months' service at any one continuous period was the principal factor, Elsie was permitted to go out without a uniform. The men enjoyed seeing a famous actress dressed like a regular American girl from Columbus, Ohio, bobbing up defiantly in an environment where all the world went uniformed.

She stops in her whimsical and entirely individual book to record the hope that:

> Some day someone with the powers of description of Hugo, Balzac, Dickens, and a few others, will try to describe the splendid work done by the Y.M.C.A.

This American girl, who had considered it a hard day's work to do

"Who Can Tell," soldier show 88th Division

two twenty-minute shows a day in peace times, tore about war-torn France and was never allowed to go to bed until she had done five and even nine shows during the day, sometimes with laps of 75 or even 100 kilometres on the day's dizzy circuit. Imagine Elsie in a little American sector in Alsace after a day of eight performances. Waking up in her hotel, she catches the strains of the song she had sung the night before, "When Yankee Doodle Learns to *Parlez-Vous-Français*"—it is echoing through the clump, clump of the doughboys' iron-shod feet as they are marching up to the front at four m the morning. Imagine her leaning far out of her window and joining in the chorus, while a thousand faces look up and shout back: "Yea, Elsie! Atta boy, Elsie!" until she withdraws in sobs of speechless exultation.

On that great Fourth of July in 1918, it was Elsie who appeared at the Gaumont Palace in Paris and symbolized j the indomitable crusader humour of the American Army. She stood on the platform in the midst of a typical American crowd—in a real prize ring alongside of the wonder man, Georges Carpentier himself. When Elsie appeared on this fantastic stage, the French members of the audience looked in terror for the next exit, for from the throats of all Americans present there arose yells, screeches, whistles, and a din so terrible and so bloodcurdling that they imagined a German spy at least must have been trapped on the: platform. It was only the boys' greeting to Elsie.

It was a great spell and it held throughout the war. It can best be expressed by that husky American colonel's brief speech up on the line, when a bunch was just getting ready to go into action after one of Elsie's shows:

"The British give their men rum when they go over the top, and the French hand out cognac, but we give ours 'Janis straight.'"

The stories! How Elsie could tell them! What boy, however morose, could help being affected by this one, with Elsie leaning over the platform and employing the richest of her dialects:

> A coloured soldier is on outpost duty, and it gets a bit thick. So he comes running back at great speed and bumps into an officer.
> "Hey! What's the idea of leaving your post of duty?" demands the officer.
> And the coloured soldier replies: "Oh, Lord, boss, the shells is just raining out there. One went right by my nose."
> Officer: "How did you know it was a shell? Did you see it?"

Soldier: "Did I see it? I seen it twice—once when it passed me—and once when I passed it."

Just one more story from her inexhaustible fund:

Two Negroes in the guardhouse, talking through the bars to each other. It is Sunday. First Negro: "How long you in foh?" Second Negro: "Three months."
"What foh?"
"Stealing from the captain. How long you in foh?"
"Three days."
"What foh?"
"Killing a sergeant."
"How come you get only three days foh killing a sergeant while I get three months foh only stealing from a captain?"
"Oh, they takes me out on Wednesday—an' shoots me."

Elsie Janis succeeded because she went through the whole experience overseas in the essential spirit of a "regular American girl." She asked no favours that she could not a hundred times repay in service; she paid her own way except for meagre personal expenses, in the spirit of true sport, spending herself recklessly in the cause in which she was little less than a fanatic. And all the entertainers in France have a right to part of her glory, which she would be the last to begrudge them, for all shared the same common danger and rose to the glorious opportunities of that unforgettable time.

CHAPTER 12

The Over There Theatre League Enters

Suit the action to the word, the word to the action.
Hamlet.

The spontaneous outburst of "Americanism" which was set in operation at the Palace Theatre, in April, 1918, did not wane. It developed into a mighty force. The whole American stage and lyceum wanted to go to the front—now—today. And unable to get overseas at once, its members put their forces into immediate action at home. They visited the American camps; they threw their energies into the Liberty Loans; they took the lead in all the war drives for funds to relieve suffering. And they took hold enthusiastically of the red tape whose unwinding would enable them to join the rapidly increasing American troops in France.

The difficulties that began to develop in America—the almost insurmountable obstacles that beset Mr. McLane and the organisers of the Over There Theatre League—were but replicas in miniature of the stupendous problems that confronted the government at Washington. Here was the urgent call from General Pershing for entertainers from "home;" here were the thousands of professionals and semi-professionals volunteering their service. Here, too, were the multitudinous restrictions and complications of civil and military authorities—the inquiries, conferences, documentary exchanges, and the whole gamut of routine which necessarily develops under war conditions. The government problems were of first consequence—they must have the right of way—all else was secondary.

The difficulties met by all the subsidiary agencies and their cooperating organisations were of minor consequence when placed in the historical light of achievement itself. Nevertheless, it is well to give an insight into the details, precautionary measures, and infinite patience required in even so comparatively limited a service as that of recruiting entertainers for the army. The response to the McLane-Ames appeals had "swamped" all the channels for securing passports, for securing transportation, and for all government decisions. The theatrical world stood ready to go to France *en masse* and now. How could it be absorbed? What regulations would it be necessary to set up? What were to be the military restrictions? These are but a suggestion of the thousand and one points of detail to be carried through.

Following the Palace Theatre meeting, there ensued an inevitable period of roughing out the great work ahead through committee meetings and through what army officers call the "exploitation of documents" for the purpose of meeting all the requirements of the government. These documents were mainly the elaborate questionnaires sent to the volunteers, to be filled out with a complex and bewildering variety of information. Each item of this information was designed to settle some practical question of eligibility for overseas service.

The number of counts on which the most ardent and apparently the most eligible entertainers could be disqualified was extensive and seemed to increase weekly. There was the question of the draft, which cut out all the young and able-bodied men entertainers at the start, and which always kept back a large number of men, on the borderland of physical fitness. Then there was the question of nationality, raised by our Allies, a ban which cropped out most unexpectedly. It was a prime deterrent, especially when a drastic interpretation was made excluding even American citizens, one of whose parents had been born in an enemy country. There was also the later ruling forbidding husbands and wives to go over and the ruling holding up sisters who had brothers in the service, which was applied with varying strictness.

Above and beyond all, there was the condition which can be described only as the great drought in passports. It was the time when every ton of shipping was being concentrated not merely on the army but on the arm of the service most crucially needed in France, the infantry, plus only the bare necessities of its equipment. While artillery, quartermaster supplies, and even engineering equipment were held up on the docks to make more room for fighting men, there was small opportunity of finding places for actors and entertainers, who had so far no status with the army but their own noble and patriotic desire to serve.

The Over There Theatre League thus opened its career in the face of an inexorable situation. The actor was willing and ready to sacrifice a season if a decision could be made to sail tomorrow, or even next week or next month, but could not face the uncertainty and delay of many weeks during which all arrangements for the coming season had to be postponed and all opportunities for the immediate future killed. Hence, with the best intentions in the world and after urgent appeals to be sent "over there," many of the great of the American theatre had to forgo their hope to serve their country in France—only to turn more energetically to serving the soldiers in America. Thousands waited eagerly, as week after week passed by, for the favourable decision from Washington which must sooner or later come and break the passport ban. The first volunteers among the "over there" entertainers waited weeks at their own expense, with spirits undismayed, already trained, contracted, equipped, inoculated, and ready for the great war circuit.

Here enters another personality, one of the leaders of the American stage—James Forbes, dramatist. It was in May, 1918, that this inspiring leader took command of the Over There Theatre League. Mr. Forbes accepted the title of Chairman of the Program Committee of the Over There Theatre League, but his duties could better be described by some such title as *Czar*, Lord High Protector, Man-of-All-Work, and Chief of Staff, with other innumerable duties thrown in. Mr. Forbes confessed that he preferred the simpler but much more expressive title of Chief Doormat.

This is Mr. Forbes's own outline of his induction into the service. Telephone conversation between Ames and Forbes, as reported from Forbes's end:

"How are you?" said Ames.

"Well," said I.

"And strong?" said he.

"Yes," said I.

"That's good," said he.

"And how is the League?" said I.

"Fine. I've decided to turn it over to you," said he.

And never a word said I. My motor wasn't transmitting.

"I'm going to be its godfather," said he.

"And what am I going to do?" said I.

"The work," said he.

Mr. Forbes is a man of vigorous ideas and action. He had already got into war work long before the Palace Theatre meeting, having volunteered for the War Camp Community Service, and with Mr. Marc Klaw and others, helped to put on its feet back in October, 1917, an organisation later perfected by the War Camp Community Service and the "Y" entertainment section, whereby the soldiers in home camps should organise amusement companies themselves. Mr. Forbes went down to Washington and volunteered his services to the Government. In the late fall he instituted at the War Department a card index system covering all the talent in the American Army—a stupendous undertaking in itself. General Kuhn, Commanding General of Camp Meade, who later commanded the Seventy-Ninth Division in France, cordially supported the Forbes plan, as it paralleled very closely the organisation General Kuhn had himself witnessed on his recent visit to the British Army front in France.

The first service of Mr. Forbes for the Over There Theatre League was to set up a practical plan for ascertaining the exact requirements of the army. His plan was to give the volunteers an effective and realistic trial on this side before sending them abroad. The League found an ideal stage ready for this purpose in the big hall at Ellis Island, where thousands of sailors from destroyers, mine sweeping, and home fleets constituted a steady audience with just the kind of criticism that was needed for "try-outs." Every Thursday night a new group of volunteers was tried on the ever-willing crowd of "gobs" at Ellis Island and the results were almost always decisive. This was another instance where the navy served the army. Mr. Forbes soon discovered what he had long suspected—that the boys reserved their greatest welcome for the highest type of acts.

Among the whistles, cheers, and yells with which this audience of more than two thousand fighting men greeted the opening of every performance, many professionals discovered that they were just beginning to learn what a stage reception could be. As the program progressed the jazz dances, monologists, and comedy acts were received with discriminating good humour. The men joined in one of those great chorus songs of the war, which can be heard in all their beauty only as the great surge of men's voices swings up to the platform. This was usually the time to put on a "straight" singer.

There were thrills in those early days, but life for most of the volunteers seemed to be just one delay after another. All the volunteering, all the training, all the sacrifices were dependent on one little piece of paper with a big seal in the corner. June passed and July, and still there were no passports. The German drive was at its zenith; the Marines were fighting their dogged way through Belleau Wood; the American Army was still in the transport crisis; and the actors, a modest, almost forgotten force, were still desperately holding a line along Broadway. There is a limit to the time that even an actor, famed as he is for happy improvidence, can live without working. And this limit approached, arrived, and passed for many of the first volunteers. "There were noble souls among them," says Mr. Forbes, in relating the experiences of those trying days. "No one will ever realise the great heart of our American stage folk. They were true patriots."

Optimism impelled alike the successful actor and the still struggling one to give up all in the hope that the ever receding "next week" would see them sail. One man sold his home, his car, and most of his worldly goods, and took a small room in town, spending the weeks of scorching July weather in waiting for the opportunity for which he had sacrificed everything. There is an end to New York engagements, even for the strongest headliner in vaudeville, and after playing the Palace Theatre and the "subway circuit" as much as they would stand, one actor after another found himself stranded in the metropolis in midsummer, a very unenviable *rôle* to play among a city full of friends who would keep exclaiming: "Why, I thought you were going to France!" With fine spirit they pitched in and filled dates around the camps, but the "neither here nor there" sensation was a grievous tax on the temperament of the artist.

An unexpected revelation of the questionnaires was the large number of vaudevillians and professional people who were of German, Austrian, or German-Jewish parentage. The regulations in this case were very strict. They required that neither the actor nor his parents should be of alien citizenship. The first quartet to start for France was crippled by the elimination, right at the very pier, of the perfectly loyal American citizen of Austrian parentage, who was to act as their accompanist. This bore as hard on sons and daughters of German-Alsatians and German-Poles as on *bona-fide* Germans; it produced heartburning complications without number.

All this time the volunteers who had passed muster were being inoculated and photographed and measured for their uniforms; equipment was bought and kits got together and made ready; and the long list of entertainers was grouped and regrouped into the teams of little units which it was hoped would harmonize into complete program companies over there. The uniforms evoked a varied reaction. "Well, I should say," said one young lady, "the boys will certainly be heroes to face us now." The general remark was, "I am willing to do this for my country, but for no one else." But the real feeling, as Mr. Forbes and many others can testify, was a new "pride in belonging," which a real uniform, a uniform that already has a tradition and history behind it, cultivates above all other agencies of comradeship and service.

While the passport drought continued unabated, the "fathers" at Washington provided one or two surprise rulings which were all in the day's work in running the War, but which nearly split the little army of actors, already impatient to the point of exhaustion, from end to end. The most interesting of these bombshells was the celebrated "husband and wife" ruling, which descended in July, 1918, and forbade both members of that well-known partnership to go to France with the same army. Mr. Forbes explains:

> Vaudeville, as all those who know it understand, is a hopelessly domestic profession. The League's lists were at that time crowded with husbands and wives, many of whom had given up all their contracts and even sold or leased their goods, in the early expectation of going overseas.
>
> The government ruling came on Saturday, and after the League office in the Little Theatre had descended to a state of complete consternation, it was decided to give these hopeful couples at least a peaceful Sunday before breaking the news to them. Even then they hung on, and divorces were really considered if that was the only way to get over.

Eventually, after a frantic exchange of cables, Mr. Carter obtained rescindment of this order direct from General Pershing, and hope again came to the Little Theatre offices.

These cold statements seem trivial now, but every problem involved men and women—individuals used to quick decision and movement on a moment's notice. No one was used to war conditions or war regulations. The changes in rulings and consequent delays during that intolerably hot summer made it the most trying time in the lives of those connected with the entertainment work, but the entertainers met the trials bravely and well.

The first volunteers under the Over There Theatre League sailed on July 31, 1918, the last on May 16, 1919. The league ceased its activities on July 15, 1919.

CHAPTER 13

A Bombardment of Songs and Fun

No pains, sir; I take pleasure in singing sir
Twelfth Night.

The spirit of 1918 brought the severest test of the Allied cause since the first great German host was beaten back at the Marne in 1914. In this crucial period, when America was bending every effort to send troops to France, and while every ship that went over had every available foot of space crammed with troops, leaving even essential equipment to be gathered on the other side, Mr. McLane continued to augment the ranks of his entertainers. It was General Pershing himself who had said to Mr. Carter: "*Morale is a state of mind upheld by entertainment.*"

Between March and July, 1918, Mr. McLane responded to the emergency by sending over artists, independent of the Over There Theatre League, including Mr. and Mrs. Forrest Rutherford of Denver, among the most successful of the early vocalists; Myrtle Bloomquist, the musical comedy star of *O Lady, Lady*, fame, with her happily chosen "side partner" at the piano, Lillian Jackson; Neysa McMein, the painter and illustrator (who added actress and playwright to her *rôles* in France); James Stanley, the New York concert *basso*, accompanied by his wife, a brilliant pianist and a favourite overseas, and by Miss Geraldine Soares, reader and impersonator extraordinary; George Warwick, artist and chalkologist, who drew and chalked cheerful pictures on every front, and downed language bars by drawing whimsical Americanisms for half a score of the motley nationalities on the Allied battle line; the immortal Joe Lorraine, banjoist; the Hoyt sisters, "Smiling Sue and Silly Sally," who sang everything from Yvette Guilbert's chansons to "Kaiser Bill's a Bum;" little Mary Seller, the Irish harpist, and Grace

Kerns, soloist at St. Bartholomew's, New York, the first American girls to stir the deathless echoes in the underground citadel at Verdun; Walter Damrosch, greatest of American symphony conductors; the St. Louis Quartet, composed of Charles Flesh, Ernest Collins, Robert Stark, and Wallace C. Neidringhaus, all residents of the Mound City and far and away the most popular male quartet that ever came to France; Sarah M. Willmer, the plucky Chicago singer who subjected herself to every hardship an artist could stand, including drenchings from the weather and gas from the Germans; Paula Lind Ayers, the girl who sang the shell-shock patients to health again; Tsianina, daughter of a real Cherokee Indian chief, who danced and sang to the music of her forefathers; and finally, omitting many, many others, a splendid little army of unselfish and devoted troubadours. Miss Margaret Wilson herself, the president's daughter, who went over with her singing teacher, Mr. Ross David.

These are some of the actors in the drama. When the "Big Push" began in earnest with the great German drive on March 21, 1918, and the whole American military policy was accelerated to the utmost limit to stop what looked like a very imminent disaster to the Allied cause, whatever regularity there had been in the lives of the entertainers disappeared. In the swift movements of troops from training areas to trenches and from one section of France to another, the entertainment policy was adapted "to play anywhere and everywhere" the men might be, whether this happened to be on the road the night before they went into action, or the morning after they came out.

The S. O. S. still remained a stable area, though new camps and veritable cities, like the great 60,000 population camp around Gievres, were growing up weekly along the American lines of communication. Before this enormous multiplication of arriving troops and of new camps and troop centres, the number of entertainers seemed microscopic in the face of the huge forces which had suddenly set themselves in motion. The organisation adapted itself to conditions as best it could, especially in administering specified areas by the regional system instead of trying to follow specific units of rapidly moving troops, and it fell to the lot of every entertainer who was in France during this ominous period to play as he could under any and all circumstances that developed.

The experiences of Mr. and Mrs. Forrest Rutherford, who went over in the middle of March, illustrate splendidly what two good-humoured, thoroughly human entertainers could do for the American

Army at this stage of the War. Mr. Rutherford was a business man, to whom singing was a delightful and constantly practiced avocation. He had had many years' experience in concert singing in the West, particularly in and around Denver, his home town. His wife had been an accompanist and a very competent musician before her marriage. Mr. Rutherford had a repertoire of droll readings and impersonations which he sandwiched in liberally throughout the program. The Rutherfords usually ended with an uproarious concert in which the audience was the dominant factor, and the test of a big evening—"Did you boys have a good time?"—was answered in a thunderous affirmative through song after song under Mr. Rutherford's energetic and contagious leadership.

The Rutherfords early in April went straight up to the Toul sector. Throughout all that long spring, when the veteran divisions were battling in the practice sectors north and northwest of that great fortress town, they wove a network of shows and traced out a tireless itinerary of cheer which kept pace, as much as one entertainment party could do it, with the rapidly shifting troop movements of the time.

They gave their show "anywhere"—sometimes in real huts and real halls. Usually when they drove into a town in their three-ton truck, it was simply a case of stopping in the largest open space and telling the boys, subject to censorship by the officers, that there was going to be a show in an hour. They then went to the nearest hut, if there was one, or to any house in sight with a roof on, prinked up a bit, foraged for a meal, and came back to that particular puddle in the sea of mud where they had left the truck. Here already a crowd of doughboys would have gathered with some live spirit beating out ragtime on the piano—it seemed a shame to disturb them by an entertainment.

Mrs. Rutherford struck the first notes of "On the Road to Mandalay"—and the boys were convinced that a real show was on. Soon the whole town, French soldiers, civilians, and the usual troop of black-eyed youngsters, re-enforced the silent ranks of appreciative Americans clustered around the truck. Then Mr. Rutherford would lean over the side of the truck and tell some real American stories. During the handshaking farewells which followed, some honest-to-goodness doughboy would exclaim fervently: "Gee, I'd rather hear the old stories well told than all the new ones in the world!"

The chauffeur cranked up the truck and they slowly oozed through the mud and lurched around the corner toward the next town, with the strains of "Glory, Glory, Hallelujah," or some other splendid refrain, ringing in their ears from hundreds of manly throats. The Rutherfords, clinging to each other and to the jolting piano, wiped the tears from their eyes and declared: "This is the greatest life in the world!"

What experience could be more romantic than that of Joe Lorraine and his bull-necked banjo? "Smiling Joe" came over in April, 1918, with a party of secretaries on the S. S. *Victoria*. Being a "one-man show," he simply slung his banjo over his shoulder on arriving in Paris and limped away. He stayed in France five months and gave over six hundred performances, not counting the times when he gave a show "every time a boy who saw the banjo over his back asked him if he could play." Joe's method was to go up with the troops wherever they went, eating and sleeping where he could, and playing and singing almost literally all the time. Imagine him sitting on a fallen tree trunk in the Argonne, for instance, while an artillery unit under camouflage lay in a circle all around him and joined in the choruses of the Southern lullabies and the old-fashioned *coon* songs, which never sound quite so beautiful as when they are twanged on a real old banjo.

The best proof of Joe's travels was this banjo. All over it on every inch of space there were scrawled and scribbled and printed the names of his auditors. He had over 700 names on the banjo, almost all of them fighting men from the front line. There is the name of the young American captain, for instance, who fired the first shot from an American gun on captured German soil; there is a Senegalese; there is the Marchioness of Marshfield, said to be the richest woman in France; there are privates from Dallas, Texas, and Cohoes, New York, and Walla Walla, Washington; and in the midst of a little white circle there is the name of Sergeant Charles Cunningham.

You may not know the story of Sergeant Cunningham—it is one of the prize stories of his division, but the reporters did not get hold of it. While out with a raiding party in No Man's Land he came upon eight Germans. He shot four of them and wounded three others before a hand grenade laid him low; and then he crawled back. Joe Lorraine met him in a hospital and was told by the doctor that his wounds were fatal. Cunningham, smiling, stretched out his hand to grasp Lorraine's and said: "String up the old banjo and let us have a tune, Buddy."

Joe sung a little Negro lullaby. Then Cunningham asked for another, and Joe played it. The nurse held the boy up, and, the doctor

Thomas S. McLane

Winthrop Ames

James Forbes

Johnson Briscoe

helping him to guide the pen, Cunningham wrote his signature falteringly in a little unoccupied space at the head of the banjo. There was a smile on the boy's face as he was laid back on his cot, but there were tears in the eyes of the nurses. And the smile was still on Cunningham's face as he died.

There is a little white space still left about Cunningham's name, the only vacant space left now on either side of the head of Lorraine's war banjo. "I never again played the tune Cunningham asked for," said Lorraine, "without looking at that little space and thinking of the smiling hero who 'went west' with the echo of the music still in his ears."

Lorraine washed dishes for canteeners, helped find beds for doughboys in Paris, and in various other ways interpreted the word "entertainment" with generous liberality. Although he was lame, and by no means husky in physique, he kept up with the infantry during the Argonne, riding on the ammunition wagons and in the big trucks. Many a terrific jam around a shelled crossroads corner heard the familiar twang of the bull-necked banjo, and as the drivers listened with a weather ear for the well-known whistle of the next German shell they said to one another: "There's that little 'Y' duck with the banjo back there somewhere."

Joe Lorraine was there once too often. One day in the folds and hollows of the captured land there lurked a little too much mustard gas. He didn't know he was gassed, however, until he tried to whistle and found his lips would not pucker, but he could sing and play, and so he went on giving shows. But his face gradually became paralysed on one side. Then he had to give it up and go back to the hospital. At the hospital they told him he had "a narrow squeak," and ordered him to go home as quick as he could get there.

So he came back to America, but he could not remain. In April, 1919, he sailed for France again, and spent three months in the great demobilization centres, returning in July. The next heard of Joe Lorraine was that, not satisfied with being a troubadour in France, he must try Russia also! With one of the early groups of "Y" folk, who went to Archangel to help cheer the lot of the little American force existing there in the dark during the winter of 1918-19, was recorded the name of Joe Lorraine, banjoist and entertainer.

Among those who met and loved Joe Lorraine in France on his wayward journeyings is George Warwick, cartoonist and chalkologist. The two travelled together for a number of weeks. Warwick, like Lor-

THE STAR-SPANGLED BANNER OVERSEAS

raine, was a whole show in himself. He also came over early in June, 1918, and wandered around through the army like a *jongleur* of old France, except that he made pictures instead of songs. Warwick broke down language barriers that singers could not overcome, for everybody understands a picture. He stayed overseas for a year; he drew for the Twenty-Seventh Division at Kemmel Hill and for the Seventy-Seventh Division in the Argonne. He was at St. Mihiel and on the Marne; he worked along the Picardy coast among the naval aviators and the naval base camps, and he was one of the headliners of the "after the war circuit" in Germany. Near Verdun, he entertained 500 men of the Twenty-Sixth Division just before they went into a drive in which only sixty of them came out unwounded.

Warwick gave shows outdoors and in dugouts. He drew the *Kaiser's* picture in every conceivable place where his audience could throw things at it. Meals were irregular and sleep was a luxury. Like many Montmartre artists in Paris, who draw their pictures on the walls of the Chat Noir and many another restaurant for a free meal, Warwick encountered rolling kitchens on the front where the cook demanded examples of his art for a hand-out of army beans. "I gave them all the pictures they wanted," said Warwick in telling of it afterwards, "even if the cook was a horseshoer by trade."

Warwick's performance generally began with pictures of the *Kaiser* in comic relief, with his numerous progeny; then, in a more serious vein, he drew striking sketches of President Wilson, General Foch, the inimitable Teddy, always a favourite with the soldiers, and other war-time figures. Then he came to even more important subjects—he could probably draw food better than any living artist.

"Now let's have a banquet," he would say. "What will you have, boys?"

"Draw a plate of hot biscuit," shouted a boy from Alabama, and, presto! there they were. Then George would draw roast chicken, waffles, salad, and strawberry shortcake with whipped cream and great big red strawberries. The boys would yell at every stroke of the chalk, for these were the days when army stew, slum, corn willy, and other famous jokes of 1920 and after were not jokes at all, but day-by-day realities with nothing else in sight. After Warwick had finished up with ice cream and a cup of real American coffee, somebody would shout from the audience: "Say, there's one thing you have forgotten. You ought to have a sign over that banquet, 'For officers only!'"

Then as a grand climax—and this was a special hit in Germany—

Warwick would draw a transport flying the Stars and Stripes with the Statue of Liberty looming out of the west. Did you ever hear real applause—terrific applause? You never did unless you heard the doughboys at this moment. In the midst of this tumult he would draw the "little gray home in the west," or that little house in Dixie, or Indiana, or Cape Cod, or wherever the majority of longings among the audience were being directed in those long, lonesome days. There was a moment of tense silence—then deep gulps and an outburst of thousands of voices in song and cheers swept over the crowd.

Neysa McMein was an artist, too. She was another early June product who played with special diligence and success along the hospital circuit through the summer of 1918. Miss McMein was a real artist—not only with her crayon and brush, but as an impresario, actress, playwright, and scenario writer, all of which vocations she employed to delight the doughboys. Her principal side partners during the summer were Anita Parkhurst Wilcox and Jane Bulley. These clever women put on one of the most original shows the boys had the good luck to see.

And this is how they did it: They arrive in a village, let us say, just as the band is concluding "The Star-Spangled Banner" at evening retreat. Miss McMein jumps out of the little car, as the groups are just unstiffening from "Attention."

"Boys, do you want a show tonight?"

Nobody had expected them. But the doughboys are quick on a trigger. "We sure do!" comes back the response from the surprised camp.

A show on the spot results. It is first necessary to find a place to give it. Somebody calls, "Fall in!" About 500 men follow along through the winding streets to an old barracks suggested as a good "theatre." By the time the crowd reaches the theatre it is about three times too large. So Miss McMein orders: "About face!" and leads the way to the village square. The mob heaves an old manure wagon up in front of a big barn door. The artists nail their sketching papers and movie curtain to the barn door, put two boxes on the wagon for table and chairs—and all is set for the show.

Like the offerings of Homer for the Greek villagers in ancient times, the show added a little at every performance. Its usual title was *Orlando Slum, a Man of Mystery*. It was an amateur play cast in a movie scenario art form. Mrs. Wilcox was the heroine, Susie Coughdrop of Bird Centre, Iowa, U. S. A., a lady of large eyes and many adventures. Miss McMein was the villainous vamp and the rest of the cast was selected from the audience. Miss McMein, cruising around among the audience, suddenly pounces on a blushing victim and calls loudly:

"Jane, can we have a villain with blue eyes?"

"Stand him up so I can look him over," replies Jane.

Needless to state, 500 brother soldiers are perfectly ready to "stand him up." Thus Orlando, the Man of Mystery, is found and cast in his part. On the other side of the field Susie Coughdrop calls:

"O, Jane, this one has a lovely profile for a hero—just look."

Mid another uproar, Harold, the Hero, is chosen with loud acclaim. A beard, some make-up, a row of medals, a pair of bone spectacles for the villain, and a red sash for the vamp, and the stupendous plot is ready to unroll. One by one the thrills are reeled off, until at last the vamping villainous lady spy eats corn willy and dies.

One can imagine the way anywhere from 300 to 1,500 men just out of the trenches howled at a performance like this. When Neysa and her *troupe* gave it for the marines—which they did for a month devoted to cornering through the Marne sector—one company of marines followed them for four or five shows in near-by towns and "laughed their heads off" at the last performance as unrestrainedly as at the first. The marines' famous battle hymn, "The Halls of Montezuma," is the greatest tribute the marines can pay to any visiting pal, and it rang out scores of times on the tours of Neysa McMein.

Neysa's principal performance was, of course, her own sketches and *impromptu* drawings of all sorts of things which "came into her head" at the front. She sketched on blank walls and tents; she worked with her chalk by flashlight, candlelight, and searchlight, as well as by intermittent daylight. Also she put on one of the most whimsical and farcical movie productions ever seen on any screen. Windsor McKay drew it. The heroine was "Gertie, the Dinosaur." Gertie had many adventures with the Germans in the war, and her prehistoric temperament unfolded its gargantuan humour through a thrilling series of episodes before the Flood, at the end of which Gertie completely "strafed" the Him and returned to her dinosauric nest chortling in Jabberwockian glee.

Jane Bulley, who accompanied Neysa on some of her tours, tells of a characteristic McMein performance during the hectic midsummer on the Marne:

> The night we played for our pet battery things were expected to happen at any minute, and the major issued us gas masks

directly we arrived. However, it isn't the thing to start anything before dark over there. They decided that if we had our show directly after dinner, even if the Hun meant to get busy that night, we could all be finished before he began.

They let the men congregate in an old barn and they surely were a beguiling crowd of generous enthusiasts. They seemed to be leaking into the building from all directions. As we became accustomed to the dim light, we picked out bunches of them on rafters, heads and shoulders coming through old windows in the back wall, and through cracks high and low on the sides.

What daylight squeezed in round the edges of the men dwindled away before Miss McMein had finished her third sketch. When she came to tackling the handsome young French lieutenant, acclaimed for sacrifice by overwhelming popular opinion, we had to pick out his features with little pocket flashlights. We'll have to 'hand it' to the McMein—all things considered, the resulting 'portrait' wasn't half bad.

After that Gertie pranced on to the scene. Windsor McKay probably didn't have the European front in his mind when he drew the 12,000 pictures that constitute the movie film of *Gertie the Dinosaur*, a great prehistoric monster who cavorted over the landscape trying to behave like a little trained beasty. But 'Gertie' has done her bit in twenty camps already, and is still going strong.

Our pet battery took Gertie straight to their hearts—so warmly indeed, that we had to make a desperate dash back to that camp next day in a Ford that had rheumatic springs and no brakes at all. For it was decreed that Gertie should serve the battery as a mascot. So next morning they took Miss McMein out to the guns with three cans of paint and some brushes that you'd like to have seen anyone offer her back in the States. With the entire battery lined up on the sidelines, she painted violent orange, blue, and green Gerties on six fine big guns.

Some of us watched her operations through a long range glass up in an observation post. By and by we swung the glass over to a point about five miles away where we could see German shells exploding in a little French town that they were tearing to bits. There seemed to be a strange mixture of good nature and nastiness abroad that morning.

Miss McMein's own account of her work is becomingly modest, but an artist certainly deserves success who writes, as she wrote to Mr. McLane in July:

> In my whole life I have never worked so hard nor been so happy. I had no idea of the importance of this job nor of the size of our 'Y' organisation when I came over here. As I told you before I left, my whole idea was service. My plan was to join Margaret Mayo, as she had asked me to do, but when I got here the Paris office had other plans, so with Jane Bulley and another New York artist we've evolved a 'show' of our own, in which we make pictures, dance, sing, show *Gertie, the Dinosaur*, and put on a melodrama—needless to say we have a perfectly magnificent time.
>
> Incidentally, I used to be rather fussy about my work, but here I've made pictures in cow-pastures, on manure wagons, on the walls of hospitals, on operating tables—and usually a barn door or a canteen table—and while this war may have put the jinx on my career as an artist, it has made me a first-class roustabout. I can build an easel or push a piano around with equal ease.

CHAPTER 14

Strenuous Days for the Troupers

*Hang out our banners an the outward walls;
The cry is still, 'They came,'*
                Macbeth.

We have seen the Liberty Quartet, the first entertainment unit to be sent over by Mr. McLane's office split up in the early spring so that the soldiers might make the most of their services. We followed the adventures of Miss Beulah Dodge, who kept on singing long after her voice had succumbed to the climate and who did such splendid work at Aix as canteen worker while she was recovering. We have also seen how Albert Wiederhold went on tour through the First Division with Mary Rochester during the spring and summer. We now find them all through the summer right up with the guns at the front.

The third member of the quartet, John Steel, the *tenor*, is continuing his service by joining forces with two very able musicians, Miss Myrtle Bloomquist, *contralto*, and Miss Lillian Jackson, pianist, forming an ideal little concert troupe called "Three of a Kind." They are playing the front line divisions, specializing on the lines of communication among the railway troops. We see them singing for a heavy artillery regiment in the Verdun sector, in which their concert is given from the flat car on which the big Yankee naval gun is furnishing a magnificent background, while the audience is lined up along the tracks.

Mr. Steel figured with pardonable pride that at least 600,000 soldiers had come within the sound of his voice during the six months he spent abroad. Most of the summer tour of the "Three of a Kind" troupe was spent within fifteen miles of the front line. Over and over again they sang in camouflaged huts two miles or less from the German trenches. On one occasion they used a piano that had been hit only a few days before by a German shell—not to speak of the many pianos which, Miss Jackson said, should have perished in this way.

Mr. Steel went home in the late fall. Miss Bloomquist and Miss Jackson after the Armistice admitted Miss Elsie Stevenson, a very capable violinist, to their little family, and rechristened the party the "Amex Trio." These three girls then entered into another, if less spectacular, chapter of adventures. They were assigned to the Aix-les-Bains Leave Area, where they cheerfully filled in as canteen girls on a "nothing to do until tomorrow" schedule—that is they went on at eight o'clock in the morning and went off sometime near midnight. In the meantime they made all their own evening gowns and kept up their entertainment schedule. At their last performance in Paris in June, 1919, Miss Bloomquist and Miss Jackson were able to claim the record of serving fourteen months as entertainers in France without cancelling a single engagement.

The achievements of the women equalled those of the ancient Spartans. There was the tour of Miss Mary Seiler, the well-known Irish harpist, and Miss Grace Kerns, the petite *soprano* soloist of St. Bartholomew's Church in New York. These two early robins went over in May. Miss Seiler soon became known far and wide on the lines as "The Little Minstrel of the Trenches." Miss Kerns, who stands on a stool when she sings in church and who at home contested with Emma Trentini the title of being the smallest *soprano* in America, sang her way into the doughboys' hearts with her wonderful repertoire of favourites, ranging from "O, Laddie, My Laddie" and the magnificent aria from the second act of *Louise*, to "Dear Old Pal of Mine" and "The Rose of No Man's Land."

We find these two wandering minstrels singing their "ballads, songs, and snatches" up as near the front as women were allowed to go. At one performance an air raid brought the usual precaution of dousing the lights; after the German *Taubes* had passed over, leaving half a dozen explosive souvenirs in close proximity to the barracks. Miss Seller found that one string of her precious harp had been neatly snipped by a flying fragment. It takes more than German shrapnel to put an Irish harp out of business, however, and Miss Seller continued her performance on the remaining strings.

Miss Kerns and Miss Seller were probably the first American girls to give a recital in the immortal citadel at Verdun. The American divisions which passed through Verdun in September, 1918, when it was used as one of the jumping-off places in the Argonne Drive, never forgot these two plucky little troubadours, and went into battle with fragrant memories of the two self-reliant little musicians giving the best of the beauty that was in them on this exposed and ruined front. Miss Kerns came back in the late fall to resume her engagements in New York, but Miss Seller stayed through until June, 1919, and carried the lilt of her harp from Aix-les-Bains and Nice up through the lonelier sectors of the Coblenz front before she finally "called it a war" and came home.

The Hoyt sisters, Grace and Frances, were two American girls, properly and conventionally billed as singers and elocutionists, who went over in July, 1918, but before they had been in France many weeks, became known wherever they went as "Smiling Sue" and "Silly Sally." These sisters had a cosmopolitan quality, coupled with an unusual amount of charm and American "pep," which insured them a tumultuous welcome.

On the steamer the Hoyt sisters sang at the church service; they sang for seasick passengers; they taught some Polish soldiers in the steerage "The Star-Spangled Banner"; they led fifty Bohemian soldiers in the chorus of "Over There;" and when they left the boat, in their most exquisite manner they sang, "Fare Thee Well and if Forever" to the sailors who had steered them safely to French soil. You simply couldn't keep those girls from singing.

The sisters' own accounts of their performances are full of humour and appreciation. This is one of Grace's stories:

> Last week we gave a performance for about 2,000 men who had been in the trenches since February. Our stage was a boxing platform in a beautiful grove. The piano was two tones below pitch. My sister sat on a soap box to play and the army mules broke loose during one of our songs. The men sat and stood in mud at least three inches deep—all who were not festooned in the trees over our heads—but we were all happy. The nights in this part of France are very cool, but we wear our fluffiest white gowns when we sing, for the boys say it's a relief from seeing uniforms. They keep us so busy that we don't have time to feel cold. The old peasants and children—there are of course no young men—come to the outdoor performances and we always do some of their folk songs, so that they can sing the choruses with us.

Another note from one of Grace Hoyt's letters illustrates their wholesome and characteristically American approach to the army:

> They (the soldiers) take a great amount of interest in our gowns. Instead of wearing tight and very short skirts as the French girls do, ours are quite full and fluffy, and the boys tell us frankly they are glad to see some good-looking slippers again.

During this same memorable summer an event occurred which made musical military history. It was the arrival in France of one of America's greatest musicians. Dr. Walter Damrosch, the distinguished leader of the New York Symphony Orchestra, who sailed on June 15th. Dr. Damrosch was imbued with an intense ardour to serve America. His desire was to head a company of musicians, largely recruited in France, who would give a series of orchestral concerts in the large centres along the American line of transportation. This generous plan was made possible by the joint initiative of the Y.M.C.A. and a special fund given by Mr. Harry Harkness Flagler, president of the Symphony Society of New York.

Military exigencies required some readjustment of plans, which finally resulted in enlarging the important service rendered by this international artist. Dr. Damrosch was so honoured by the French that he became the first non-French orchestra conductor to be invited by the French Government to play at the historic Salle de l'Ancien Conservatoire. His concert at this famous hall was part of the festivities on Bastille Day, July 14, 1918. Among the audience were M. Pichon, Minister of Foreign Affairs, M. Alfred Cortot, Acting Minister of Fine Arts, and many other distinguished French and American guests.

An inspiring feature of Dr. Damrosch's concerts in France was the rendition of "The Star-Spangled Banner," as arranged by a committee of American composers headed by Dr. Damrosch and John Philip Sousa. This martial arrangement set the blood of every true American tingling and the heart beating, while the feet kept time. Its thrill swept through the army, it was adopted by the American Navy, and has steadily gained headway among military bands and orchestras throughout the country as the most dignified and artistic rendering of America's great anthem.

Dr. Damrosch was an indefatigable worker. While in France, in addition to his musical services, he continued his generous activity as president of the Society of American Friends of Musicians in France, an organisation formed for the purpose of obtaining funds to aid French musicians and many foreigners who were studying music in

France, and who had suffered on account of the war. Several months after his election as president more than 65,000 *francs* were sent to the various societies to be distributed among artists in straitened circumstances. Dr. Damrosch thus combined his mission of music to the soldiers with substantial aid to his fellow-musicians in France. Besides his work in France, he gave many concerts in home camps and cantonments in America.

The American Army also had the historically suggestive experience of being entertained by a native American Indian singer, a Cherokee girl, daughter of a former chief of that tribe. Her name was Tsianina. She had been educated at Eufaula Indian School and at Wolf Hall in Denver. Tsianina, or, as the boys delighted to call her because of her proud and erect posture, Princess Tsianina, sang and crooned the old Indian lullabies of her forefathers and did many of the stately Indian dances. There were 15,000 Indians in the American Army, and Tsianina, both in America and overseas, did her best to bring to each and every one of them the message of aboriginal music and culture, to the study and expression of which she has devoted her life.

Tsianina had two brothers fighting in France. Consequently, she could not go over until the rule was abrogated which refused to allow women entertainers in America to go to France if any member of their immediate family was fighting abroad. One of her brothers was killed, and the other, a member of the signal corps, saw action throughout all the major battles.

Another Cherokee girl played Pocahontas to the American Army. This was an Oklahoma girl, Galilohi, whose American name was Anne Ross. It was Galilohi who was chosen to pose for the Zolnay statue of Sequoya, one of her Indian ancestors, who was the inventor of the Cherokee alphabet and one of the great leaders of American Indian culture. Sequoya's statue now stands in the Hall of Fame at Washington, and Galilohi was fittingly chosen to unveil it when it was presented to the public in 1918. The Indian name Galilohi means "one who does things well," and this Indian princess lived up to her ancestral name by singing and dancing for the soldiers of the Ninetieth Division, which contained hundreds of Indian soldiers. She also, as plain Miss Anne Ross, filled in her time as a tireless and diligent canteen worker and a girl of all work.

A distinguished personality of these strenuous days was the eldest daughter of the president. Margaret Wilson went to France on October 23, 1918, after spending the spring and summer touring

JAMES W. EVANS　　GEORGE W. DOYLE　　C. A. BRAIDER　　A. M. BEATTY

throughout camps and army centres at home, singing to more soldiers than have been reached, probably, by any other single entertainer. Her splendid energy and enthusiastic devotion carried her through a similar trip which covered, during the seven months she spent abroad, practically every centre that the American Army was then occupying. It was a remarkable effort by a woman who knew how far the magic of her name and the semi-official character of her mission carried a real message from the American people to the men in France.

Miss Wilson was accompanied by Mr. Ross David, her singing instructor, who had traveled with her on most of her tours throughout America and who was himself an accomplished baritone and genial platform singer. Mrs. David was the accompanist, and this remarkable woman, herself a composer and a poet, raised the task of accompanying Miss Wilson's songs to a very fine art indeed.

Throughout this whole period leading up to the victory (Armistice Day), and on till the last American soldiers left France to return to their homeland, the troupers were in constant action. Through the hospitals and convalescent camps their songs and laughter were ringing. The entertainment forces, now hundreds strong, threw out their barrage of good nature along the lines. What magnificent tales of adventure could be told of this whole loyal army of entertainers if the limitations of space would only allow! Tales of self-sacrifice, fortitude, courage, patience, and all the noblest qualities of manhood and womanhood, but we must now turn to the oncoming invaders under the indomitable James Forbes—the Troupers from the Over There Theatre League.

Joan of Arc Pageant at church near her birthplace

CHAPTER 15

Keeping Step With the Doughboys

O, what men dare do! What men may do!
What men daily do, not knowing what they do
                    Much Ado about Nothing.

It was in the late summer of 1918 that the American Army began to upset the idea that this war could be fought only in the trenches. Wherever the American Army went, open fighting took place—open fighting in which for the first time in the whole War the tide of victory began to set steadily and surely against the enemy. In similar fashion Mr. Forbes and his much-tried volunteers had been forced to "break through" the obstructions back home in America before they could begin their first drive in France. July dragged on; and at length Mr. Forbes, figuratively speaking, addressed his fellow-volunteers in this wise:

> I have told you, you were going to France to act for the soldiers; and yet after thirteen weeks you are still waiting—and still here. This is magnificent, but if it is war, then Sherman was right. And so I am going down to Washington to fight it out on these lines (apologies to General Grant) 'if it takes all summer.'

Thus began the siege of Washington.

The general staff was organising the first strokes of the counter-offensive that stopped the last German drive in the middle of July. But General March found time enough to be interviewed and finally surrender—to Mr. Forbes, General Churchill, then Lieutenant-Colonel Churchill, head of the Military Intelligence Division, signed, sealed, and delivered forty-four actual, authentic, and long awaited passports.

The fact that there were no steamship reservations available was a small obstacle before the accumulated momentum of three months' impatience. To save Mr. Forbes from the imminent danger of being stampeded by his own *troupers*, the Women's Department of the "Y" postponed enough canteeners, and the Men's Department vacated the places of sufficient secretaries to make a little gap in the passage lists on various ships just large enough for the first of the Leaguers to creep in. Thus it was that on July 31, 1918, the first contingent of American players, five in number, to be sent abroad by the Over There Theatre League, set sail, closely followed by twenty-three others. The departure of the first unit was an event—and from then on the invasion of France by the professionals was a constant, forward movement. Mr. Forbes says:

> No one will forget the unique experiences of the early period. One young lady of the first contingent, who shall be nameless, burst into the office of the League at eleven o'clock, three hours before she was to sail. She protested in tears and complete despair that she could not go after all. The office by this time was beyond any reasonable accountability for its actions; so it simply waited dumbly for her to state the trouble.
>
> 'Haven't you been telling me all along,' she said, 'you must have ten things to go to France? Well, I have only nine. Look for yourself,' and she dumped the contents of her handbag on the desk; while she related how she had unpacked her trunk and hand luggage twice and had worried all through a sleepless night, she checked off the following list:
>
> Passports with French and British visas,
> War zone pass,
> Y.M.C.A. certificate of identification.
> Certificates of inoculation and vaccination.
> Orders for steamship tickets,
> Twelve extra passport photographs.
> French and English money,
> Baggage labels,
> Contract with the League and with the Y.M.C.A.,
> League salary card.
>
> The missing item was No. 8, baggage labels, and they were on the excited young lady's trunk!

Fortune, that most fickle and exasperating of stage managers, had piled one anticlimax on another until she bade fair to make the contribution of the American actors' great drama in France one long, heartbreaking rehearsal in America. It must be admitted, however, that when she finally got them cast and on the way to the scene of action, she then proceeded to evolve a series of situations that satisfied the most exacting temperaments among the actors and their soldier audiences. Picture, for instance, the soldiers who were waiting for "real home stuff" greeting the first company that arrived under the banner of the Over There Theatre League. Will M. Cressy and Blanche Dayne were the leaders of this company.

There are very few Americans who have not seen or heard of that most familiar of all American stage classics, *The Old Homestead*. Who does not remember the corn huskings and spelling bees and countrified sagacity of that rock-ribbed old American drama? Who, especially, could forget Cy Prime, the greatest of all story tellers of the cracker barrel brigade, every one of whose stories could be proved "if only Bill Jones were alive!"

Well, Cy Prime was Will M. Cressy, and Will M. Cressy was Cy Prime, and so much has Mr. Cressy mingled himself with his first and greatest characterisation that he still lives on a little New Hampshire farm. He has lived on the same farm, in the same town, with the same wife, for thirty years. He met Blanche Dayne in *The Old Homestead* and they have lived in it ever since. Mrs, Cressy is also the heir of another great American stage tradition. She was—yes, you have guessed it—little Eva in *Uncle Tom's Cabin*, and for six years played the unforgettable part of Rickety Ann in *The Old Homestead*. For twenty years they have played in vaudeville and have carried their country types, born out of their own shrewd observation and their own native hills, to every city in America.

Certainly, then, it was a generous fate which cast these two genuine Americans for the Over There Theatre League's pioneer party, which sailed for France on the S. S. *Megantic* on July 31st. The supporting cast of that little company included three exceptionally able theatrical folks: George Austin Moore, a vaudevillian and Winter Garden star, who had travelled throughout the Orient with Donald Frawley's famous "China Coast Players;" Howard T. Collins, musical director in Victor Herbert's, *The Only Girl, Nobody Home, Very Good Eddie*, and other successes; and last but not least, Helene Davis, a little vaudeville singer who was another of the bright stars to graduate from the first production of *Everywoman*. Later the party received a breezy re-enforcement in the person of Stella Hoban, who had sung her way to success on Broadway in the *Oh Boy* and *Love o' Mike* productions.

On the *Megantic* going over, there were 3,200 boys of the Wildcat Division, National Army boys from the Southern Atlantic States, who later made that division one of the most picturesque units in the American Army. During the nine days' passage the Cressy Company made life exciting even for the Wildcats, and turned up with twelve good generous shows. The company, on arriving in England, had the honour of giving the first regular Over There Theatre League show at the big Eagle Hut in London.

These pioneer leaguers arrived in France on August 20, 1918. Five days later they were headed out along the old Neufchateau-Toul circuit. On the Keith circuit in faraway America the Cressys used to skimp along in the old days with a carload of scenery to put on one sketch; in France they had repertory of a dozen plays and they got along on a suitcase apiece. The most unwieldy property was the inevitable organ, the exact counterpart for a generation back of the familiar sitting-room ornament in *The Old Homestead*. Occasionally there was a piano; and Mr. Collins, who had to live up to his description in the program as "at the piano," kept it as clean of rust and mud as possible under the circumstances. The Cressy Players quite deserved the name of "that dead game bunch." How they made good so emphatically, Mr. Cressy's own words may help to explain. This is how he describes the exciting days of their first trip to the front:

> This is a great route we are playing. I started in my career of crime, via the footlight ladder, about as near the bottom as anyone could. My weekly remuneration, if I could get it, which I couldn't always, was six per week. Now, twenty-five years later, I am getting twelve—and paying expenses out of it. And, in addition, living in such dirt and general filthiness as I did not know existed. I am writing this by the light of a candle in a dirty room in an awful French inn, where the furniture consists of two lame chairs, two beds, and a wounded table. We don't talk the language, and don't have to, but take what they bring us to eat, which is black bread, string beans, carrots, and some kind of meat, the original shape and name of which we do not ask. But at that, there is not money enough in all America to make one of us quit our job. Oh, if you could see what we can do for these boys! We are now playing to men who have been up in the front line trenches in the midst of such hell as you cannot

imagine—hungry, dying, seeing their best friends die at their sides—for weeks and are now back before going at it again. When I start in to talk—I open the show with a 'single'—their faces are drawn and tense. But gradually they begin to relax, the lines go, the smiles begin to come, and then, when I think the time has come, I go after a real, man-sized laugh. I may not get it the first time, but by the time I hand them over to Helene Davis they are feeling better, and from then on the laughter and applause and cheers are such pay as no living player ever received in America. And then, at the end, to see the changed men that go out of the Y.M.C.A. huts—well, God has been good to us to let us have this opportunity.

Mr. Cressy was a great lover of the doughboy. He knew the man who wrote home to America, "I am touring France in an *hommes-chevaux* four-wheeled car;" and the legless doughboy who received a pair of socks as a Christmas present, but proved he had not had his sense of humour amputated by getting up a little presentation ceremony and presenting them to a man who had lost both his hands in the same hospital. With all these lovable, inimitable, fun-loving, and lion-hearted boys, Will Cressy made good. You can see him as he stands with his arms around a group of "your sons and mine," leading the vociferous hymn which was among all other songs the darling of the doughboys' hearts:

"We are, we are the Doughboys,
With the dirt behind our ears;
We are, we are the Doughboys,
Our pay is in arrears;
The Caval-ree, Artil-ler-ree,
And lousy Engineers,
Oh-h they couldn't lick the Doughboys
In a hundred thousand years!"

The Cressy show was a simple affair which, after the company had got into the swing of a circuit, practically ran itself. Will Cressy generally opened the program by stepping to the front of the stage and giving his famous monologue. One of the best features of this monologue was his own little poem, *The Boy Next Door*, for he says in one of his letters:

That is what these kids over here are to me, just the boys next door, and that little poem never failed to make us friends at the start.

Then he would indulge in that famous theatrical sport known as "kidding the set," that is, he would introduce the piano and tell how the only way that last night's show was given was by means of four husky doughboys holding a tarpaulin over the said piano in the midst of a terrific downpour; he presented the various wounded chairs and incapacitated tables serving as furnishings of the New England country home; the scene of the night's drama would likewise be "kidded" into proper perspective.

He would say:

> These two soap boxes are the dear old family sofy, and here is the supper table—imagine it has four legs instead of three—with the old red checked table cloth, and among other things the good old-fashioned New England cream pitcher with real cream for real Yankee coffee.

This was the signal for a deafening outburst, for most American boys who went abroad had by that time forgotten that real milk had ever existed. In the Riviera Leave Area "kidding the set" became a totally different kind of pastime, but none the less a laugh-getter; for the New England homestead had to be played at Nice, Mentone, Cannes, and similar "swell" places, in a room decorated with Louis XIV furniture and gilded French mirrors.

Mr. Moore was a capital singer and an invariable success, and beside his own special part in the performance, he was usually cast for a strong part in the playlet which followed. Almost all the plays were of Mr. Cressy's own writing. Their alluring titles included *Bill Biffin's Baby*, *The New Depot*, *Town Hall Tonight*, and *Wyoming Whoop*.

The Cressy Company was one of the first Over There Theatre League *troupes* to cover the Riviera district after the Armistice. For three months more they continued their unabated war speed of four or five shows a day. From dawn until dark they could be found in the hut, and when the time came for them to start for home late in February, 1919, they left a splendid record of ungrudged and generous service behind them.

Will Cressy had that happy faculty which a great many more actors possess than the world gives them credit for—the ability to get on with the people with whom he was working. This is what he said of his relations with the Young Men's Christian Association:

> Of course, soul saving was entirely out of my line. My religion had always been a good deal like the one white shirt that was issued to me along with my two O. D. shirts. I had it with me all the time but I didn't use it much. But I do not believe there was anybody, man or woman, who saw more of the American soldier boys or the workings of the American 'Y' in France than Mrs. Cressy and I. For seven and a half months we banged and bumped around the eastern front, playing at from three to seven different camps a day. We played at over four hundred different camps. We played to something over eight hundred thousand boys. And all under the auspices of the Y.M.C.A.. And if we do not know the organisation, I don't know who does. To put the facts in one small bundle, I want to say that anybody who finds fault with the Y.M.C.A. as an organisation is mighty mean or mightily mistaken.

None of these actor folk, least of all modest old Bill Cressy, want to be called heroes. In Mr. Cressy's case a wreath of honour should be placed upon his reluctant brow. Like many of his comrades, he went into the gas zone whenever his job called him there. He was gassed, like many others, but how badly he did not realise until almost a year later when the axe he was wielding on his New Hampshire farm slipped and made a deep gash in his leg. The gas poisoning in his system then operated on this surface cut and brought about an infection which it may take an indefinite period to heal. It is as honourable a wound as any soldier endured in the cause which he went overseas to serve.

But for the fact that this narrative has of necessity been constructed in a series of parallel lines, along which the players in this great drama seem to lead a much more consecutive kind of life, independent of one another, than was really the fact, the adorable and whimsical career of Margaret Mayo would have flashed across these pages long ago. At one time or another this energetic little playwright and actress met everybody on, the circuit and everybody met her. She took over "The Mayo Shock Unit." It goes without saying that the author of *Polly of the Cu-cus*, *Baby Mine*, and *Twin Beds* had a sound idea as to what would amuse the American soldier. Certainly her company was a splendid witness of her instinct for the right people in the right place. It was a great company that could include, beside Miss Mayo, two such feminine stars as Elizabeth Brice and Lois Meredith.

Elizabeth Brice is the girl who, just as in a novel, stepped out of obscurity one night into the satin slippers of the star—one night when Grace Van Studdiford was taken suddenly ill—saved the performance, and became an unmistakable star herself. She twinkled her way to the reputation of one of the most roguish and fetching musical comedy stars of the day.

Lois Meredith came to Broadway from the Alcazar Stock Company of San Francisco, but didn't stay there long, for one of the road companies of *Peg o' My Heart* claimed her talents in the name part; then she went on to more fame in the movies. The men included Will Morrissey, the famous vaudevillian who has recently been Miss Brice's partner in *Buzzin' Around*; Thomas J. Gray, the vaudeville comedian who sang himself to fame with the song, "Any Little Girl That's a Nice Little Girl Is the Right Little Girl for Me," and who has written over 200 playlets and short stage pieces; and W. Raymond Walker, pianist, music publisher, and accompanist.

When "The Mayo Shock Unit" went "*trouping* with the troops," it strove to play straight to the doughboys. The *troupe* played for more than ten weeks in the thick of the steady but terribly costly advance of the American Army. Miss Mayo herself gives a typical setting of these performances in a passage from her breezy and very personal little book, *Trouping for the Troops*. (This book is given in full at the end of this one, after the Appendix). They had arrived in the midst of a forest. Although there were thousands of American troops within a few miles, the encampments were so densely camouflaged in a thick woods that from her own little lookout absolutely nothing could be seen of human occupancy.

> Each day our local secretary would take us in a car to some thicket where within twenty minutes we would have such an audience as none of us shall probably ever see again. Sometimes we would mount a truck for our performances, for wagons, artillery, and horses were also concealed in these woods, but more often we would play on the ground. The officer in command would give the order for the first few hundred boys to lie flat, those behind them were permitted to kneel, those at the back could stand, and those who were 'left over' would 'shinney' up the trees like squirrels and drape themselves across the branches and hang suspended in strained attitudes during the entire

show. If we happened to be playing in a young forest we were sometimes almost dizzy with the swaying of the slender saplings waving back and forth under the weight of human bodies. Sometimes our performance would be cancelled or cut short by the men to whom we were playing being suddenly ordered forward. On one occasion when our conductor had happened to leave us to the colonel of the regiment, who had volunteered to send us home in his car, the whole division was ordered forward in the midst of our performance. The colonel had no alternative but to move with them. We were obliged to walk to the nearest railway station and beat our way 'home' huddled together on a meat chest in a box car. We arrived about midnight, hungry and chilled. As we picked our way through the mud and the darkness up the hill toward the barracks, our musician drew his foot out of a hole and paused long enough to remark that he was sick of life. He didn't care whether his gas mask fitted or not. . . . But the next morning we were all going back down the hill in the sunlight with the despised gas masks and helmets—off toward Verdun.

The Mayo party gave from start to finish a light-hearted vaudeville show, a regular "little night at home" by itself. Will Morrissey told stories and played the fiddle, Tommy Gray sang, Lois Meredith danced and sang her song-hits, and Miss Mayo herself resumed her career as a comedienne to put on a bright little informal act all by herself. Also there was usually a skit in which everybody took part. Miss Mayo never claimed to have the latest jokes. "The old jokes well told," says Miss Mayo, "are better than all the new jokes on earth."

Maybe the best chance the company had to see how the boys felt about it was the one time they played in a real theatre up near Argonne. It was crowded to the roof with buck privates and *poilus*, shoulder to shoulder. The *poilus* were quiet during the time-worn gags from back home. Will Morrissey, with his vaudeville jokes, got only a polite murmur from them. Tommy Gray, with his alfalfa whiskers, amused them very mildly. Pretty Lois Meredith won real but sedate appreciation; and even Elizabeth Brice, singing "Buzz Around, Buzz Around," with all the pep in the world, was welcomed quietly, so far as the French half of the audience went.

But the doughboys! The doughboys made up for all that. Not since the time when the theatre was divided into three parts had that gallery so resounded! Whistling! Clapping! Stamping of feet! But the next morning while the *troupe* was at breakfast, a delegation of French visitors, including the mayor of the town, called upon them. They wanted, they explained, through an interpreter, to compliment the company upon the most excellent performance of the night before, and to present their profound apologies for the rudeness to which the players had been subjected. They were grieved to the heart that there should have been whistling during such a charming production.

And so the Mayo Shock Unit weaves throughout the army its web of cheer and encouragement. Its members sing one day in a base hospital. On another they make a dash to Paris at a gala show at the Tuileries Gardens; next day they play at a barge canal, at a little camp behind the lines where a lonely service unit has just finished putting up a little platform for the first entertainment they have ever had; next day they are in the midst of the front, playing in a barn somewhere south of Montfauçon; another day they are in a nice little theatre just as far front, but, to their amazed eyes, having all the appurtenances, footlights, dressing rooms, and real scenery of an up-to-date playhouse; now they are playing in the drenching rain under a camouflaged stone rest-billet for the forward artillery; now they play for the gas units, and afterward eat a friendly meal in the gas chamber itself, an ugly little structure which looks like an iron-lined hogshead, but which their presence makes as bright and cheery as the snappiest cabaret in Paris.

In late October or November, 1918, they make a triumphal little tour through the rest areas and leave cities of eastern France. While they are there, Margaret Mayo's presentiment that the war would be over before they got back to the front comes true. Late in November the little company breaks up, a shock unit no more, but a group of individuals who have given abundantly.

Chapter 16

Pushing Up To the Front

To be generous, guiltless, and of free disposition is to take those things for bird bolts that you deem cannon bullets.
Twelfth Night.

It is said that the only complaint Marshal Foch and the Allied staff ever made of the American Army was, "You can't hold them back." That, too, was the only real trouble with the actors—they wanted to play right up to the German trenches.

There never was a group more thoroughly expressive of the American "never-say-die" spirit. The streets of Paris soon began to look as familiar as "dear old Broadway." Here on this August afternoon in 1918 we find our old friends—Irene Franklin of "Redhead" fame, and her husband, Burt Green. Here, too, are Corinne Francis and Tony Hunting, likewise twin luminaries in married stardom. They are just starting on a conquest which is to result in an unconditional surrender of the armies. They sailed on August 5, 1918.

Stage folk, when confronted by the harlequinade of getting about in this bizarre daylight world, are the greatest satirists in creation; and Irene's account of what was perhaps the most exasperating voyage of any made by members of the Over There Theatre League is a little classic voyage of satirical humour. Miss Francis and Mr. Hunting, by the way, had started two days before and were spared all this. Miss Franklin says:

> We left on the S. S. *Quilpue*. It was her maiden trip across the Atlantic. Well, finally, to skip a lot, we arrived at a port somewhere near the North Pole (it was only Scotland, but that's near enough). The harbour looked like a Russian toy shop gone mad. All the ships were covered with bright screaming camou-

flage. Not a single colour was omitted.

'Now, look here,' I said to Burt Green, 'if we are going to stay in this place two days, I'm going to give some shows,' so we went ashore and found a theatre which we rented. Then I asked the captain if he would wigwag to the captains of all the boats in the harbour and ask if their men could come to the show. I guess that was the first time that a program with all the acts and names of the performance was announced in real shipshape sailor fashion. All the captains except one agreed. That one commanded a special mother ship to submarines or something of the kind and everybody was strictly kept off her mysterious decks. Everybody? Well, now listen.

That afternoon I hired a tug, and Mr. Green and several of the other entertainers went out to that ship. The stern captain came to the side and said nobody could come aboard. He looked so sorry, that I thought I might take a chance, so, standing on the rope ladder, we started one of the strangest shows that you ever saw on sea or land. I don't know what watch it was, but before we finished everybody was watching us. Finally, just as I had thought, the stern captain relented and I led a troop of boys to the back deck, where I shut my eyes and said I wouldn't tell what I'd seen, and then for about a half an hour we gave a regular show.

Irene Franklin and Burt Green made a remarkable team, and the fact that Miss Franklin's physician had warned her of a nervous breakdown a few weeks before they started for France only made her work the harder. After a short period out on the front line circuit, they met Tony Hunting and Corinne Francis. The four of them, "The Broadway Bunch," put on a combined show during the big weeks of the St. Mihiel offensive. They were playing just south of Verdun when that offensive got under way, having just "detrained" in the midst of the Woevre Wood, all loaded down shoulder high with bedclothes, costumes, gas masks, helmets, make-up, and other equipment. "We looked like a couple of caravans," says Miss Francis, "as we rolled off the train, but our entrance got a big Yankee laugh and that made our aching limbs a lot less tired."

A vivid idea of the kind of show these four clever entertainers were giving may be had from the account of an enthusiastic soldier critic in the *Plane News*, a weekly sheet issued at a big aviation centre.

There are shows and there are shows, and there are just productions. The true classification of the 'Redhead' show, however, is that it is one of the biggest and greatest productions on the stage in the A. E. F. And the most remarkable thing about it is that only four people make up the entire cast. Irene ranks first; she is ably accompanied at the piano by her husband, Burt Green, who also is the single-handed orchestra for the other big part. Miss Corinne Francis and Tony Hunting are real comedians. The curtain rises if their stand happens to be in a place where such a thing is available. Burt Green is at the piano, and after they hear his first selection the audience usually wishes that the evening program might be entirely musical. But Corinne and Tony soon cause this feeling to disappear and create an uproar. Their comedy is about as genuinely American 'as they can make 'em.'
Miss Francis displays fine talent with instrumental and vocal selections and Tony clogs himself up into further fame. When this couple has finally satisfied the bench warmers and escaped from the continuous cry of 'Encore' Miss Irene reappears as the little 'Redhead' in bloomers. It is impossible to describe the effect of her song and expression. Time flits by all too quickly, and almost ere one has had a chance to appreciate fully her splendid effort, the curtain has separated the audience from the finest entertainment that ever struck France.

This is straight-from-the-shoulder doughboy criticism. And the fact that it deals with superlatives is no reason why it should not be applied to many another show, for in the generous atmosphere of France every show that really made a hit was "the best that ever came over."

Like their teammates, Miss Francis and Mr. Hunting gave an informal and extremely adaptable vaudeville show, in which either partner could do almost anything people generally do in vaudeville, from playing musical instruments to dancing and singing. Hunting and Francis so fell in love with the work that they decided to stay over as long as there was any work to do; and as they gradually became veterans they accumulated in an unusual degree the store of experience which was life's greatest compensation overseas.

Perhaps their most unique show, best illustrating their exuberant generosity and good will, was given one day when their car overtook an ammunition train of fifty-eight motor trucks. These had pulled up

DOUGHBOY MASQUERADERS AT COBLENZ

REHEARSING THE HEAVY VILLAIN

by the side of the road for a few minutes' rest and overhauling. About four hundred men were in the convoy, and a lot of them were in bathing as the entertainers came by. The boys spotted Hunting and Francis at once as entertainers. There were cheerful greetings, then somebody shouted, "Can't you give us a show?" And Corinne Francis replied, "Sure, let's give it right here." So the grimy motor drivers who hadn't been in bathing, and the clean ones who had, all gathered around in a large circle. Hunting and Francis, vaudeville headliners and distinguished comedy artists, got down in the chalky-dusty road and gave their show for all it was worth. Ear-splitting yells greeted their sallies and songs. With the shouts of the doughboys echoing their choruses to the horizon, they got back into their machine with tired lungs and voices but full hearts and drove away.

At another time in the Argonne they gave a show on a little homemade stage down in the valley, with 3,100 doughboys looking down from the hillside. This time, as on many other occasions, they had no piano. Miss Francis strummed the guitar. After the show was over she went out among the groups of men and sat down on the steps, wherever there were any, and played whatever the boys called for—proving a veritable angel of music to the men who were, within a few hours, to go back into battle.

A very exceptional performance was in a French foyer about five kilometres behind the line, where they were billed to give two shows. The first show went off all right, but in the midst of the second there came a blistering air raid. Bombs actually dropped all around the hut. Miss Francis was singing and playing the guitar when the raid started. She never turned a hair, but continued to sing and play, calmly passing from one song to another. The French *poilus*, who were fond of American songs under all conditions, caught the spirit of the American girl. Their voices rang out in the choruses of "Smiles," "You'll Never Believe Me," and the always infectious "Pack Up Your Troubles," until the air raid was finished and Miss Francis declared both shows over.

A young French captain who was present said it was the finest example of American nerve he had seen in the war, and declared that he would put in a claim for a decoration for Miss Francis at once. The organisation soon afterward went back into the battle lines, however, and the great veil of the war dropped over their lives again forever.

"The Broadway Bunch" made a specialty of "girly" dresses. This made them welcome even before they spoke a word or timed their instruments. It must be added that it was not only the doughboys who

At Versailles

Counted Out

were glad to see these pretty dresses. Nobody ever gave "The Broadway Bunch" a more enthusiastic hand than the nurses, those stout-hearted American girls who braved the privations of the front and the deprivation of feminine clothes for many long months. All they could wear for variety was a coloured sweater, and they cheered heartily whenever their eyes were filled with the delight of real clothes worn by the women entertainers.

Hunting and Francis played at Verdun and St. Mihiel, at Dun-sur-Meuse, one of the last towns captured by the Americans, and at the Verdun citadel. Immediately after the War they undertook the very heartening work of playing to the returning prisoners. They made a specialty of this at Verdun, and many a group of ragged, footsore, soul-weary Britishers, who had been confined in German prison camps for two, three, and four years, got their first welcome into their own world through this fun-radiating pair at the shows in the old Verdun citadel.

"The Broadway Bunch" was recruited up to strength again by the addition of Edgar H. LeVan, and, at different times, Tsianina and Marguerite Perry Bailey. In December, the long triumphal visit to Germany began, which lasted for six months.

There Miss Francis created a record. She and her partner arrived there in the middle of December, 1918, among the very first of the troops of occupation. How they did it is still more or less of a state secret, but, like the great example of the Americans in the war, they got there in time. On December 13th the American Army crossed the Rhine; and on December 15th Corinne Francis sang "The Star-Spangled Banner" in Coblenz. This was the first tune that song had been heard in Germany since 1914. With this send-off, Hunting and Francis played the entire Army of Occupation circuit and in time were given charge of the booking office of the Coblenz Area. Here they came to manage the numerous theatres and entertainment huts in the great leave and administration centre around Coblenz. They sang in Luxemburg and Lorraine, along the Saar and the Moselle, and in royal castles under the ancient arms of Rhenish robber barons.

Corinne Francis again showed the spirit she had manifested in action when, under the strain of continuous entertainments and vindictive weather, she found that she still had the will to sing but with a comparatively evaporated voice. She might have justly taken six weeks or two months' leave to safeguard those vocal cords on which depended not only all her joy in life but her livelihood. Mr. Steele offered her a leave, but it was returned with thanks. She said to Mr. Steele:

I can't sing a note, but just try me in the soldier show development section as a coach. If I can't put on a show, let me help the boys who can. That's where the need is and I want to be in it.

Miss Francis was in it for a month or more, during which she carefully nursed her voice back into health again, but gave all her intelligence and skill to the continuous dress rehearsals of the soldier entertainers. When she came back to Coblenz and sang again, tuneful, fresh, and irresistible, she got a reception the like of which was seen on only a few other occasions in the army.

Any show that contained Leo Donnelly, Will J. Kennedy, and James F. Kelly just had to be called *The Shamrock Show*. Leo Donnelly is one of the best comedians. Will Kennedy is one of the best known funny men on the popular-priced vaudeville circuit known as the Columbia Wheel. James F. Kelly and Emma Pollock, who have toured together for many years in a comedy singing and dancing act, have never failed to captivate the strong Irish and Irish-admiring public wherever they went; Miss Pollock especially has a reputation of long standing in this field as a soubrette entertainer in the good old Irish plays of the Harrigan and Hart management. Helen Goff, the fifth member of the show, has played to Al Jolson and supported Kitty Gordon.

The Shamrock Show arrived in France on August 12th, and, controlled by home contracts, stayed abroad during the four crucial months of the emergency period. During that time, however, they accomplished great results. The enthusiasm of the troupe was kept at fighting pitch by its inspiring and hard working leader, Leo Donnelly, who wrote home from the thick of things:

> I never was so dirty, tired, and happy in my life. I wouldn't change places with any actor in America for the biggest salary ever paid. I am having the time of my life. It is the greatest real work that I have ever done, and believe me, I sure am happy.

Donnelly spread a good deal of this happiness about France.

Will Kennedy had an extraordinary knowledge of the outside appearance and the particular individual quality of every large city in the home country. After a show, the boys would flock around Kennedy just to ask him questions about what the latest news was from Oshkosh, or Little Rock, or Los Angeles, or Portland, wherever they happened to come from. Kennedy would come back with gossip about the folks, the elections, and the record of the local baseball team. As a travelling purveyor of home town gossip, Kennedy was a walking wonder. He could remember the exact situation of the best lunch-cart in town; he could describe the local grill room which the real people always patronized; he could discuss the flavour of *chile con carne* or *frijoles* or the aroma of the immortal baked bean with equal felicity, and in those days when home-cooked food was the ultimate of all earthly bliss, his after-the-show reminiscence act was a most enduring winner.

Helen Goff's songs were memorable. A member of the league writes:

> Helen is a riot with the boys, because she knows how to handle them. Her songs go with a bang. Above all, she is typically American and the boys just love her and her work.

And then after this little comedienne had finished her jazz music, Emma Pollock stepped forward and sang "Maggie Murphy's Home," with Jimmie Kelly acting as a whimsical foil to this uproarious old melody.

The Shamrock Show got up to the front in the days of the great advance, and started on a tour which the Seventy-Seventh Division, the New York National Army Unit, at any rate, will never forget. They played in the Argonne and the Woevre, and they went out on the great circuit from Verdun. In the areas where German bombs and long range artillery—and an occasional leakage of gas—penetrated, *The Shamrock Show* continued its work, as vital to the success of the division, as one staff captain put it, "as a regiment of infantry." The armistice period found them "mopping up" in the leave areas; and the beginning of January, 1919, found them embarking at last for the homeland, veterans who had fought a good fight and had added their bit to the war prestige of their profession's honour.

From the wealth of the war experience of these Over There Theatre Leaguers it is possible, because of space limitations, to give the merest suggestion of what was accomplished with the American Army throughout the area of the war. Take the unit, for instance, called so modestly "A Little Cheer from Home." It set sail from America, August 9, 1918, and was composed of Inez Wilson, famous during the past few years on the Canadian stage; Henry Souvaine, a concert pianist who has accompanied Caruso and Galli-Curci; Eleanor Whittemore, a violinist; and Ethel Hinton, monologist and reader.

Their program opened with an ensemble number, followed by snappy songs by Inez Wilson, violin solos by Miss Whittemore, and monologues and impersonations by Miss Hinton. Mr. Souvaine played the accompaniments. The party got into St. Mihiel ten days after the Germans had been driven out. Here they gave a show in the old Roman fort, *Fort du Camp des Romains,* to thousands of French soldiers. Miss Wilson sang in French, and the piano was an abandoned Boche instrument. They found meat in the icebox, soup on the stove, and bags of potatoes on the floor—real food, which was the surest evidence that the Hun had been caught unawares.

During one show a shell dropped 200 yards away; they kept on without a hitch. They entertained on another occasion 8,000 Polish American soldiers. The Poles sang their national anthems with heads bared, the most impressive sight the troupe saw during the war. On some nights the whole sky was illuminated with fire, and the shelling became so heavy that the commanding officer ordered them back.

The most protected place in the Ford, even in the drenching rain, was always given to the old piano. They travelled in ambulances and on foot, in trucks, narrow gauge railway cars, and flat cars; and they gave shows in camps which had not seen an American girl in thirteen months. They gave one historic performance on the immortal Dead Men's Hill at Verdun. On another occasion they had a thrilling experience in an advanced American artillery position a few kilometres from the front. Mr. Souvaine writes:

> The Americans were brigaded with the French, and we had a few hundred Americans sitting around the piano, the French forming a fringe on the outside and hanging all over the roofs of the adjoining huts. All during the show the Boche and French artillery near by gave me a real symphonic accompaniment, which sounded just like 'old times' Wagner recitals. Three Boche planes came over to see the show after we had started, but the boys were very poor hosts and sent them home with a barrage of air shells.

Frequently, when the crowd was too big to get into the hut, Mr. Souvaine took the piano outside and played to the crowd that couldn't get in; he put on this feature at a great Polish American camp where 7,000 men climbed on trees and houses in a vast crowd around him.

This unit was one of the few parties chosen to tour Italy. During the final stages of the Italians' last great offensive, they followed the Italian Army into Austria. Here they rendered magnificent service to the American regiment attached to the Italian Army and to the ambulance drivers and aviators whom America loaned so liberally to the

Italian front.

January, 1919, found "A Little Cheer from Home" being dispensed in Germany. They were assigned for a good part of their stay with the Thirty-Second Division, the Ohio National Guard unit—the Red Arrows, as the world has come to know them. Here they circulated throughout the region around Rengsdorf. When they left in February, Major General Lassiter, commanding the Thirty-Second, sat down and wrote this straightforward little tribute, which expresses in its way the finest and most characteristic type of appreciation, such as a real entertainment group unfailingly got from the high American command:

> I should like you to know how much this group of talented people has done in maintaining the cheerfulness and contentment of the officers and men of the division. They have put up with all sorts of hardships without murmur; they have entertained the men of all the little garrisons we maintain throughout the Coblenz Bridgehead; and always they have made light of the difficulties in the way and have won the hearts of our men. The entertainment which they have given has always been of a high class, never appealing to anything but the better instincts of the men, and I think it has been very interesting to observe that this has been the type of entertainment most enjoyed and appreciated by the soldier men. Everyone in the division hates to see them go. I feel that they have shown a spirit in carrying out their part in this war worthy of the best type of soldier, and I cannot too much thank you and the Y.M.C.A. for putting their services at the disposal of the Thirty-Second Division.

D. C. McIver was what they called in the British Army a "dugout." It took the war to bring him out of the quiet of a new profession and thrust him back behind the footlights. For many years McIver had been an illusionist and magician in vaudeville, but some five years before the war he retired from the stage and went into mining in Arizona. When the war broke out, he figured that he was worth more to the soldiers as a magician than as a mine operator. Abandoning his mining, he assembled a little company called "Magic, Melody, and Music," McIver took over with him his former accompanist, Miss Madeline L. Glynn, and rounded out the quartet with Alfred Armand, the tenor, Hal Pierson, the bass, and Louise Carlyle, of that famous vaudeville organisation, the Manhattan Trio. They sailed on August 5,

1918. Mr. McIver reports early in September:

In the seven days since our landing, August 25th, the Magic Unit has given twenty shows, five of which were under shell fire, some with piano and some without. We have given them with fully equipped stages and also on truck bodies, in airplane hangars, hospitals, and stables. Miss Glynn is one of the best soldiers in the world. She goes everywhere we go and undergoes all the inconveniences without a murmur. The two boys, Hal Pierson and Alfred Armand, are great, and my own work is going very nicely with the boys. We leave today for the front, with full equipment—tin hats, gas masks, knapsacks, and blankets. No baggage except the egg bag and music rolls.'

In Troyes, about half way between Paris and the front, the McIver Unit found a wounded American aviator alone in a local hospital. They loaded him into a truck and took him to town to see a real show on a stage, with footlights and piano. It was the first show he had seen in France. "He was so happy that he cried," reports McIver.

Amparito Farrar was a picturesque artist who went over in what afterward came to be known as the second wave of entertainers. She sailed August 9, 1918. Miss Farrar is an Oregon girl who spent most of her early life in California; she studied in Paris, Berlin, and London, and became a noted lyric soprano. She was of immense service abroad not only because of her beautiful voice—she had sung in grand opera at the Royal Opera in Vienna, and in light opera in New York—but also because of her remarkable fluency in languages. She spoke with equal facility English, Spanish, French, Italian, and German. She was accompanied on her trip by her mother, Mrs. Guadalupa Farrar, who is an accomplished pianist.

Miss Farrar gave a very successful series of Franco-American concerts, specializing in the American troops brigaded with the French, where the mixed audiences welcomed her and fell in love with her on about even terms. She writes home:

I have sung in motor camps, huts, bakeries, hospitals, and even at the bedsides of the boys, one at a time; everything from grand opera to 'Tickle Toe.' I even dance a little. Such a spirit! They want to get right out of bed and go back at the Boches. And they want the best you can give them—nothing is too good for them.

Miss Farrar also sang in municipal theatres, where her European reputation secured her a constant welcome among the French and other Allied soldiers along her itinerary; but always dearest to her heart were the audiences of doughboys on whom she centred her efforts as far as possible. She writes:

> They seem to love us, and I know I love them. It never fails to bring a throb to my heart to hear Americans on the street when they catch sight of us as we go by. They always say 'American girls! Gee, those American girls look good to me!' Well, I am certainly glad I am an American girl, and I never was so glad of it before.

CHAPTER 17

Knights and Ladies

The expectancy and rose of the fair state
The glass of fashion and the mould of form,
The observed of all observers!
    Hamlet.

Many an American girl discovered that there was no place in the world where she was safer than in the American Army. It is not to be wondered at that some of the most successful of all the entertainment troupes were those; which were composed of women only. These travelled about France with no escort, manager, or male protector, whatsoever.

The experience of these American girls is one of the finest tributes that can be given to the soldiers. Moreover, it forms the basis for a psychological study into the character of American youth as it expressed itself under the strain and stress of war. One of the hundreds of American girls who could bear such witness is Vera Barstow, who ran the gamut of the A. E. F. up to the firing line; and she declares:

The American doughboy was the truest gentleman I ever met. First, last, and all the time he was a gentleman wherever he met an American girl.

The unit known as "The Musical Foursome" sailed from New York on the transport *Lapland* on September 16, 1918. It was composed of Miss Barstow, violinist; Maude Allen, *soprano*; Lucie Babcock, accompanist; and Mildred Evans, reader. Hardly had they passed the Statue of Liberty when, with another unit aboard, they began to entertain the soldiers on deck, most of whom were marines from a camp in Florida. An epidemic of flu broke out, which resulted in much sickness and a number of deaths. Miss Barstow, too, got the flu. In Liverpool the unit gave its first overseas entertainment for American soldiers. From there they went to Paris for two weeks and entertained at the hospitals and the nearby camps. Miss Barstow says:

> The first day we played was in the hospital at St. Denis; there were two thousand badly wounded cases. We played for the boys three hours and I never can forget how grateful they were, and how their faces lit up. In the evening we went to an anti-aircraft station and played for the men. They had been there; six months and had not seen an American woman; in fact, they had seen nothing in the way of entertainment. These boys were so excited over the fact of our being there that they didn't know what kind of an entertainment they wanted—the chief thing to them was that there were four American girls there.
> When Miss Mildred went on to tell her funny stories they were shouting before the point came out. We shook hands with all the boys. We always made it a point to do that wherever we were. One night while we were in Paris we went out with about fifty other 'Y' girls to dance with an outfit in a near-by camp—and they treated us like long lost sisters.
> In the Argonne Forest we were attached to the army. The army had to billet us, feed us, and look after us in every way. When we joined the division we were permitted to take with us only one suitcase apiece. We also had an army cot, blankets, and a gas mask. Water was terribly scarce and we didn't have a bath until we got back to Bar-le-Duc—three weeks later. We had very little to drink and occasionally it was a toss-up as to whether we should scrub our teeth or drink the good water that we happened to get. Usually we got up too late for breakfast. We would go straggling along the road until we came to an army kitchen and then make friends with the cooks.
> In that way we fared very well. Incidentally, this was a good way to become acquainted with the doughboys, which was part of our duty as entertainers. We had instructions before we left Paris not to favour the officers and we always made it a point from the very beginning to mix with the doughboys.
> Once, when we were with the Eightieth Division, there was a bunch of men—they were muleteers—who never seemed to be able to hear the entertainment. We told them we would

entertain them during their lunch hour and promised there should not be one officer present. Several officers appeared on the scene and we shooed them away, very much to the delight of the men. The buck privates enjoyed immensely our jokes on the officers, especially when the officers were present.

Leaving the Eightieth, we penetrated deeper into the forest to join the Seventy-Seventh. This was right in the heart of the Argonne. Here we were billeted in German dugouts. We could hardly tell from day to day where we were or what we were doing. The first night we were nearer the front than we realised. We had no cots, but I was completely exhausted and slept all night long and didn't hear a thing. The girls did not sleep at all. Our first German dugout was an underground theatre which seated about three hundred people. The walls were whitewashed. They put us in the dressing room. We had a stove and were quite comfortable. This was after we had gone to join the Seventy-Seventh Division; the men were all in the line. The colonel told us he would try to get permission to take us into the field hospitals. They didn't allow women in these hospitals; they did not even have women nurses. We went up there and gave an entertainment. The wounded men seemed to like the violin music. It was quiet and helped to distract their minds from the pain. We played in the treating 'rooms'—it was just a tent, of course. The wounded were brought in on stretchers and the stretchers laid right down in the mud.

We took turns going into the shock 'rooms' to write letters and take messages from the dying men. We played three days in succession at this hospital; the second day they brought in the wounded men from the Eightieth Division, and the third day they commenced bringing in German wounded. Most of them were just young boys and they were very thinly clad. The material in their clothes seemed like fibre. It was bitter cold weather. They wore just a uniform of this fibre-like material and their top coat, neither of which was heavy. I remember one boy with a shattered leg; they ripped open his uniform and I saw that he had neither socks nor underwear.

Many are the stories of their experiences that these girls could tell. One day, while the boys are fighting their way step by step, driving the German invaders before them, we find Miss Sarah Willmer, a Chicago girl, riding ten miles in a terrific storm that was almost a cloudburst to a camp of soldiers where there were to be 5,000 men in her audience. She arrived with her pretty white frock soaked. When she mounted the platform it looked, as a soldier said, "more like a last year's nightdress left out in the rain" than an evening gown. But there was no time to change, and she gave her show with the abandon and enthusiasm which come when you feel that nothing worse can happen whatever you do. Months afterwards, when she was giving out cigarettes in a hospital back of the lines to the boys who were being unloaded from a fleet of ambulances, an Illinois boy, noticing her uniform, said:

> The last 'Y' girl I saw was up in the night before the St. Mihiel drive. Her name was Sarah Willmer—I remember her because she came from my state. I shall never forget as long as I live the blessed white dress she had on the night she recited to us. We had not seen a white dress, it seemed to us, in years. There we were with all our gas masks at alert, all ready to go into the line, and there she was talking to us just like a girl from home. It sure was a great sight, you bet; and don't forget to tell her if you ever see her.

There was one ward in a big hospital where no entertainers had been allowed to go. Many of the men who had been brooding, or muttering, or simply lying despondently on their backs ever since they had been brought out of action were perilously near losing their reason. One day a young singer. Miss Paula Lind Ayers, asked the surgeon if she could sing them some lullabies just to see what they would do. She sat outside the ward and sang the most familiar song she knew, 'The Little Grey Home in the West." There was absolute silence inside. Then came another, "Just a Baby's Prayer at Twilight." Then she sang old Southern lullabies and Negro melodies which every American knows by heart—"My Old Kentucky Home," "Way Down upon the S'wanee River," "Old Black Joe," and finally "Abide with Me." Before she had finished this wonderful group of heart songs—all of them crooned rather than sung—almost the whole ward was joining in the words.

Men who had not spoken since they had been stricken at the front were singing. There were no more incoherent yelling or nerveracking mutterings for the rest of the day. The doctors had her come back again and again, until the "lullaby cure" came to be one of the most successful medical discoveries of the war. No ragtime or catchy

Broadway melodies could have done this. When the boys did want something livelier, the doctors said they were cured, and put them in the evacuation ward.

The work of Miss Ayers was duplicated by scores of others in the big hospitals and constituted one of the great spiritual services of the War. Miss Alice Woodfin, one of the pioneers who came over early in the spring of 1918, gave many song recitals at hospitals, and used as one of her chief specifics the teaching of dancing to ambitious convalescents who possessed both feet. At the end of one successful evening's singing, Miss Woodfin sat down at the piano and began to play an enticing air that made everyone want to get up and hop around.

> This is one of the best dance tunes ever written, boys. I am going to teach it to you right on the spot—the music as well as the dance steps that go with it. It is called the 'Tickle Toe.'

There was a snicker, then a gale of laughter. Miss Woodfin hesitated, but her audience applauded uproariously, so she went on, thinking they were laughing with pleasure at the prospect before them. But the snickers and giggles kept breaking out, and at last, after the lesson was over, Miss Woodfin turned around and said to her accompanist, "Now tell me what the matter is."

So they told her she had taught "Tickle Toe" to the Flat-Foot Camp.

Another "woman party" which upheld the banner of self-reliant womanhood was the little unit composed of Marian Dana, of Chicago, and Hazel Bartlett of St. Paul. They went over on an unwieldy old ship that hit the autumn seas heavy and hard and sprang a leak a few days out. For six days there was water on the lower decks, which finally reached a stable depth well above the ankles. The boys in the bunks below figured that heavy seas and decks awash would keep silk-stockinged entertainers up in their proper places in the passengers' cabins, but these plucky Middle Western girls took off their shoes and stockings and went right down.

They went down every day, and with their feet covered with brine sang, "If He Can Fight Like He Can Love, Then Goodbye Germany," splashing about in the water to the tune of that rollicking chorus as if they did that sort of thing every day.

There sailed from New York in October, 1918, a group of four girls, "Just Girls"—Garda Kova, a classic and aesthetic dancer who undertook the management; Margaret Coleman, soprano soloist at

St. Matthew's, New York; Marguerite Stunner, singer and story-teller; and Diana Kasner, pianist. They landed in England, dividing their time between London and King Llynn. They then went to France and were in Paris when the Armistice was signed They entertained the Twenty-Sixth, Seventy-Seventh, and Eighty-First Divisions around Chaumont, then went to the Riviera and Marseilles, back to Paris, and to all the larger camps again. All this was in midwinter.

If a single group were to be selected for mention as typifying the spirit which sent the entertainers over dangerous seas and through sunless days in cheerless billets, none would be more surely representative than "Just Girls." Their engagements were so continuous and so exactly met that the unit was finally destroyed by the illness of two of its members. Margaret Coleman returned to America, her health seriously impaired. The unit was later revived by Diana Kasner, with three new members, and it followed the Third Army to Coblenz and played three months in Germany.

Out of all the companies which remain, let us take a final glance at the unassuming but eventful record of one of the most tireless little units of all, "The Electric Sparks." Headed by Harry Israel, its membership included Annie Abbott, the Georgia Magnet, who had a *jujitsu* act in which she guaranteed to lift or throw the largest sergeant in the audience (and invariably made good); Doris Thayer, a New England girl who did character singing and monologue and made the song "*Oui, Oui, Marie*" universally known throughout the American Army; and Gladys Sears, who did almost any kind of dialogue from Swedish to Italian, but fixed her principal attention on Irish songs, and rose to universal appreciation by the manner in which she rendered the classic lines of "Knox 'Em Down, McCluskey."

"The Electric Sparks" went over on October 26, 1918, and Armistice Day found them the big feature on the bill at the gala performance at the Eagle Hut in London. They entered France by means of the much travelled Brest route, and for many weeks played the lonely towns in Brittany surrounding the great Brest embarkation camp. Here they put a new breath of life into the thousands who were chafing under the first disillusion of the long delay in getting transportation home. Brittany was primitive enough for any American quartered there, so "The Electric Sparks" soon become accustomed to playing on a dirt floor, in barns having no windows and with what the doughboys called "ventilated" roofs, to let the Brittany rain in. The pianos universally suffered from that richness of tone which the

'Y' MINSTRELS IN ACTION

Brittany sea air and seven days of rain a week gave to mediocre instruments which were never tuned.

Their long spell of unremitting work took its usual toll. Miss Abbott was forced to remain at Brest to recover from an influenza-threatening cold, while Miss Thayer was operated upon at the same time for an eye affliction. This necessitated the regrouping of the company, but while in Paris Mr. Israel was fortunate enough to enlist in his company the services of Robert Woolley, a Y.M.C.A. Secretary from Schenectady, N. Y., who had come over in September as a religious worker and had been through the thick of the war as one of the best known vocalists and song leaders in the Battle of the Argonne.

The show had a lively final number composed of a medley of catchy song hits, working up to a climax in which the whole company, and the whole audience usually, joined in "The Darktown Strutters' Ball." At first Mr. Woolley was off the stage when this great number was put on, but one day he asked if he might not take part in it. So "The Electric Sparks" taught him some dance steps, lively ones but with due regard to his professional restraint, and at the next show Woolley appeared in the centre of the stage and danced his steps in the finale. The result was a crashing, smashing hit, and the show closed amid the stormiest doughboy approval they had yet seen.

Thus did the Church and stage cooperate to the profit and edification of the friendliest critic either of them ever had—the American doughboy. It was a partnership multiplied in many other sectors, in the give-and-take fraternity of the World War—and many a doughboy got a religious message from a loyal old stage veteran like Will Cressy, and learned what a good laugh really was after seeing Robert Woolley on an A. E. F. stage.

A ROYAL STAIRWAY

THE FAMOUS PALAIS DE GLACE

CHAPTER 18

Two Makers of Entertainment History

If this were played upon a stage now, I could condemn it as an impossible fiction.
   Twelfth Night.

Two events occurred in the autumn of 1918, while the American Army was engaged in the great offensive, which carried the troupers to new conquests. The first event was the arrival direct from America of a dynamic personality, a man so charged with magnetism that he became loved not only by every entertainer in France, but by every soldier with whom he came in contact. The second event was the arrival in France of a woman who was to "conquer" the Army of Occupation, after it conquered the Germans. A. M. Beatty arrived in France early in September, 1918; and Dorothy Donnelly, vice-president of the Women's Stage Relief Society, arrived toward the last of September. Both immediately began to make history.

Beatty is intimately known, perhaps, by more actors than any other man who went to France. Because of this important qualification, and his ability to make new friends, he was placed in charge of the Personnel Section at Entertainment Headquarters in Paris from the time of his arrival until June, 1919, when, at the request of Walter H. Johnson, Jr., who then returned to America, he was appointed his successor as chief of the whole entertainment organisation.

Familiarly known everywhere as "A. M.," Albert M. Beatty—theatrical manager by profession, diplomat by training, and a regular fellow, whose friends early discovered his inexhaustible vein of golden humour—sat on the lid in the entertainment department during all this period. Sometimes the lid rocked, often it was shaken, and there were many rumblings underneath. But when you saw Beatty you knew at least "one reason" why it was held down, and why the energies of hundreds of stage people were so well directed that the whole enterprise came out of the war with the universal approval and gratitude of the American Army.

Beatty's job was to direct the personnel. These are simple words, but they express a complex maze of duties far too numerous to recapitulate. One can only appeal to the imagination and endeavour to grasp the job of a man who had to fit the tempestuous moods and artistic temperaments of actors into a program for entertaining a fluctuating army in a country where transportation and accommodations were the most uncertain quantities in the whole uncertain war. Beatty had to do this, and he had to do it patiently, firmly, uncomplainingly, and successfully. The fact that he did it, and that everybody in any way connected with the operation acknowledges that he did it wonderfully well, is as great a tribute as can be paid to any man in a responsible position. Beatty's personal qualifications for his job included a physical frame which should not be omitted in setting before the reader this picture of the man and his work. It was a combination of John Bunny and Irvin Cobb—big, but none too big to contain Beatty's heart, and that is the main point in this story.

When Beatty first arrived in France, the performers were being sent out on regular schedules and were being capably and methodically handled, but there was no one who really "belonged" to the actors, who talked their own language, and provided a shoulder broad enough for them to weep out their troubles on. Beatty stepped into this gap and filled it completely. He also attended at once to some very vital details. He found that the entertainment *troupes* consisted mostly of parties too large to be taken in one car on tour. These he broke up into mobile units of not more than five persons. The total number could cover a wider field and entertain more men, and yet the units were big enough to put over something good "even with one member sick."

Now matching up actors for units is no easy matter. One ship would bring over theatrical recruits with a preponderance of piano players; another would land thirty artists, of whom twenty would be singers, and in Paris getting balanced parties ready for the road was a task to turn a man gray. But Beatty neither grew gray nor lost his *avoirdupois*. He insisted on keeping his smile. He made it a rule that anyone who couldn't smile at the close of the day's work in the office needed either a rest or a release—and they got one or the other. The units were first sent around the circuit near Paris for a few days, where Beatty could "dash out of an evening and get a look at their work with the boys." This also gave the players time to quarrel, which, being human, they sometimes did, and that called for readjustments. After the try-out was over, and the readjustments had been made, the units were booked for the big circuits and sent forth.

Expense accounts are fearful and wonderful things in the hands of theatrical folks. Beatty explains:

> They simply don't know and can't understand them, and I couldn't deal with that phase of the work at all. But fortunately we had two 'Y' girls who could, and these women handled all our actors' expenses with a finesse that was another modem miracle. They conserved the funds and yet hurt no one's feelings, which was a delicate task. Another 'Y' girl ran our complex card-indexing system, by means of which we knew the movements of every unit and the records and affairs of every individual actor.

Let us observe the imperturbable chief awaiting the entrance of a typical "actress with a grievance" during the big days of the final drive in October, 1918. She has just come back from a tour in the Argonne, giving four or five shows a day; she is physically worn out and has a long list of grievances of which she says, "I want nothing more than justice, but the moment anybody starts to argue with me there will surely be an eruption." After a few moments' wait in the anteroom enter worn-out actress through door at left, determined to blow up the manager, resign, and go home. Business of hand shaking and sitting down for talk. Then Beatty gets in his deadly work.

> Well, well, I'm mighty glad to see you, but you look tired, and I know you are, because I've been following you through every mile of that nasty mud. I've known all about those awful billets. I know the food isn't what you ought to have, and yet they wire me you've put it over in spite of everything and that you go strong. Now, you've had a wretched time, but how those boys have laughed! I've heard about it, and it did my heart good! We're all tickled to know what you've put up with without a grumble and we're going to book you for a run into the S.O.S., where you can get a little rest and sleep in a real, honest-to-

goodness hotel with a bed in the room and warm water, and have coffee with real sugar in it. Now I can see you're not yourself after this tour at the front, so just go to your hotel, and take twenty-four hours of complete rest. I'd have my meals served in the room. Just lie around and read and rest and have your clothes cleaned and pressed, and then tomorrow, say in the afternoon at two, after a good luncheon, come in and we'll talk things over.

She had been trying desperately to slip in her kick, but Beatty beat her to it on one long breath. Before she knew it Beatty was shaking her by the hand and patting her on the back, and she was saying:

Mr. Beatty, I wouldn't take a million dollars for my experience. It was too wonderful for anything. I did have a horrid time getting about, but I didn't suppose you knew how awful it was, and I didn't know you were keeping such a sympathetic watch over me. You're a perfect dear, and I'm going back just as soon as you'll let me to give those boys all the songs and dances I can crowd in. Please let me go back as soon as you can.

Nobody could have blamed these actresses, for, though deep in their hearts they held an unswerving loyalty to the cause they had come to serve, surely this was no easy life for them. The reader who does not know the life of the stage cannot imagine how difficult it was for theatrical people suddenly to adapt themselves to the system of booking and travelling which necessarily prevailed in France. Beatty said, in discussing this problem:

In America, we managers do everything for the actress. They are told to have their trunks packed at five in the afternoon, and to be at the station at six. The porter takes the trunk from the hotel room to the sidewalk. The property man takes it to the station. There the manager checks it. He stands on the platform and says, 'Your berth number is 19.' In the morning he furnishes a list of hotels and tells how to reach them, while the property man sees that the right trunks go to the right hotels and rooms. The manager has informed them of the hour of the rehearsal or the curtain raising. The same thing goes on in endless succession. But 'over there' it was different. The actress had to be her own property man and she had to worry about her own transportation—generally in a Ford. Nobody had time to worry for her. She studied her own time tables, and they were written in French; she got her meals where she could and more often went without them, and made the circuit on her own luck and initiative, but was held to the schedule. It was all very new and difficult for theatrical people.

But there was another side to the experience, and Beatty saw this too. He acted on the principle that a good personnel officer should get out into the field to see the conditions which his personnel was up against. And so we find Beatty getting away from Paris for a time in the thick of the fight, seeing his entertainers at work, watching the last shows given to the boys about to go into the line, and meanwhile writing inimitable little accounts of his impressions.

> One afternoon in the Argonne, I had one of our finest women violinists and a splendid contralto soloist sing and play for the boys of a machine gun battalion. It was in a natural amphitheatre, with the women on the bottom of an overturned wagon on the hillside. The lads with their fighting equipment by their sides were pressing close around us—a thousand or more. We knew, and they knew, that at dusk they were going forward, and that in the early hours of the morning they would jump off for the great adventure. Part of the outfit had just come in as replacements and faced their first action. They knew they had taken the places of casuals.
>
> The veterans had in mind the fact that a man may go through one or two scraps unscathed, but with every additional zero hour his chances of not being hit grow less. We could hear the rattle of machine guns. Shells were dropping occasionally not far away. Overhead our aviators were patrolling the sky to keep the German observation planes from coming over into our rear. The boys didn't want jazz music then! they didn't want coon songs. The girls gave them the old tender ballads, things the mothers of these boys had loved. Finally the soloist said: 'Boys, I'll sing one more. What shall it be?' And what do you think they wanted? 'The End of a Perfect Day.'
>
> I thought that girl would never carry on. I couldn't look at her myself, for fear I'd let her see a quiver of my lip. But she just nodded and to the sweet accompaniment of the violin sang it as splendidly as if it were at a concert in Carnegie Hall. I knew she was using every ounce of her physical and nervous powers to

hold her woman's heart strings from snapping. Then an officer of high command stepped out and said, 'Miss, would you sing just one more? We want awfully to hear "The Rosary."' And then she sang that. It was too much for me, and I went over and got very busy fixing things in the bottom of the automobile.

One of the outstanding sentences in Walter Johnson's report in March, 1919, on the whole entertainment organisation under his command reads:

> As a result of his (Beatty's) lovable personality and tactful management, he has held a great many entertainers in France whose contracts would otherwise have expired.

Mr. Steele also goes out of his way in his final report to say:

> A. M. Beatty rendered invaluable service both during my tenure of office and that of Mr. Johnson as head of what we might call our Entertainment Personnel Division, receiving the incoming entertainers, grouping them into units, regrouping them when necessary, adjusting difficulties, straightening out tangles, and acting as a father confessor to many of the temperamental performers. Being a professional theatrical man himself, Mr. Beatty was admirably qualified for this work.

Consequently, when Mr. Johnson returned to America at the end of June, 1919, A. M. Beatty was the logical choice as the new head of the entertainment organisation overseas. At that time the entertainment section had grown to an organisation possessing 850 theatres and huts, with a total seating capacity of more than 750,000, 181 of which were first class, fully equipped, full-sized theatres.

It was Beatty who maintained this organisation at its highest pitch until the time came to ease off its activities with the rapid demobilisation of the American Army. Even then, especially in the Paris and Le Mans areas, new demands for entertainment arose here and there, and the entertainment section was not able to finish its official work until August 16, 1919, remaining to the end as one of the last units of the whole American Army to be demobilised and sent home. It was with a full heart that Mr. Beatty closed the final report on August 30, 1919, with these words of just and proper pride:

> We have a sense of having been of real benefit to the personnel of the army and a feeling that our time has been well spent and

that we can, in honour, write *Finis*.

Now to our "second event"—the achievement of Dorothy Donnelly. Of all that army of fine dramatic artists who went to France, it is fair to say that no one laboured more diligently and self-sacrificingly, or accomplished greater results than Miss Donnelly, authoress, play collaborator, and one of the real personalities of the American stage.

Dorothy Donnelly is best known to the American play-going public for her performance a few seasons ago in the title *rôle* of "Madame X." Long one of the organisers and leaders of the Stage Women's War Relief, Miss Donnelly was slated to go overseas as a dramatic coach and organiser of soldier drama activity as soon as war conditions permitted. Unfortunately her plans were subject to the same delays that unavoidably deterred the Over There Theatre League, but Miss Donnelly left on September 17, 1918, and spent in France and Germany almost a year of untiring effort which made her one of the best known and best loved figures in the American Army. She took with her as collaborator and *confrère*, Mrs. Patricia Henshaw, a California girl who was a concert singer, pianist, and *ingénue* actress of ability and charm, and who became known and adored as Patsy throughout the ranks of the A. E. F.

Miss Donnelly's activities up to the close of the war chiefly centred around Chaumont, where the General Staff was located. Here she and Mrs. Henshaw originated and put together the first and one of the best soldier shows, known by the irresponsible title of "*Ah, Oui, or Y Not?*" This production was inspected by General Pershing, who thought so favourably of it that he invited the King of the Belgians and the Prince of Wales and other privileged persons to special performances in their honour, but most of all he recommended his oldest and best friend, the doughboy, to go and see it. So "*Ah, Oui,*" had to make a triumphal trip to Paris and spent a happy week at the Champs-Elysées Theatre. It then embarked on a tour of France.

The most touching performance of "*Ah, Oui*" was given at Chaumont itself, however, not for General Pershing or for any other American, but as a Christmas "jazzerina"—a word patented by the "*Ah Oui*" company itself—for the kiddies of that little French provincial town. When they arrived they found, not strange American ragtime antics, but a beautiful little Christmas play in French, written for them by Captain Joseph Hanson of the American Army and acted by Dorothy Donnelly herself. At the close of the performance, which had to be put on several times so that all the children could see it. Miss Donnelly presided, also in French, in giving out the presents.

Her own soldier actors, by now her fast friends, all pitched in and helped her, and formed an awed group of auditors for the little show in French. By this time they regarded Miss Donnelly as their own personal property and James Forbes, who was in the audience, just arrived from America, heard one of them say in a breathless undertone: "Gee, listen to the way our Dorothy spills that stuff." "It was the best instance I saw while in France," said Mr. Forbes afterward, "of the absolute identity of interest and of 'belonging' to the army achieved by a member of the Over There Theatre League."

Besides coaching and staging "*Ah, Oui*," and providing innumerable dresses, costumes, and lighting effects which helped to make that performance memorable, Miss Donnelly and Mrs. Henshaw found time to give a series of shows in the camps and army centres which clustered thickly around Chaumont during the closing days of the war. In spite of all their other prepossessions, Miss Donnelly and Mrs. Henshaw kept up almost a full-time program day by day, not excluding Sundays, always entirely sympathetic to the audiences they knew so well.

Mrs. Henshaw had her own approach, which was none the less sure and triumphant. Not only was she one of those rare persons who can sing almost any song that ever has been written, but at one time or another during her stage and concert career she had packed away its words in her memory. Patsy Henshaw would sit down at the piano and play and sing the song you asked for just as the person you had in mind used to sing it on that romantic occasion you never could forget.

On one occasion there was a crossroads service for a regiment of Negro troops, the last before they went into the line. A Negro chaplain had moved the hearts of his hearers with a stirring war sermon which ended with this fine appeal:

> So now you coloured soldiers, free citizens of America, at last have the opportunity to justify that freedom which white soldiers fought for and won for you sixty years ago. They are now watching to see if you, too, are worthy of the fight to keep that freedom alive in the world. Go in and win honour for yourselves and victory for America, and God be with you.

Then he announced in the most perfect stillness that "this little lady" was going to sing some of the songs which they had heard at their mothers' knees, their own songs that they could remember as they went into the ordeal ahead of them. Under the spell of this emotion-charged introduction, Mrs. Henshaw stepped forward and sang one after another of the Negro spirituals, arranged by the great Negro composer, Burleigh—"Going to Jerusalem, Just like John," "Sometimes I Feel Like a Motherless Child," "Deep River," and the finest of all these primitive melodies, "Swing Low, Sweet Chariot."

Little by little, as she sang these beautiful harmonies, other voices stole into the refrain and as she concluded "Swing Low, Sweet Chariot," a choir was following her, singing the eight bar harmony in accurately placed male voices, swelling the melody to a beauty which no one who heard it could ever forget. The auditors stood silent after the song was over, many of them with the tears rolling down their dusky cheeks, but in the yell which arose as the little automobile drove away there was no weakness. It was a real war cry, and it will ring in the little singer's ears forever.

The American Army was not an army of men alone. There were the army nurses who were fighting a battle of their own, none the less glorious, under conditions where an evening's relaxation and a little unadulterated fun might set up again the tone of the whole hospital personnel. The Roosevelt Hospital Unit from New York, which made up the bulk of the nurses of Base Hospital 15, just outside of Chaumont, was the first large group of nurses to arrive in France. By Christmas, 1918, it had been in active service for eighteen months and was proudly displaying three service stripes among an army most of whose members could still boast of only one. So when these nurses of Base Hospital 15 wanted to get up a show all their own and turned to Miss Donnelly for assistance, she let everything slip for the time being to help them do it. The nurses' *Follies* ensued.

It opened with a rousing chorus of "Hail, Hail, the Gang's All Here," coming out strong on the second line, much to the joy of the patients and the doctors who crowded the hospital concert hall to suffocation. Miss Huntington, a plucky little nurse who had served in the advance dressing station along the Marne, wrote the show, and a wounded lieutenant arranged the music; so it was exclusively a home product. The chorus, diligently coached by Miss Donnelly, grouped itself attractively behind Miss Huntington as she sang, in a natty lieutenant's uniform, "They Go Wild, Simply Wild Over Me."

But the most telling number of the evening was that of the nurse who dressed up "eagles, moustache, and all," to look exactly like the colonel. She rode a bicycle across the stage and called down recreant nurses in a manner exactly like the original, who sat in the audience beneath. It only showed how much "lady soldiers" can get away with in war. The show was so funny and so admirably arranged and staged by Miss Donnelly, however, that there was no official aftermath save good-natured congratulations.

In January, 1919, after a short rest in Paris, Miss Donnelly and Mrs. Henshaw went up to Coblenz to undertake the second and last chapter of their service to the American Army. There Miss Donnelly directed for five months the soldier shows of the great Third Army. To say that she directed the theatricals of the Army of Occupation, however, is only to suggest the bare outline of the immense work she accomplished during this period which was so trying for all. Miss Donnelly deserves a substantial share of the credit for the sportsmanlike behaviour of the American Army in Germany; for not only did her little stock companies, led by her own Third Army Stock Company of Coblenz, put on a series of plays, but the entertainment program with which the Third Army, largely on Miss Donnelly's initiative, was fairly deluged, had a potent effect in every town in keeping the Americans, figuratively speaking, in step and with their heads up.

The danger that the Americans in Germany might have to rely on German music and German theatrical companies for their entertainment was averted, and the tide of German artists who thought they were going to reap a harvest was successfully rolled back before the widely enlisted array of American stage ability that Miss Donnelly drew from the Third Army. The boys put on everything from *Box and Cox* to *Hamlet*, and their own orchestras played everything from "Just a Baby's Prayer at Twilight" to chamber music of the highest class.

In fact, the little units of the American Army which are still left in Germany continue to reap the benefit from the entertainment program so competently carried on by Dorothy Donnelly. There were many able administrative heads whose cooperative effort made this achievement possible, but the genius, the inspiration, which brought forth the spontaneous response of the great American doughboy, belonged unforgettably to Dorothy Donnelly herself.

CHAPTER 19

Spreading Joy Along the Line

> *It would be argument for a week, laughter for a month, and a good jest forever*
> King Henry IV.

The examples of endurance along the front would require a Hall of Fame to perpetuate them. Every one of the entertainers faced deprivations and hardships that under ordinary conditions would have interrupted their bookings. There is the "Some Pep" Unit, for instance—it went "over" in this same autumn of 1918, headed by two of the best known acts on the vaudeville stage, Rita Walker, the dancer, and her partner-husband, Johnnie Cantwell. Travelling with them in this unit were Bessie Carrette of the Hippodrome, *High Jinks* and *The Pink Lady* and George Botsford, one of the greatest jazz pianists in America.

The "Some Pep" Unit put on real jazz vaudeville stuff all along the lines. They were waiting one day to catch their train at a big junction on the American line of communication. A long freight train came in, full of doughboys *en route* for the front. The entertainers on the platform were not hard to spot. The boys yelled for an entertainment. They got not one, but a series of shows all along the train. Johnnie Cantwell and George Botsford sang all their songs half a dozen times. Bessie Carrette sang and danced, and little Rita Walker danced her jazz from one end of the train to the other.

Johnnie Cantwell gives an alluring picture in real actor language of the way in which the *troupe* left for the front early in October, 1918:

> We left for the field today loaded down with equipment. Can you imagine Rita Walker loaded down with a blanket roll, five blankets, a grip, banjo, musette bag, canteen, tin kelly, and a

This is that so famous scene "over there." Arriving in a strange town, preferably late at night, and finding nary a "Y" representative or an army man to meet us—and asking in our best ought-to-be French, "Ou est la American 'Egreek M. C. Ah headquarter?'"

gas mask? And she insisted on carrying them all. As she started to walk down the platform to get into one of those trick railway coaches the sight of that blond apparition loaded for bear was too much for the French audience watching her, and the French people as a rule don't pay any attention to you no matter how you are made up. Soon two American doughboys tripped over each other and relieved her of most of her bundles. You will wonder why we did not help her, but the fact of the matter is that we were all loaded down, and if you didn't know George Botsford you would think that he was carrying equipment for a squad of doughboys minus the rifles. Well, we finally got into our compartment, after tripping over a couple of French generals."

They finally arrived at their destination. To go on with Mr. Cantwell's story:

I was standing in the lobby of the hotel while Felix, the porter (by the way, all the porters in France are named Felix for no reason at all) was telling me the history of the war, and I called his attention to some of the shell marks in the lobby. He told me that right where I was standing three people were killed by a bursting shell. Bessie Carrette said, 'Let's get the air,' so we left Felix flat on the spot, before he had a chance to relate some horrible details of the war and spoil our whole day.

The "Some Pep" Unit fixed up their show so that they could give it on the road, or on top of a box car, or on any sort of trick stage which turned up. This adaptability, backed by their physical exuberance and endurance, certainly served them well, especially in their tours through the hospitals. On one occasion, Mr. Cantwell wrote home:

We played a big hospital up near the front in the afternoon. It was quite a large place and when we made our entrance into one of the large wards and they realised that we were American vaudeville artists, well, I wish that you could have heard the cheering. For a moment, I forgot that I was in a hospital. We put on the show and put all the 'zizz' on, too. After we had gone all through the place, and had counted up the house in every ward, we found that our company in an hour and a half had sung a hundred and twelve songs, and Rita had done her dance

ON A SIGHT-SEEING TRIP

A FEW STADIUM CHAMPIONS

twenty-seven times, and when I got through I found out that I had turned into a beautiful tenor.

When they got back to the officers' quarters after giving their show, they heard one of the officers say, "Well, Sammie would certainly have enjoyed this." It turned out that Sammie was an aviator who had started on a dangerous mission that morning and had not returned. Just as the entertainers were finishing their sandwiches and coffee preparing to go back to their barracks, a pale face was thrust through the door and a voice said, "Well, boys, what have we here?" It was Sammie! He had crashed, and come back in a friendly ambulance unhurt save for a few scratches. The returned aviator heard so much about the "Some Pep" show that there was nothing to do but to stage the whole performance all over again just for Sammie. Then the tired quartet went back at last to their hotel to prepare for more shows in the evening. Mr. Cantwell says:

> Talking about the morale of the army, and how our shows affect the boys—we played in a camp where the boys had not seen an American show since their arrival in France. There were about three thousand in the audience, and they were hanging all over the rafters, and looking in the windows. The lights were not working that night and the best we could do was a row of candles for footlights and two lanterns for 'borders;' then they rigged up an auto lamp for a spot light and away we went after them—and those boys thought that 'theatre' was lit up like the Hippodrome. I have never in my life heard such cheers as we all received that night. I happened to meet the colonel who was in charge of that camp in Paris a few days later and he told me almost with tears in his eyes that he would never be able to repay us for that entertainment we had given the boys; that they were all like new men, happy and contented, and that their efficiency had gone up a hundred *per cent*, and they were all telling our jokes over again.

When the roll for "endurance" is called, there is one pair of mere men who should be allotted a substantial share of credit for the extraordinary nerve and pluck they added to an unusually successful and picturesque act overseas. These are Harry H. Perry and Frank A. Vardon, two Denver boys, who went over in October, 1918, and in 175 days of practically continuous entertaining gave 335 performances, each packed full of an hour of live-wire music and singing. Vardon and

Perry were true troubadours—wandering minstrels. They produced the music by means of two instruments slung over their backs, a little guitar and a big bull guitar, but every boy will testify that those instruments certainly did create harmony. Vardon and Perry played to the American troops in England, France, Luxemburg, Germany, Belgium, and even in Holland. Their enthusiasm was so great that the strain and hardships were too much for Harry Perry. He developed a very serious throat disorder on his way home, and the ship's surgeon declared that only by means of an immediate operation could his voice be saved. The operation was successful, and Perry and Vardon came home in June, 1919, a tired but thoroughly rewarded pair of full-time entertainers.

The unit which went with them through the war zone was known as "The Live Wires." It included Helen Colley as accompanist, who had accompanied the well-known baritone, Henri Scott; Dora Robeni, vaudeville and stock company actress in the Middle West; and the charming little Kentuckian, Margot Williams, whose over-night success in the first production of *Experience* established her on Broadway some years ago.

Miss Williams gives a little picture of the audiences they played to, in one of her letters home:

> They told us that one show of the Y.M.C.A. was worth a week's leave of absence to the boys, and I can readily understand it when I remember how the boys after each performance had begged us to send some other shows to them as soon as we got back to Paris. The most satisfactory work we ever did was with the sick and wounded. We would go to hospitals and give a performance on each floor and sometimes in each ward. Wounded soldiers would take me by the arm and beg me not to leave without singing again. One I remember particularly; he was blind, and our singing, his friends told me, had been the first thing that had interested him in months.

Another of these original joy spreaders in the army at this time was Burr McIntosh—actor, lecturer, raconteur, war correspondent. He went over to France early in November, 1918, just in time to go straight up into Germany and become one of the veteran entertainers in that entertainment-hungry sector. A writer who was touring the American Army shortly after it moved into Germany gives this graphic description of the type of entertainment Burr McIntosh selected from among his talents to give the doughboys:

> Picture, then, a big room, probably once the dining-room of a hotel where rich Germans and foreigners came as tourists to take a 'cure.' This high, square place is crowded with boys in khaki, sitting on the benches and the window sills, and standing against the wall.
>
> Up there on the platform is big Burr McIntosh and behind him a knot of amateur performers. Big Burr is just talking—just rippling along, with here a story full of laughs, there a bit of homely advice which received the tribute of silent attention, then a question about what those boys are going to do with their future which stirs the hearts and ambitions of his listeners. Perhaps he rises up and teaches the audience, 'Will yez all be wid me when I tackle Paddy Ryim?' Perhaps he shows some of those marvellous card tricks of his which used to impress King Edward.

Burr McIntosh varied his program with a lecture which he called *The Beast Hunters*," a straight-from-the-shoulder warning against anarchy and Bolshevism, which was a serious interlude in the midst of his funny stories. One of his most frequent hits was a little poem he wrote himself called *The Doughboy*. He lectured constantly, never missing a night, and would have been at it all the time if rheumatism had not gotten hold of him. He was ill with rheumatism in Coblenz for five weeks and a half and later in Paris for three weeks and a half. But during the time he was able to be on the road he was an inspiration to the boys, who never failed to admire his type of upstanding adventurous American.

No reminiscence of this period would be complete without a tribute to "The Laugh Barrage." Here we find Kate Condon as the leading spirit, one of the finest Gilbert and Sullivan actresses of the American stage. She is ably supported by Amy Horton, formerly pianist at Oscar Duryea's celebrated dancing school; Harry Adler, the vaudeville ventriloquist; Florence Nelson, whom everybody remembers as the "banjo girl;" David Lemer and Paula Sherman.

Here, too, we meet on the roads of France "The Gloom Chasers," a gallant sextet composed of Ray Walker, Ida Van Tine, Olive Palmer, Hinda Hand, Bonnie Murray, Eddie Fredericks, and Dunbar Averitt, one of the greatest encouragers of sunshine the gloom-infested area of Le Mans ever had.

Here we greet "The Quaint Quintet," including the twins, Mary and Marie McFarland, who had a splendid interchanging vaudeville act; Jack Cook, one of the best chalkologists in vaudeville; and an anonymous (as far as the records go) accompanist. And here, too, we listen to "Tricks and Times," which includes the lyric *soprano*, Nella Allen; the pianologist and magician, Henry Markus; and his charming partner in vaudeville, Erminie Whittell.

While chronicling, we must follow for a moment one of the breeziest of all the companies that came over—"The Manhattan Four," headed by Carol McComas, the Broadway actress who graduated from musical comedy to dramatic eminence. Walter Dale, formerly one of the ablest juvenile actors on the American stage, supported her, and the two other members of the company were Jane Tuttle, soloist at the Flatbush Congregational Church and Calvary Baptist Church in New York, and Eleanore Rogers, from the Society of American Singers' revivals of Gilbert and Sullivan at the Park Theatre in New York.

"The Manhattan Four" upon their arrival in France were given the privilege of going straight to Verdun. Here they entertained the many units of the American Army that were in radiating distance of that famous citadel. The most genuine approval of their performance comes from a detachment of the Fourteenth Engineers, who addressed the following little panegyric on the Manhattan Four "To the Whole World:"

> Never in our experience on this western front has anything pleased us as did the Manhattan Four last evening. Eighteen months' absence from the theatre and entertainment may sound like a short time to the average man, but only those who have done without amusement as we have can describe the yearning that comes over one to see, hear, and be thrilled by the songs and patter of clever entertainers. And so we looked forward to the Manhattan Four—and we judged them long before we ever saw them. 'Let's go,' we said. 'It will be good just to see American talent but, of course, we cannot look forward to the stuff we had at home.' Well, sir, we take it all back.
>
> That entertainment was the stuff to give the troops, and it was the stuff that cut the distance from here to the U. S. A. from three thousand miles to zero. Miss Jane Tuttle's songs were rendered with a tone that was as smooth and mellow as that hammock scene she described. Could we hear better at home? We

could not! Miss Eleanore Gala Rogers also was very charming, and it will be many, many days before her beautiful voice and those songs, which made such a hit with us, are forgotten. Miss Carol McComas and Walter Dale? Oh, Boy! More action than the British artillery, and if they didn't remind us of the good old days back home, I'll hope something!

Gentle Reader, our words are weak—yes, they are weaker than army coffee—in trying to express our appreciation of the Manhattan Four. We are modest and all that, but, outside of boasting of our third gold stripe, the thing we are the most proud of is the fact that we saw the Manhattan Four.

CHAPTER 20

Soldier Shows After the Armistice

This is the very coinage of your brain:
This bodiless creation ecstasy
Is very cunning in.
    Hamlet.

November 11, 1918, brought to men and women of all races and religions release from the tension and horror of war. The effect on the soldiers was more indirect, more subtle, but no less positive than had been the dangers of war.

The American Army, with the rest of the world, dropped down into the long wait before the home-going—the months that dragged on and on before the victorious soldiers began their last, long journey home. The motives which had dominated the lives of officers and men had, in large measure, been removed. All joined in the most popular and appealing refrain of the war, "We want to go home." Officers were to be demoted or permitted to resign, men were to be demobilised. The war was over, the motive for training and discipline was gone, but the courage of 3,000,000 homesick men had to be maintained 3,000 miles from the homes which some of them were not to see for months to come.

During these dangerous months of waiting the entertainers entered upon their last and greatest campaign. While the days of adventure and danger at the front were over, there was a new enemy to fight—the most dangerous of all—homesickness. "Your work has only just begun," was the order that ran along the lines of the entertainers.

You helped to win the war—now help to keep the boys happy and fit until the great day of the movement homeward.

It was at this crucial moment that the campaign for soldier shows was set in operation— and the whole army either became players or the willing prisoners of the players to whom they surrendered. There was talent enough in the A. E. F. to furnish an unlimited number of shows. The problem was to discover and assemble that talent, coach and costume the acts, and furnish theatres as soon as the companies were ready to appear behind the footlights. So Uncle Sam became the senior partner in "the greatest theatrical business in the world."

Carl J. Balliet of Buffalo, New York, had first gone overseas in December, 1917, as a Hut Secretary. He was called back to France in November, 1918, and became Entertainment Secretary at Base Hospital No. 1, at St. Nazaire, where he started in organising soldier shows. General Orders 241, by command of General Pershing, directed "the attention of all concerned to the importance of encouraging the development of all kinds of appropriate talent." Not only did the order provide for the detailing of an officer from the General Staff as Army Entertainment Officer, but specified that such officers should be detailed in "each corps and division." It further ordered:

> Commanders of regiments and other similar units will also detail suitable officers to supervise the entertainment activities of their units. All commanders will give every encouragement, consistent with military requirements, to the development of soldier talent within their commands: First, in the production of theatrical shows within the division or other unit, and second, for the training of small groups of entertainers suitable for giving entertainment in the neighbouring units and for touring the A. E. F.

This order appeared December 29, 1918, and was supplemented by Bulletin No. 1, January 28, 1919. So prompt was the response that within thirty days 1,000 members of the A. E. F. who had been professional actors had been card indexed and sixty soldier actor units had begun touring France and occupied Germany.

Here let us give credit where it is due. The notable success of this entertainment campaign is due to the outstanding ability and tireless labours of Colonel John R. Kelly, Army Entertainment Officer, and Lt. Col. R. B. Gamble, Entertainment Officer of the services of supplies. There were no men in the army better qualified for these responsibilities—and their achievement is one of the finest records in the World War.

This soldier talent movement had started from a very small beginning. Before the Armistice *The Crimson Cocoanut*, a play by Ian Hay, had been produced by two Englishmen attached to Base Hospital No. 1 in St. Nazaire. Carl J. Balliet had used *The Crimson Cocoanut* as the nucleus of a vaudeville show with soldier actors, which gradually worked itself into a musical comedy bearing little resemblance to the original drama. Mr. Balliet's continued utilization of army talent for entertainment in the St. Nazaire region provided a model for the entertainment directors of the rest of the areas of France.

In the fighting days before the Armistice Clarke Silvernail, who was an actor before he became a soldier, presented the Cohan and Harris show *What Happened to Jones* with soldier talent. This play was a milestone, for it proved that the boys at the front wanted to see shows with "women" in them, even though the "chorus girls" had masculine voices and wore hobnailed shoes. The idea soon spread, until every soldier show had its heroine and some even had pony ballets. Under Army Order 241, not only soldiers and Y.M.C.A. girls but Red Cross nurses and Knights of Columbus and Salvation Army workers could be detailed for entertainment duty, so that real girls were finally secured from these organisations to act in soldier shows, as well as the professional actresses brought over from America.

The development of dormant talent in the A. E. F. had started during hostilities, but after the Armistice work on a big scale really began. In transforming 15,000 doughboys and sailors, with now and then an officer, into singers, dancers, and spotlight favourites, George W. Doyle, assistant and successor to Carl J. Balliet, played a prominent part. Under his direction men fresh from the lines, motor mechanics, marines— in fact, men in every branch of the service—were recruited to play before doughboy audiences. The old-fashioned amateur night proved the best means of discovering talent in the army, not only the professional but the undeveloped talent.

Under the direction of Colonel John R. Kelly and Lt. Col. R. B. Gamble, all the army entertainment officers in divisions and regiments effected liaison with "Y" secretaries, having their desks in the same offices wherever that was possible. Through them, under plans developed by Mr. Doyle, announcement was made in every company that there would be a try-out in the local hut, that prizes would be given, and that the men who made good would be chosen for army shows.

No one was quicker to appreciate and encourage the efforts of a comrade in these try-outs than the soldier, but it was hard to "put anything over" on him. For instance, in one camp a would-be monologist, whose ancient jokes were received in silence, tried to rally his auditors.

"What's the matter?" he said. "Can't you guys follow me?"

"Speed up, bo, we're fifty years ahead of you," was the prompt retort from a man in the third row.

Those soldier audiences were competent judges, too, for a large number of able-bodied men of fighting age were on the American stage when America entered the war. These were not slow about volunteering, and many of these soldier-actors were men who would not have been in the draft. In nearly every regiment there was at least one man with stage experience and they were eager to get into the work.

The best talent brought out in a company show went into a regimental show, where it was given professional coaching. When the coach considered the troupe "good enough" it was tried out all through the division. Then if it seemed good enough for the A. E .F. circuit it was outfitted, costumed, and given its travelling orders. The army entertainment officer took the men selected and ordered them detailed for entertainment duty, supervising their transportation, discipline, and all military matters. The "Y" furnished coaches, costumes, stage sets, musical instruments, plays and parts where they were not written by the soldiers, sheet music, and expense money.

At the Play Factory at Tours soldier shows were manufactured almost while you waited. Here, on the side door of one of the buildings which forms the big square of barracks and headquarters offices of the Services of Supply, was a sign reading: "Entertaining Training Studios, A. E. F.—Y.M.C.A.."

The sign was not misleading. Those studios certainly were entertaining, apparently a riotous scene of turmoil, and a pandemonium of pianists, pirates, dancers, and acrobats. The real name of the place, however, by which it became known to all the A. E. F. entertainment workers, was "The Play Factory." For there, plays for the entertainment of all the soldiers in France were originated, written, cast, equipped, rehearsed, and staged, with a speed and effectiveness which would make Belasco or the Shuberts open their eyes in admiration.

Lt. Col. R. B. Gamble and his staff occupied half the office. In the other half were Howard L. Acton, of New York, "Y" Entertainment Director for the Services of Supply, and his assistants. Colonel Gamble and Mr. Acton worked out all the general plans for soldier entertainment in France. With Colonel Gamble's approval, Mr. Acton suggested and created the Play Factory. The soldier talent here was taken in charge by two professional coaches. George Spink, of East Providence, Rhode Island, who used to write sketches for Jesse Lasky and is also a popular song writer, sitting at the piano fired a continual stream of directions, criticisms, and encouragement, and never missed a note. Miss Isabel Kennedy coached not only doughboys but "Y" girls. Red Cross nurses, and occasionally French girls. Though the army was proud of the A. E. F. "chorus girls" and every regiment was sure it had the greatest boy-girl in the world, yet there was a crying, sometimes a swearing, need of real girls.

Much of the coaching was done by a twenty-three year old sergeant, Teddy Symans, who before the War turned out vaudeville sketches for the Western circuits. At nine o'clock he would be rehearsing a trio of dancing and singing artists in the ways of jazz; at ten he would be rehearsing a skit on the Russian Bolsheviki written by him the night before; in the afternoon he might train A. E. F. "chorus girls"; and from seven to ten he rehearsed "The Black Babies" in a revue written by him on Southern plantation life. "The Black Babies" had offered their own contribution, an original skit entitled *Your Man Friend*, but since this plot was hung too lightly on the familiar triangle situation, Symans had to rewrite the show.

The result was "The Black Babies" in a two-hour revue—cakewalk, jazz, buck and wing, and everything—which promised to be sent forth on the road in a week's time if the piano jazz artist could be released for art and service. For he, it must be stated, was kept from rehearsal by the harsh confines of the headquarters guardhouse. He could play the piano, but he would also fight. "As soon as Henry gets out of the guardhouse," explained Symans, "you fellows go on the road."

Nine complete original soldier shows were produced in the last three months of the Play Factory's existence, and in addition several times that number were reconstructed and freshened with new songs and dialogue. Hundreds of individual acts were tried out. Captain Sadler wrote three *librettos*—*The Hindustan* produced by the Eleventh Infantry, Twenty-Eighth Division; *One for You and One for Me,* produced as the official show of the Services of Supply, and the major part of *She Should Worry*, the Twenty-Eighth Division show. Spink was the author of *Home Again*, produced by the Thirty-Third Engineers, and *The Moppers Up*. The Tours Players, who so pleased General Pershing that he aided the soldier actors in the show to obtain transfer from the army to the Y.M.C.A., were organised and coached there.

The Le Mans Company, famed for its "Wild Fire" production, was also coached there. Both of these organisations were made up entirely of professional players, the men being from the army and the women from the Over There Theatre League. For the try-outs of shows before soldier audiences, the Trianon Theatre was operated, the largest playhouse in the city. The Play Factory was so successful in raising the standard and increasing the number of army shows, that the idea was expanded and Paris, Bordeaux, and St. Nazaire had similar "factories," all clearing through the head offices in Tours.

In this vast cooperative theatrical business, there was so great a demand for coaches that a special class at the Carnegie Institute of Technology, in Pittsburgh, gave intensive training to prepare soldier talent directors. When the specially trained coach arrived in France he was sent to a division, taking with him an assortment of costumes and stage properties suited to the needs of that division. He would then organise a dramatic club, using soldier talent almost exclusively. These shows would visit near-by divisions, which would repeat their performance one after another in turn. And there were "Y" girl dramatic coaches, too. In Finisterre Mary Sedgwick and Rose Glass trained the bluejackets of that region for vaudeville and minstrel shows.

Keen competition was encouraged and many soldier-actor plays were produced. U. S. ambulance sections with the French Army organised jazz bands, and various regiments and divisions put on musical shows and vaudeville skits. Soon the Soldier-Actor Division had 500 special theatrical units, ranging in size from ten to one hundred, touring the A. E. F. circuit. Each theatrical unit of importance went through the Play Factory at Tours, where the finishing touches were given before the road trips began.

When a show was hammered into shape by the coaches and had gone through some one of the play factories, it was costumed and outfitted. This was a vast business in itself. From March, 1918, to May 1, 1919, 23,138 costumes were provided; musical instruments and accessories 18,136, including 1,590 obtained by the Third Army; sheet music 447,908 copies, including 350,000 published by the Third Army; orchestrations 18,100, including 8,000 from the Third Army; music books 11,124; and plays 4,205.

Before the Armistice Orlin Mallory Williams, formerly of Westminster, Colorado, had the always strenuous and often unenviable job in Paris of Y.M.C.A. costumer to the khaki troupes. It was his task to see that there were frills for the Elsie Janises of the army and wigs for the martial chorus girls. Many of these garments were contributed by actors and actresses back in the States. Winthrop Ames sent over twenty-six trunks of costumes in June, 1918. Here were Indian outfits, period robes, Uncle Sam suits, cowboy rigs, hoop-skirts—everything that a khaki actor might require.

The soldiers had their own wardrobe mistresses, too. A staff of French seamstresses renovated the costumes and other properties, and their task was far from being an easy one. "Ten inches bigger at the waistline this has to be made!" you could hear one of them groaning as she held up the ball gown of a well-known actress back home. "They simply can't learn not to step on their trains," another would say, exhibiting a rent that at first glance looks beyond human skill. "My boys are the finest actors of their kind in the world," asserted Mr. Williams, "But I have to admit that chiffon flounces don't last very long with them! They forget that they are. ladies and take long steps when they have them on!"

Appeals for supplies were varied. Negro wigs were unknown in France until the doughboy came, and thousands had to be brought over, enough to camouflage an army corps. Letters like this would come in:

"The —— Machine Gun Company wants six ukuleles, three bass viols, twenty wigs, lots of grease paint, and six pairs of bones, and the colonel says the 'Y' will send them. We've got the greatest nigger show on earth! Now shoot, Mr. 'Y' man and we'll show you the real thing! (Signed) Private John Henry."

Then there was the call for gowns for the A. E. F. "chorus girls"— that grew to be a big business. Some of the gowns were creations by the most famous dressmakers—Lucille, Paquin, or Worth. During one month alone (March, 1919) 36,118 men were costumed for 4,000 productions, divided into 134 units that played in 281 different theatres. These costumes ranged all the way from policemen's uniforms to debutantes' ball gowns. In fact, the A. E. F. debutante of the 1919 model was especially successful. "She" may have fought in the Argonne or Château-Thierry as training for her "maiden effort," but her back-of-the-footlights manner retained nothing of the offensive.

"Are you a lady?" inquires the beautiful young gentleman in the dress suit. "Gawd, I try to be," she answers in perfect New York.

"I want a costume for a lady," said the entertainment officer of the 316 F. A. of the Wild Cat Division.

"Sleeping cars! Insomnia!" Words not in the entertainer's vocabulary. After a few months, one could travel atop a supply truck and sleep as soundly as in one's own trundle bed. One even learned to take a few winks the while one danced with an unsuspecting "buddy"; and to change trains in the dark silence of the night without waking was a stunt easily acquired. As for those stop-overs from 2 A. M. to 4:07, there was always an inviting sack of meal or a friendly chicken crate or two, upon the platform to snuggle up against.

"What size?" asked the "Y" costumer.

"About a perfect forty-two," he ventured.

Two "gobs" chorus ladies were sent up to Paris to select their own costumes. They fared very nicely until it came to the choice of the shoes. "*Des shoes pour moi,*" the younger and fairer urged of the shopkeeper. A sturdy pair of hobnailed buckskins were presented. "*Non, non, comme ça,*" he pointed to a pair of high heelers. Then followed an argument in which the sanity of the sailor was openly questioned by the shopkeeper. The chorus ladies departed *sans* slippers.

"Gee, they're a race without imagination," he maligned, "they can't even recognise a blushing heroine when she admits it."

At Nantes, one of the most famous costuming establishments in France worked exclusively for the soldier actor section and at Coblenz a complete German costume house was taken over. Scenery departments were established in every area. In St. Nazaire German prisoners painted scenery for doughboy shows.

Music was an inseparable part of these soldier shows. Many of them were musical revues, and dancing skits that made music absolutely necessary. There was plenty of musical talent in the army, but the crying need was for instruments. Because of an army regulation, the boys in general could not take their instruments to France. Instruments were very expensive there, because their manufacture had been suspended during the war, so the boys' pay would not permit their buying them. In the Army of Occupation sheet music was put out in bulk by a photographic process. German composers were hired to make orchestral compositions, which were also photographed and put out in enormous quantities.

After the Armistice a number of army show units were taken over into the "Y" service. The American Ambulance Jazz Band saw six months of active service with the Italian Army. It also gave special concerts under the auspices of Ambassador Page and Princess Yolando, appearing in Florence, Rome, Bologna, Naples, and Venice, where it gave a gondola jazz concert on the Grand Canal. Its concerts so amazed and delighted the Italians that the biggest phonograph concern in Italy offered to pay a high price for records. Owing to army regulations, however, the contract was declined, but the band played for fifteen records, which are immensely popular in Italy. Later, they were granted several months of additional time in France to tour the leave areas and base ports. Their fine war record and their ability to put pep into the Yankee troops made them a great attraction.

To come back from the front for the three-day rest and see a regular girl again—one who could "parlez Americaine"—was the height of many an ambition. What matter though you spend that last franc! 'Twas sure worth it for the smile and a word or two (and no English-French dictionary needed) to say nothing of the smokes and crackers!

General Pershing's "Own Band" of 105 musicians selected from all the combatant divisions, which was at Chaumont for five months under the directorship of Lieutenant Fisher, represented the best musical talent in the A. E. F. It delighted many Parisian audiences at the Cirque de Paris, and at concerts for the French Homes Association. It played for the soldier athletes of twenty-two different nations competing at the International Games at the Pershing Stadium near Paris. It made its final appearance in France in the Victory Parade on Bastille Day, marching under the Arch of Triumph with the victorious Allied Armies. Later it appeared in triumphal parades in America.

The famous Scrap Iron Jazz Band, with each member a real artist in jazz, which was composed of members of Washington University, St. Louis, and Western Reserve University, Cleveland, after being attached for nearly two years to the British forces toured the American camps and leave centres of France for several months. These were only a few of the organisations, large and small, which made American marches and American jazz known and popular throughout France.

Many of the soldier shows, as we have seen, had former professional stage men in them—actors from the trenches—as well as amateurs; others made much of the fact that not one of the cast had ever been on the professional stage, such as the *O. U. Wild Cats,* the Eighty-First Division show which became one of the most popular in the A. E. F. One of the earliest soldier shows was the Argonne Players of the Seventy-Seventh Division. They staged their first performance in the Argonne Forest in a German built theatre, twenty-four hours after it had been wrested from the enemy. Their show, *The Amex Revue,* written by Lieutenant Warren E. Diefendorf, was put on by a *troupe* of thirty soldiers who had had theatrical experience before entering the war.

On their first divisional tour the Argonne Players actually performed under shell-fire. In spite of this not a performance was postponed. After its first performance, the revue was presented in ruined cathedrals, tents, underground theatres, châteaux, huts, and on open-air platforms. President and Mrs. Wilson and the members of the Peace Commission attended the performance of the Argonne Players in the Champs Elysées Theatre, Paris. The boys of the division think that the president hastened their sailing date when he heard their song, "We Would Like to Know Just How Soon Before It's Over, Over Here"— for they sailed soon after appearing before him.

There was plenty of pathos, too, that was inseparable from France in those days. In a hospital near Tours, for instance, a show was given

"For men on crutches only." The stage was on operating tables. Wings and curtains and scenery were made of sheets. There was no music, lest it disturb other patients. Yet the performance made such a hit that the one-legged men passed their crutches out of the windows so that the soldiers not "fortunate" enough to have had their legs shot off could get in.

Then there were "The Convalescent Entertainers," a group of eleven privates organised while all its members were patients in Base Hospital No. 46 at Bazoilles. The men were strangers before they met in the hospital, though all were professionals before their enlistment. One drizzling day, one of the men sat up in bed and asked for an accordion. When he began to play another man sat up and stared.

"I may be crazy," he said, "but you sound a lot like Val Marconi of Marconi's Wireless Orchestra."

"Discovered," admitted the accordionist. "And haven't I seen your face on the screen?"

"I did juveniles for Keystone Comedies a couple of years," confessed the other. "I'm 'Sunshine Hall.'"

In a few minutes nine others of the listening patients who had been stage professionals introduced themselves, and before they left the hospital they had evolved a show of their own and produced it for the other patients. It made such a hit that, after touring France, they spent a week entertaining at the Palais de Glace and in other Paris centres and hospitals.

A soldier show contest was held at Is-sur-Tille among all the companies in that camp to determine the best show. More than 150,000 men saw the contests. The choice was made on a percentage basis, taking scenery, costumes, music, and pep into consideration. The winners were Supply Company 321 and A. S. O. No. 1, for the show "*A Day in School at Hicksville.*" They were awarded the prize which was a dance at the Officers' Headquarters, where all officers were excluded and plenty of American girls were furnished.

In New York, theatres have been built for stars, but in France one theatre was built for the first presentation of the soldier play, "*Ah, Oui.*" It is apparently much simpler to build a whole new theatre than it is to rehearse one play," observed the coach. Miss Dorothy Donnelly. The auditorium was started on Monday morning and Friday evening it opened its box office. The morning of the performance of the "*Ah, Oui,*" the orchestra looked over the new theatre and revolted. "We have no orchestra pit," they objected. "Then build one," suggested

Miss Donnelly. Ten hours is, after all, a long time. Accordingly, they dug a pit, cemented it, and when the curtain rose at 8.15 that evening, Lieutenant Fisher rapped for attention in one of the best appointed orchestra pits east of the Marne.

Liberty Bells was the Thirty-Third Division show, which had the distinction of being the first American soldier show to play in Belgium and Luxemburg before French as well as doughboy audiences. A Luxemburg paper said of this musical comedy:

"The performance was perfect in every way. The management was that of a field officer. Fifty *per cent* of the audience stood for an hour and a half, shoulder to shoulder, with stretched necks. . . . And the orchestra was a revelation with its accompaniments; the rhythm was clean cut. I had but one fear—that the head of the orchestra director might drop off from his exertions while leading the music."

Evidently their American jazz pleased the dramatic critic of Luxemburg's leading paper.

Largest of all the soldier shows, with its cast of 160, was the Eighty-Eighth Division play, *Who Can Tell?*

The dialogue was written by Dinnie McDonald and Elbert Moore of the Over There Theatre League, but many of the lines could probably be traced to the uncensored conversations of one buck with another.

"Where did you get your training to be a detective?" asks Mrs. Gondrecourt of the would-be searcher for her jewels.

"I was six weeks with the Salvage Corps," he replies.

"Are you from Scotland Yard?" demands the Englishman of the detective.

"Scotland Yard, where?"

"England."

"I don't know anything about Scotland Yard in England," admits the detective, "but I've slept in every barnyard in France."

"I never have any trouble with my French," boasts Mrs. Gondrecourt.

"No, but the French people do."

The costume effects of *Who Can Tell?* were of unusual beauty. The Jewish Welfare Board donated 75,000 *francs* to the show. This was spent entirely on costumes. They played a week's run at the Champs-Elysées Theatre. President Wilson, General Pershing, and representatives of fifteen nations at the Peace Conference attended.

As the A. E. F. extended into Germany, the theatrical circuit widened. Soldier units were likewise sent into leave areas and the smallest organisation in the A. E. F. had an opportunity to see the soldier actors at work. It was the ambition of every soldier show to play in Paris. This was a leave area for thousands. Here the Palais de Glace, the Theatre Albert Premier, and the Champs-Elysées Theatre, all under lease to the "Y," with a combined seating capacity of 15,000, were turned over on certain nights to the soldier actors and here musical comedies, minstrel shows, and vaudeville were given. *A Buck on Leave, O. U. Wild Cats, the Mo-Kan Minstrels, Let's Go*, and hundreds of others were among the attractions, each a complete show, staged, written, and produced by *soldiers*. No tickets were issued. The posters announced, "Your uniform is your pass."

As a result of this joint entertainment project outlined in General Order 241, nearly 700 soldier shows were organised, ranging all the way from small regimental affairs to such high grade productions as *Who Can Tell?* and *Liberty Bells*. The soldier actors who did duty in these shows numbered over 15,000. In March, 1919, the S. O. S. shows had an attendance of 7,350,000 for 10,158 shows. It would have taken one company five years, giving one show a day and two on Saturday, to have appeared before every audience on the army circuit when it was most extended. Despite the rather cynical observation of a middle-aged and somewhat severe colonel, who remarked that the entire A. E. F. seemed to be made up of masquerading soubrettes, there is no one who would hesitate to affirm that the job of entertainment was the biggest factor in creating contentment in the life of the army. Let us turn now to the stock companies, the real Broadway successes that played to the A. E. F.

CHAPTER 21

Broadway Successes on the Big Circuit

*For it so falls out
That what we have we prize not to the worth
Whiles we enjoy it, but being lacked and lost,
Why then we rack the value.*

Much Ado about Nothing

When the Armistice was signed the Over There Theatre League only began to fight the harder. "Extensive as the entertainment service had been," reports no less an authority than Mr. Carter, "it was speeded up after the Armistice."

The vast organisation of soldier shows described in the preceding chapter was soon supplemented by a syndicate of first-class stock companies with star castes, including some of the ablest stock actors in America. Many of the most famous shows from old Broadway were taken right into the ranks. If the soldiers could not go home, they could have something of Broadway of their own.

The legitimate phase of the stock company work began with the John Craig players. Then came John Alexander McKesson, known to Broadway as John Alexander, who organised what was known as "The Hut Players" from the men at Neufchateau. They produced Lord Dunsany's *A Night at the Inn* which was most enthusiastically received, also musical comedy adaptations and one-act plays written by the soldiers themselves. Later he organised a group called "The American Players," consisting of Theresa Dale, John Rowe, and Rose Saltonstall, who put on sketches to entertain the men in the front areas in the summer of 1918. They were followed by the Margaret Mayo

Company, in August, 1918, as already described.

A star stock company was recruited in New York and brought to France by James Forbes, direct from the Over There Theatre League. It included professional actors and actresses headed by Mary Boland. Known throughout the A. E. F. as the James Forbes Stock Company, they presented *Kick In, Travelling Salesman*, and *A Pair of Sixes* at Paris during the latter part of 1918. The company contained many prominent members of the profession—Leo Cutley, Mary Hampton, H. B. Kennedy, Madge West, Homer Miles, Albert Perry, Jack Raymond, Sidney Shields, Walter Young, Howard C. Bliss, and others. They were booked in the larger regions. E. P. Daniels worked ahead of the unit as advance agent and arranged a route in the S. O. S., playing places such as Marseilles, St. Malo, Antwerp, and Brest. They gave a Dramatic Special in Paris on December 21, 1918, at the Théâtre des Champs-Elysées with *Kick In* as the play of the occasion.

Two of the ablest figures in the whole overseas theatrical enterprise appear here in the organisation and operation of these stock companies—A. M. Beatty, whom we have already met; and after the Armistice, Oswald Yorke, the well known actor, who built dramatic units in the form of stock companies. Mr. Yorke organised and directed his work from the Paris Headquarters. It took considerable ingenuity to select plays for this purpose. He had to keep in the field as many travelling stock companies as the supply of talent would permit.

Often Mr. Yorke was compelled to oversee personally the work these companies were doing in the field and to adjust whatever difficulties menaced the stability of such units. He was aided by a corps of assistants and coaches. Mr. Yorke organised and operated seven stock companies. These companies made their headquarters mostly at St. Nazaire, Brest, Bourges, and Tours. They played *Kick In, Wild Fire, Twin Beds, A Pair of Sixes, Stop Thief,* and many other Broadway successes.

One of the most popular stock companies organised by Mr. Yorke was the Brest Stock Company, every soldier in which had seen active service on the front. They offered Eugene Walters's *Paid in Full,* along with their biggest hit, *His Majesty Bunker Bean.* The production and staging of the weekly plays of this company were under the direction of Corporal Howard Lindsay, who before the war was stage manager with Margaret Anglin. The cast included three girl entertainers sent over by the Over There Theatre League, the Misses Betty Barnicoat, formerly with Castle Square Theatre in Boston; Irene Timmons of New York, who played with Charlotte Walker in the *Plain Woman*, and was the heroine in *When We Were Twenty-One*; and Phyllis Carrington of New York City.

Then there were Ruth Garland, Alice Guthrie, and others. From the various branches of the A. E. F. came Sergeant Bernard Nedell, John Alexander, Sergeant Tod Brown, and Private Arthur Kohl. The Municipal Theatre at Brest burned down and they continued their performances on the stage in one of the largest huts. They also appeared at the Champs-Elysées Theatre in Paris. This theatre was reserved for divisional and regimental shows and most of the stock companies appeared at the Albert Premier.

From the Play Factory which we have described came the Tours Dramatic Theatre at Tours. Maida Davis, a canteen worker, changed her career in France and became an actress with this company. Their other offering was *Officer 666*. Hugh E. Wallace, Marie Falls, Alice Baxter, Howard Hall, George Leary, Ethel Martin, W. J. Roe, H. B. Turnbull, Mary Lena Wilson, and Howard Wysong were the professional members of this company.

In the Le Mans region, Madison Corey, New York producer of such successes as Mrs. Fiske in *Erstwhile Susan* and John Barrymore in *Justice*, recruited and directed talent for soldier shows and stock companies. Under his direction the Le Mans Stock Company presented big successes with a professional caste and soldier talent. This company included Dallas Tyler Fairchild, leading woman and playwright. They also played *Under Cover* in various points in the field and gave one week's performance at Paris. Walter Bull, F. Esmelton, Frances Golden, Marian Tanner, Elizabeth Paige, Pauline Whitson, and Bertha Alice Wyatt were the professional members.

The Paris Stock Company was the outcome of the "Playlet Players." It was assigned to produce plays such as *The Bishop's Candlesticks* and *Words Mean Nothing*. They gave two weeks of performances in Paris m the Palais de Glace before 20,000 soldiers. They played at Aignan, Le Mans, and Coblenz. Annette Tyler, Frances Golden, Harry J. Mates, George P. Smith, Jack Storey, Louise Hamilton, and Jeannette Grant were members of the company.

The American Players, made up of some of the members of the Craig Stock Company, were sent to the fifth region and played at the leave areas. They were in charge of Frederick Cowley. The company included Ivy Troutman, Rose Saltonstall, Theresa Dale, Rawn Rapsher and W. C. Swain. They presented one act plays such as *Strenuous Rehearsal* by Claude Gillingwater, *Bills* by William Francis, and *After the War* by J. W. Stevens. They were booked at Nice, Nimes, Lamalou-les-Bains, Val-les-Bain, Grenoble, and Aix-les-Bains.

Dorothy Donnelly organised and rehearsed the Third Army Stock Company composed of professional soldier actors and actresses, which played *Seven Keys to Baldpate*. Harrington Reynolds was the stage manager. Rosalind Fuller, Helen Scott, Patricia O'Connor, and Harriet Sterling were members.

About April, 1919, Charles Silvernail, an actor, secured permission from Cohan and Harris to present *What Happened to Jones*, with soldiers to be used as talent in the cast. They were known as the Paris Players and they added to their repertoire such plays as *Under Cover, Officer 666, Kick In, A Pair of Sixes, Hit the Trail Holiday, The Miss Leading Lady*, and *Beverly's Balance*, playing before 45,000 soldier spectators at Paris. Frederick Truesdell, Beverly Sitgreaves, and Garda Kova were professional members of the cast. They toured Toul, Marseilles, and Tours, giving one week's performance at each place. Marlyn Brown, Maurice B. Du Marais, J. G. C. LeClevcy, H. L. Jones, Joseph Diffendal, J. R. Mackay, Guy Bollinger, Gerald Sullivan, Read Rocas, D. Fullam, Harold Grigg, and Paul Sorg were the soldier members.

Then there was the Caserne-Carnot Stock Company, organised by Clara Blandick, a professional with an Over There Theatre League contract. Miss Blandick had been with May Irwin and under David Belasco's management. This company was formed of enlisted men, two professional entertainers, and members of the Women's Auxiliary Army Corps. They played American plays by well-known American playwrights—real Broadway successes. Captain E. A. Butterfield secured Clara Blandick from Nevers; the American actress was reassigned through the entertainment headquarters to Bourges to act as stage manager. On February 24, 1919, rehearsals were begun for the first production of *Forty-Five Minutes from Broadway*. This stock company opened in the Municipal Theatre. Dorothy Chesmond was reassigned to appear in this play and in the second production entitled *Believe Me, Xantippe*.

The vast cooperative entertainment schedule promulgated by Order 241 not only organised these well-known actors and actresses from America, but developed the plan originated by Carl Balliet for producing shows written—both lines and music—produced, and acted by soldiers, which the preceding chapter has described.

CHAPTER 22

Famous Casinos in a New Role

*This castle hath a pleasant seat; the air
Nimbly and sweetly recommends itself
Unto our gentle senses.*
                Macbeth.

The gigantic task of entertaining our army in the World War expanded to such proportions that it soon became "the greatest enterprise of its kind that the world has ever witnessed. When the Red Triangle went to France it was for but a single purpose—to serve the soldiers wherever, whenever, and however the service could be best utilised by the government and the army. It was ready and willing to do for the soldiers anything and everything it found to do and to the best of its ability.

It never expected, however, to become the Shuberts or the Klaw and Erlangers of Europe and corner the management of all the leading theatres—any more than it ever expected to take over the leave areas for the army, assume the canteen burden for the army, inaugurate the educational system for the army, institute the unprecedented system of athletic contests which culminated in the Inter-Allied Games, or conduct a soldiers' remittance and banking business. It assumed the unparalleled task of all these and many more duties whenever the army called upon it for service, even though it knowingly and willingly under took the "impossible."

The incomparable record of the leave areas, while a great story in itself, is so interwoven with the entertainment service that the two are here inseparable, for it was in the theatres and casinos where the Americans were on leave that the actors played before their biggest houses.

It was a glimpse of the Grand Cercle, the big casino at Aix-lea-Bains, while searching for a suitable spot for a leave area, that first started this great syndicate. Immediate grasp of its recreational possibilities determined the selection of the place, whose name practically became a synonym for the word furlough throughout the A. E. F., and began the enterprise which proved to be the most successful of all the American undertakings in France. It was a strange fate that this magnificent temple of chance with its splendid theatre should, through the exigencies of war, come under control of the Y.M.C.A., with the result that some of the biggest playhouses in France and Germany were later taken over.

The night of its formal opening was an auspicious one. E. H. Sothern was there and consented to read Hamlet's soliloquy and a poem from *If I Were King*. Among the *permissionnaires* attending was an artilleryman who was a member of the company which fired the first American gun at the Boches. In private life he had been an actor and a member once of Mr. Sothern's companies. He was selected to introduce his former chief. Although he had written out his speech and memorized it, when the time actually came to present Mr. Sothern the young man was seized with stage fright. However, while the audience held its breath, he did manage to declare it was the "proudest moment of his life," and bow to Mr. Sothern, making probably the hastiest exit of his artistic career. Later there was dancing in the ballrooms, with music by the military band and local French orchestra.

When owners of rival institutions at other resorts heard of the war-time use of the Aix casino they all seemed eager to have their own serving the cause in similar manner. Many visited this noted watering place to see for themselves. They were so favourably impressed with the excellent care and management, under the supervision of Mr. Franklin S. Edmonds of Philadelphia, assisted by Mrs. Theodore Roosevelt, Jr., that nearly all of them offered their own casinos to the Association. When the Prince of Monaco saw the Grand Cercle during the American occupation of Aix he was convinced that the "Y" was a good tenant, and expressed a desire to have the famous resorts of his own domain—Monaco, Monte Carlo, and Condamine—leased in similar fashion.

But there were international precautions regarding neutral boundaries which prevented any immediate step in accepting the Prince's invitation. The time finally came after the Armistice when Monte Carlo could be taken on; needless to state, it became one of the most popular retreats of the Americans. France has nearly as many casinos as it has watering places. Almost every resort, whether by the seaside or in the mountains, has its amusement centre where gambling is a licensed pastime and theatrical attractions ranging from *opera-bouffé* to vaudeville provide continual diversion throughout the season. Thirty-nine such places were taken over for leave centres and entertainment, and the casinos were converted into soldiers' clubs where the little army of entertainers came and went in endless procession.

Most of the casino owners and lessees were pleased with the idea, offering their properties without any profit on the same patriotic terms as did the proprietors at Aix. A few were found to be grasping, as is always the case, demanding such high rentals that the French Government stepped in and settled matters. Besides the noted Riviera casinos, the "Y" conducted the famous St. Malo Casino, the High Life Casino at Dinard, that glittering spot far-famed as the "Nice of the North," and the casino at Bagnères-de-Luchon, the finest in the Pyrenees. Others leased were at Challes-les-Eaux, Lamalou-les-Bains, Eaux Bonnes, Grenoble, La Bourboule, and Cauterets. At Cauterets the capacity of the big casino was so taxed by the large number of *permissioinaires* sent on leave to the Pyrenees that it was augmented by the rental of a smaller place near by—the Casino des Oeufs.

In the resorts of lesser magnitude where there were no casinos, the theatres afforded the principal amusement. These the "Y" rented, as at Nimes, where the Grand Municipal Theatre, and at Annecy where the Theatre Municipal were taken over in lieu of casinos. And here the American actors were hailed by the crowds. When the Brittany coast area was opened at St. Malo, its famous casino was in use as a French military hospital. Until the French Medical Corps could find other quarters for its patients in order to accommodate its American allies, the municipal theatre was rented for soldier entertainments.

Of course the great St. Malo Casino was vastly preferable to any theatre, because of the unusual combination it offered in recreational facilities. Under its roof were a beautiful theatre, dining rooms, and dancing halls, besides the big bath house on the beach, the Hotel Jacques Cartier, and other hostelries which went with the lease.

At some resorts there were hotels with small concert halls or there were storage buildings in which a proscenium arch could be improvised. When Biarritz was opened in February, 1919, the casino owners were fearful lest any lease might cut into their profits of the approaching season. So at much pains and no little expense the building of the

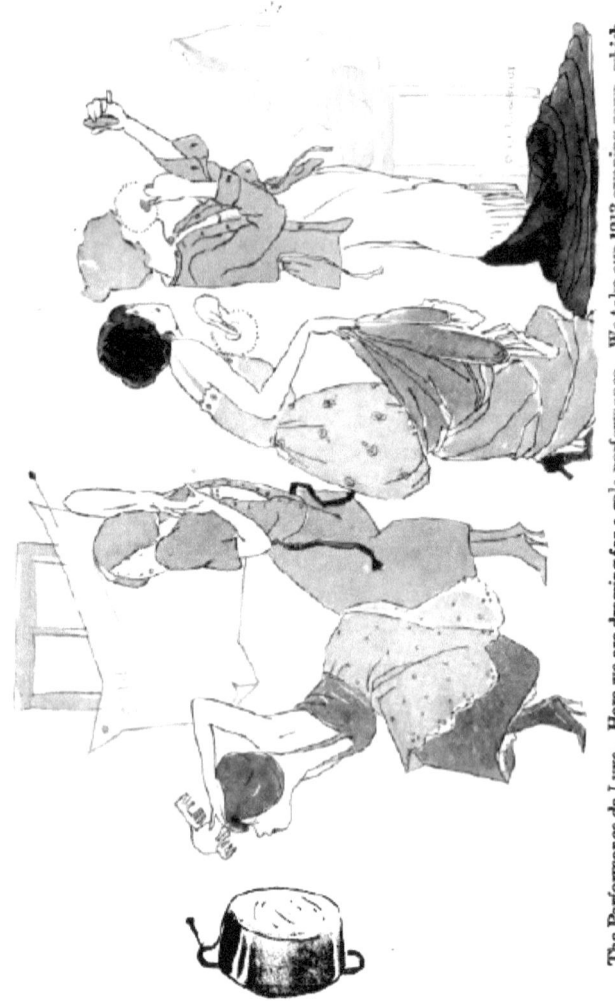

The Performance de Luxe. Here we are dressing for a gala performance. We take our 1913 evening gown, which, after having carted it about with us for the last sixteen months, we are at last going to have the opportunity to wear. What matters a few rips and wrinkles! Aided by a pin or two, a much-appreciated dish pan "mirror," and a lot of chatter, one can (even in a six by ten room) make oneself a wondrous sight for the boys who have seen naught but uniforms for many a month.

Syndicated Initiative, an exhibition building, was taken over. An ample stage was erected to suit the requirements of almost all the shows and movies routed through the place.

At Chambéry, the Apartement du Boigne was the only available place in town besides the Chambéry Club. So the entertainment program there was largely confined to the screen and smaller productions. The ground floor of the Hotel Majestic at Chamonix was made to fill all needs. Cinema halls and concert rooms with small stages and limited seating capacities were equipped in the Officers' and Enlisted Men's Clubs at Nancy and in the building of the famous Nancy Thermal Baths.

When the Stars and Stripes crossed the Rhine in December, 1918, the Red Triangle went along—or, rather, tried to be there m advance to receive the troops. In response to a request from General Dickman, sent through W.W. Gethmann, the chief secretary with the Third Army, Mr. Edmonds and the late George W. Perkins hastened to Coblenz for a conference regarding the establishment of leave centres and entertainment at five of the principal points in the zone of American occupation.

Nine complete divisions comprised the United States forces in Germany. Having just finished a strenuous campaign which closed the war, General Dickman and his commanding officers felt that the men were in real need of relaxation of the proper sort. An universal opinion prevailed that inasmuch as these were all combat divisions, the best was none too good for them. The officers, too, felt concern for their men lest if proper diversion was not provided the enemy might make insidious overtures to fraternize. Entertainment was vitally important.

At once the great Fest Halle and the Leseverein Theatre at Coblenz and the big Kurhaus at Neuenahr were taken over. The Casino at Andemach was converted into a soldiers' club, and to entertain its overflow two movies a day were run at the Hotel Dahlmann. At Neuwied, the Hotel Hohenzollern was turned into a cinema hall, patronized by the crowds that poured into that centre on leave. All these amusement places seated great numbers. The Neuenahr Kurhaus easily accommodated 2,500, while the Coblenz Fest Halle was much larger.

On its first floor was a small stage for concerts and there was a large concert hall with a splendid organ on the second, where evening gatherings were held. It was soon found that this stage was too small for both professional and soldier talent *troupes*, so under Tony Hunting a large, finely equipped stage was erected which accommodated the

Dancing is generally conceded to be a pleasure, but when one has, in the space of a few months, danced 78,571 miles,—or 3 1-7 times the distance around the earth,—it ceases to be such. With smiling faces and aching limbs, in heavy shoes and hot uniforms, before breakfast, through lunch hours, on stone, on wood, on cinder floors, or on no floors at all, they danced biggest productions. The Gemeinde Haus, renamed the Little Playhouse, was rented later for rehearsals of soldier shows during the day and professional vaudeville at night.

Paris became after the Armistice the American's Mecca. It was a herculean task to keep the boys properly entertained during this American invasion. Many thousands pressed in to the city daily. Extensive plans were launched forthwith for their diversion. The Theatre Albert Premier, with only a seating capacity of 700, which had been used for various theatrical productions, was now found entirely too small for growing demands. So the Palais de Glace was taken over. This was one of the biggest single ventures.

In addition to its theatre, accommodating 4,000 seated and 1,000 more standing, it served as a clubhouse and canteen for men and women in any of the uniforms of the Allied nations. Over 1,000,000 persons, mostly soldiers, were entertained here. There was a constant stream of distinguished guests—among them were President Wilson, Ambassador Sharp, General Pershing, Premier Lloyd George, Secretary Daniels, and Samuel Gompers. During its period of operation, from March 31 to June 30, 1919, its wet canteen served more than 675,000. Over 200 theatrical performances were given during the time, and thirteen cinema shows were run every week.

Noted actors and A. E. F. boxing champions appeared on its stage. Homer Rodeheaver and other religious leaders conducted services on Sundays. Its closing program on the night of June 30, 1919, was an all-star vaudeville bill. The feature number was the song "America to France" dedicated to Marshal Foch. It was written by Henry Hadley, with words by Louise Ayers Garnett, and sung by Ida Brooks Hunt who had sung "My Hero" in the original production of *The Chocolate Soldier*.

Another of the mammoth Parisian playhouses conducted by the Entertainment Department was the Théâtre des Champs-Elysées, one of the most elegant in appointments on the Continent. New, spacious, and elaborate, it was richly decorated and upholstered and had a comfortable seating capacity of 4,000. The stage was so large that an ordinary company was obliged to bring its settings away "down stage." For the large musical show it was ideal, and for general equipment it was unsurpassed. It delighted the A. E. F. chorus "girl" who complained that other surroundings cramped their style. The opening performance was a gala night—*A Buck on Leave* earning the *sobriquet* of the big *Winter Garden Show of France*, with seventy-five American soldiers in the company, fifty in the band, and an orchestra of thirty. It was put on by the Motor Transport Reconstruction Park of Verneuil.

The next attractions were "The G. H. Q. Players of Chaumont," "The Merry Makers" and "The Ordnance Review." The Cirque de Paris capped the climax so far as accommodations were concerned. Its seating capacity of 6,000 was increased to 8,000, entertaining in two performances 15,000 men a day. The stage was equipped with facilities for large and small productions. There was also a regulation boxing ring besides many rest rooms. With the seating capacities of all the amusement places under the management in Paris, including the Hotel Pavilion with its 450 chairs in its concert hall, about 25,000 soldiers were entertained every day between March 31 and June 30, 1919.

At various other points theatres were taken over, especially at Chaumont, Tours, Le Mans, and Trèves. All were fairly well equipped with curtains, lights, scenery, and commodious auditoriums. At Toul the municipal theatre was engaged and outfitted and it made a splendid show house for the Second Army productions. The Trianon Theatre at Tours gave long and valuable service, housing at different times every important A. E. F. attraction.

The largest theatre in France under the control of the Young Men's Christian Association was one it constructed itself, the Victory Theatre, at Bordeaux. It covered three acres of ground in the Embarkation Camp and could be seen for miles. Besides a large stage and auditorium with boxes and graduated seats, there was a huge dancing floor. The equipment included eleven dressing rooms, four floodlights, two spotlights, numerous "sets," and a curtain on which was painted the most colossal eagle in France, the work of Lieutenant Robinson. Franklin Hall was another theatre in Bordeaux.

The large municipal theatre at Le Mans was secured whenever there were no French shows billed. There were regular performances there, too, at the Salle des Concerts. At Antwerp, the Theatre des Variétés was transformed into an American amusement place, which was operated under the supervision of Captain Donovan, entertainment officer for the area embracing Antwerp, Brussels, the Hague, Rotterdam, and Apa. Here the Knights of Columbus furnished the theatre, the Y.M.C.A. the entertainment and costuming, and the Jewish Welfare Board the orchestra.

The greater part of the entertainment work in Italy was carried on in hospitals. A few theatres were rented such as the playhouse at Treviso, the Teatro Sociale di Palazzola sull 'Oglio, the Teatro Politeama di Como, the Teatro Politeama di Monza, and the Teatro Lirico—all in Milan. A medieval palace in Florence containing a private theatre was probably the most pretentious place taken in Italy. Near Bologna, Castel Maggiore was rented for entertainments.

The actor in the World War was always on duty: his "cue" was twenty-four hours a day wherever the doughboy "called" him; and his theatre was wherever he could find an audience from front line trench and dugout to some of the finest houses in Europe.

CHAPTER 23

Entertainment in Camps at Home

*You shall have better cheer
Ere you depart; and thanks to stay and eat it.*
                                            Cymbeline.

Let us now review the reserve army of entertainers who were holding the "fort" back home in America.

More than half the American soldiers, called to the colours never left our shores. Nearly 3,000,000 men, whose service stripes are of silver, share the honour in which America holds all who donned the olive drab. So among the entertainers it is estimated that more than 20,000 actors, professional and semi-professional, with lyceum workers, singers, and amateur entertainers, appeared before the soldiers in American camps.

The need of entertaining the army at home was almost equal to that in France—and the American stage rallied to the home service. It must be remembered that every soldier, whether he went across or not, spent some time in one of the thirty-two cantonments. The whole army, 5,000,000 strong, passed through these camps. This called for a volume of entertainment—an army of artists, singers, and actors—exceeding the numbers needed overseas. If there was drudgery in France, there was also novelty; if there was discomfort and danger, there was also excitement and activity. It may be doubted if any man was ever more homesick in France than he was in those first days when, fresh from the comfort of home, he was thrown into the roughness of training camp life.

The process of reshaping American individualism into a harmonious unit, of adjusting widely differing personalities into a disciplined, smoothly working machine, was not accomplished without painful experiences. The best medicine was a good laugh, a clean hour of distraction and forgetfulness.

In these American camps we find thousands who volunteered at the historic Palace Theatre meeting when the Over There Theatre League was organised and who, unable to get overseas because of restrictions, limitations, contractual obligations, or other obstructions, literally invaded the American camps—still eagerly waiting for the opportunity to go abroad with the soldiers.

"Come and hear Madam Schumann-Heink."

"Madam Louise Homer will sing at the Big Y tonight."

"Free concert by the New York Clef Club Orchestra."

That was the sort of invitation extended night after night to the boys in the home camps. It was possible because the greatest artists of the American stage and concert would give their time and talents freely for the entertainment of the army. The roll would fill this volume and make of it a catalogue and directory of the profession. Think of any form of entertainment you like—it was given by its foremost exponents before soldier audiences. Vaudeville, in all its variety of monologue, dance, sketch, acrobatics, juggling, tight and slack rope dancing; opera and concert; musical comedy and farce; instrumental music of every sort from the soloists to the greatest bands and orchestras—whatever the American public has stamped with its approval by crowding the theatres of America, that the soldiers of America saw in the great auditoriums or in the huts of the welfare societies scattered through the camps.

The list is endless. Nothing was too good to show before the soldiers. Mischa Elman and his magic violin, Harry Lauder, David Bispham, Evan Williams, Reinald Werrenrath, Freda Hempel, Nora Bayes, Irving Fisher, Richard Carle, Grace Van Studdiford, Maud Powell, Andrew Mack, Maude Adams, Jefferson de Angelis, are only a few of the names which come to mind. The Coburn Players, the New York Symphony Orchestra, and the New York Philharmonic Orchestra were some of the organisations whose names are familiar. The French Veterans' Band, every one of whom had seen active service and most of whom had been wounded and decorated, was brought to America and toured the cantonments, financed and routed by the "Y."

The places for entertainment comprised an immense variety of buildings and improvised stages out of doors. There were the great Liberty Theatres, thirty-two of them, erected by the Commission on Training Camp Activities. In these, metropolitan successes were booked. Bookings for the Liberty Theatre at Camp Dix during the month of February, 1918, included William Courtenay and Thomas A. Wise in *General Post* from the Gaiety Theatre, New York; the Liberty Comedy Company in *Baby Mine*, and *Kick In, Flora Bella, The Beauty Shop, Fair and Warmer, Turn to the Right, Princess Pat, Daddy Longlegs, Prince of Pilsen,* and *Mary's Ankle*. For these shows the commission fixed a nominal charge of twenty-five and fifty cents.

Then there were the big "Y" auditoriums seating several thousands, designed like the Liberty Theatres, for audiences drawn from the whole camp. Here great concerts were given by artists of international fame. The Philadelphia Orchestra, the New York Clef Club Orchestra, The Elsa Fischer String Quartet, and the Edna White Trumpet Quartet were among the organisations which were thoroughly enjoyed and appreciated, while a number of university glee clubs, and such organisations as the Tuskegee Singers and the Fisk University Jubilee Singers gave their always popular programs.

In many camps what was called "the outdoor Y" was added to the big auditorium. This was usually a stage so arranged that thousands of men could gather about it on all sides. It served equally well for a boxing match, an acrobatic exhibition, a speech, or a concert. With a booth erected for the movie machine, and with a screen of boughs and flags along one side for a background, it enabled larger audiences to watch the pictures or a vaudeville program than could be gathered in any building.

At Camp Sheridan, an old state fair ground auditorium known as the Buckeye Coliseum was repaired and used for entertainment. This was capable of accommodating 12,000 men, and ex-President Taft addressed there a crowd that filled the building. This is but a sample of the audiences that were addressed by Mr. Taft at other cantonments. Under the auspices of the "Y" he visited all but two of the cantonments in America, addressing a total of over 300,000 men. He presented before his soldier audiences the case of America *vs.* Germany from the standpoint of an international lawyer, presenting both sides of the case and drawing his conclusion so that there could be no possible doubt in the minds of his audience of the justice of their cause.

Just as space does not permit mention of all who entertained in the camps, so the names of the many organisations and individuals who arranged bookings, got together troupes, and conducted parties of entertainers to the camps far outrun the possibility of adequate record. Mr. John D. Sullivan of the United Booking Office, New York, the manager of the Keith Orpheum Circuit, Mother Davison, Amelia Bingham, Sophie Tucker, The Stage Women's War Relief, the New York Mayor's Committee of Women, and many others in every part of the country will be long remembered for such services. Mr. Charles D. Isaacson, of the New York *Globe*, served faithfully and persistently in providing concert parties of the highest quality, and what he saw of the response of the men as he went from camp to camp led him to predict again and again that the war would develop an appreciation of music such as America had never known.

The Stage Women's War Relief extended a service that will never be forgotten by the soldiers. Here we find serving the army such distinguished artists as Rachel Crothers, Elizabeth Tyree Metcalf, Louise Closser Hale, Dorothy Donnelly, May Kirkpatrick, Mrs. Shelley Hull, and Minnie Dupree. Here, too, in our American war relief we find Blanche Bates, Jessie Bonstelle, May Buckley, Bijou Fernandez, Mrs. Joseph Grismer, Gladys Hanson, Florence Nash, Mrs. Chauncey Olcott.

There are also Mrs. Otis Skinner, travelling from camp to camp; Chrystal Herne directing the work in New York; Mrs. Walter Vincent recruiting the vaudeville world; Mrs. William Farnum recruiting the cinema stars; Fanny Cannon in charge of soldiers' welfare; Mrs. Daisy Humphreys directing publicity; Felice Morris as executive secretary; Anna L. Faller as auditor; and Mrs. Eula S. Garrison as manager of all camp entertainments. Here, also, we greet Mary Boland and Carol McComas, Florence Gerrish, Virginia Fox Brooks, Lillian Albertson, Margaret Dale, Georgia Caine Hudson, and Hope Latham Keniper—every name mentioned being an officer of this vast organisation, the rank and file of which enrolled practically every stage woman in America.

Mrs. Garrison says:

> We gave 1,430 shows and entertained in more than 1,000 wards in hospitals. We played in 61 different hospitals, 58 camps and training stations, 67 clubs and service houses, and on 14 battleships. We co-operated with the Y.M.C.A. and every organisation—the Red Cross, Knights of Columbus, Jewish Welfare, War Camp Community Service, and Salvation Army—and with individuals.

No profession was more largely represented in the army itself than the theatrical. In the very first days, when entertainment was wholly *impromptu*, men would be discovered in almost every audience who could do a song, dance, or monologue with all the finish of the experienced performer. As one entertainment director described it:

> The hall would fill up after the evening mess and something had to be done to entertain the boys. We would get a pianist somewhere, I would usually start with a few songs, and then the performers would be dragged, pushed, or lifted on to the stage by their buddies. Everybody was good-natured and all seemed to enjoy the evening whether the show was good or not, and usually it was surprisingly good.

Men were found who were experienced in producing plays, canvasses were made to discover soldiers who had dramatic talent or experience, and elaborate plays were written, staged, and produced before enthusiastic audiences. At Camp Dix Mr. Leopold Lane, legitimate and movie actor, had charge of entertainment. The first play was a one-act comedy *One Hundred Dollars Reward*, written by Private Roland Southerland, 1st N.Y. Field Artillery and presented by Company A. 311 Infantry, October 29, 1918. This was quickly followed by *My Turn Next* presented by Company E of the 311th. Numerous others followed, among them *You'll Like It*, with a cast including Private William Sully formerly of the Ziegfeld Follies, Jack de Graff well known in musical comedy, Eddie Flynn from the vaudeville stage, and several others familiar to Broadway.

At Camp Upton, the well-known song writer Sergeant Irving Berlin produced *Yip Yip Yaphank,* which not only scored a hit in camp, but was eventually produced on Broadway with great success by its soldier cast. At Camp Zachary Taylor, Foxall Daingerfield organised and trained the "Soldier Players," who not only toured the huts of the camp, but were sent on tours through several states by the Government, in connection with the Liberty Loan drives. At Camp Shelby the "Thirty-Eighth Division Players," were organised and directed by Marston Allen, and at Camp Gordon the "Army Entertainers' League," at one time numbering more than 150 men, gave high class vaudeville in all parts of the camp. At Camp Sherman, for four months, the Ohio Federation of Musical Clubs furnished the entertainment.

Chambers of Commerce, Rotary Clubs, and other organisations did their part, and hardly a city or town within a half day's journey of one of the big cantonments or smaller camps could be found without some organisation or individual who had assumed responsibility for seeming talent for shows or concerts.

This is not to say that there were no difficulties. It took strenuous days and nights on the part of those responsible to keep the stream flowing smoothly so that every point would be regularly served. Many a cold ride in street car or automobile was taken by performers, to keep engagements in out-of-the-way places. Sometimes the eagerness of soldiers for more, and ever more, put a severe strain upon endurance. During the quarantine at Camp Dix, on a single evening one group of vaudevillians repeated their thirty-minute sketch seven times at different barracks, and the Orpheus Quartet sang more than eighty selections. This record was soon passed by another group of singers who gave ninety songs in one day.

Opportunities for heroism, mounting even to the last full measure of devotion, presented themselves. At Camp Lewis, two members of the Metropolitan Opera Quartet, Misses Linnie Love and Lorna Lea, arrived for a return engagement just as the camp was going under quarantine for influenza. Both girls volunteered to remain and undergo quarantine for the sake of entertaining the men. As a result of overwork and exposure, both were stricken with the disease and taken to the hospital. Miss Lea recovered, but Miss Love was so exhausted by her untiring efforts that she rapidly failed and died in the hospital, the only worker with the Y.M.C.A. who died as a result of the epidemic in that camp. No braver or more loyal heart ever went over the top in France.

There was an informality and personal exchange between artist and audience such as never could be possible under other conditions. Again and again the entertainers stayed for greetings after the show, and the shout would rise, "No seconds, boys. You can't shake hands but once," as enthusiasts tried to slip into the line for a second greeting. When Sue Harvard, singing for the first time "Have You Seen Them in France?" ended by throwing copies of the song, with a package of Bull Durham attached to each, among the audience, there was a small riot. Often the camp song-leader would spring to the platform at the end of a concert and say, "Shall we sing a couple of songs to entertain our entertainer?" Choruses would rise in "The Long Trail" and "Over There," until the artist whose voice had held thousands spellbound confessed that she had received more than she had given.

CHAPTER 24

Singing Their Way to Victory

*The man that hath no music in himself
Nor is not moved with concord of sweet sounds,
Is fit for treasons, stratagems, and spoils.*
                    The Merchant of Venice.

America has never been a singing nation, yet in each great national emergency songs have appeared that in words, melody, and rhythm expressed the emotion of the time. No one who has heard the veterans of the Grand Army of the Republic sing their songs has failed to realise what those songs meant to another generation. The great drawback in those songs was that they were sectional and tended to sharpen memories which should be softened with the passing of time.

The Spanish-American War was too short to develop a mass of songs, as true folk songs are the product of time. "Hail, Hail, the Gang's All Here," and "There'll Be a Hot Time in the Old Town Tonight" had all the care-free enthusiasm of American youth volunteering for an adventure. "The Blue and the Gray" indicated the end of sectionalism for a new generation. The one song which came out of the Spanish-American War as a national song was old when that war began, but "Dixie" is unquestionably the most popular song in America today. The interim between the Spanish-American War and the Great War did not produce a single addition to our folk songs.

While the Anglo-Saxon stock and traditions are predominant with us, the growth of our great cities, with their colonies of foreign blood not fully Americanized, has hindered the development of an art form so dependent on common standards as the folk song and folk singing. Before the Great War this was recognized by a few musicians and attempts had been made to promote block parties and community singing. Tentative efforts had also been made at sing-songs in the Plattsburg camps organised before we went into the war. It was here that the first new song appeared—"The Last Long Mile"—of all those which came to express the various feelings and emotions of America's soldiers in the camps at home and overseas. George M. Cohan's vigorous march song, "Over There," was even more popular with the public outside the cantonments, and both were constantly used by the soldiers at home and overseas.

The French had a single song, the melody of which was so inflammatory that prior to the Great War it had become the song of insurrection and anarchy all over Europe. It was then known as "The International" but the essential part, the fiery melody, had a century before been sung by "Marseillaise Battalion" when it toiled northward toward Paris to hearten the sinking spirits of those who were struggling for a new republic. The *Marseillaise* has always been dangerous to the enemies of freedom and liberty. It was sung by all the Allied Armies in France more generally than any other song.

There were other songs, not so powerful, which were heard by all Americans overseas. The whole French nation sang the fine old song, "*Chant de Depart*," the greatest bond between the glorious men of France who went to the front and the bereaved country which sent them. Then there was the most romantic of all the Napoleonic marching songs, "*Le Reve Passée*," and the present-day song "Verdun," which sets the phrase "They shall not pass" to music for generations of French to come. One new song our overseas army brought back as characteristic of the France they knew. Naughty and philandering, brave and sacrificial, with a rush of wondrous marching meter, "*Madelon*" was the most generally popular of all the new war songs. With its French words and a half dozen English versions, "*Madelon*" became as familiar to the Americans as any of their own songs.

The Americans had little chance to hear or learn the British songs aside from "Tipperary," which had become well known long before we went into the War and went straight to the heart of every city man whether he had ever before heard of Piccadilly or Leicester Square or not. Later, the Americans took up "Blighty," "I Want to Go Home," and "Keep Your Head Down, Fritzy Boy."

When the great training camps began to be organised, it was decided to have a singing member on each of the "Y" staffs, a policy which was adopted after careful investigation and in accord with the wishes of Mr. Lee F. Hamner of the Fosdick Commission on Training Camp Activities. The early song leaders were highly trained musicians, whose professional efficiency made unnecessary any special training for their new work. The intention was to send a singing army to France and keep it a singing army. Mr. Marshall Bartholomew, a trained musician, who had been in prisoner-of-war work overseas, was placed in charge at New York Headquarters. Professor Harold C. Knapp of North-western University prepared a list of songs and music to be used by the American Army. Mr. Robert Lawrence was at the head of the classes for musical leadership at the Columbia University conferences held in New York during the summer and fall of 1918 and all prospective overseas workers were given daily drills in singing. The methods developed at New York Headquarters were used in the five other training schools, the intention being to produce a standardized method of song leadership for a limited list of the best known hymns, patriotic and sentimental songs.

General Pershing, in speaking of the most inspiring moments in the war, once remarked:

> I think they were when I heard my army singing.

From that historic moment when General Pershing, with his First American Expeditionary Forces, stepped on French soil, and the strains of "The Star-Spangled Banner" greeted them, throughout their months in France until they embarked for home a victorious army, the Americans sang their way through the war.

"Keep the army singing!" This was the constant order, not only from General Pershing in France but from General March throughout the army camps in America. It is recognised by the ablest military minds that song is one of the most potent factors in warfare; and how they did keep the men singing! More than 200 song leaders were sent overseas, more than 1,000 athletic directors were trained as song leaders, and every one of the 25,000 workers "got the boys to singing" whenever the opportunity occurred. These song leaders followed the army into Italy, Germany, Russia, Siberia—they actually followed the Stars and Stripes around the world.

So great was this sing-song campaign that printing presses in America, England, France, and wherever they could be secured in Europe, were humming off songbooks and song leaflets by the millions for distribution to the army. It would probably be difficult to find a doughboy who did not at sometime carry one of these songbooks in his khaki pocket. A bag of "makings" and a soiled copy of the paper-

When for weeks you've had performances morning, noon, and night, and at last comes an afternoon with nothing to do but three weeks' laundry, a few letters, a bit of mending, some socks to darn and maybe wash your hair and file a nail or two—and along comes Jimmy something-or-other, aged nineteen, from Tulamasoo, Idaho, to pay you a call (knowing you must be lonesome!), and he stays and stays and stays and tells you of all his love affairs (oh what a devil with the ladies he is!) of the last sixteen years, but vows no girl holds a candle to you!—wouldn't you just like to forget you're a nice "Y" lady and say something in "shavetail" language?

covered *Popular Songs of the A. E. F.* bearing the slogan, "Give me the man who goes into battle with a song in his heart," were like Captain Kidd's treasures to the doughboy. This songbook, sent out along the front by the A. E. F.-Y.M.C.A., carried the words of 143 popular songs with the message:

> It's the songs we sing and the smiles we wear that make the sunshine everywhere.

A transport, crowded with soldiers, is on the "road to France." The shores of America have faded from the vision and the ship is plunging on its way toward mid-ocean and the submarine danger zone. We hear the rhythmic echo of voices—thousands of voices:

> *Goodbye Broadway, hello France—*
> *We're ten million strong—*
> *Goodbye sweethearts, wives, and mothers.*
> *It won't take us long—*
> *Don't you worry whole we're there—*
> *It's for you we're fighting, too—*
> *So goodbye Broadway, hello France—*
> *We're going to square our debt to you!*

And on that memorable morning when the shores of France first loom into view—what an outburst of song: "Hail! Hail! the Gang's All Here!" "It's a Long Way to Berlin, but We'll Get There." "When We Wind Up the Watch on the Rhine."

The great job finally became to prevent the soldiers from singing at a critical point or to stop them once they got started. The song leaders who went over to France found lots of work to do, but on the whole they found that the intensive work done in America in teaching the soldiers the words of the real songs they wanted to sing, and impregnating them with confidence and the love of real singing, resulted in much singing and some new songs.

The songs will not always bear textual repetition, but their melodies, even those which sprang spontaneously out of war conditions, were pure music. Over and over again on going up to the line in the cold dawn, or in the equally wretched hours just after midnight, officers would frequently have to call out, "Cut out that d—— singing!"

For the American doughboy had that type of buoyant courage which can be properly expressed only in a chorus.

Coming back from the lines it was often one continuous sing-song

And now and then the entertainers were entertained and 'tis hard to know which enjoyed themselves the more—the noble much-bandaged hero telling how the "seventy-fives were raining around," or the spellbound, wide-eyed "Y" girls whose nearest approach to the front had been to G. H. Q. or a souvenir-hunting trip to Rheims five months after the Armistice.

all the way. In the huts, where men would occupy the seats hours before the performance began so as to make sure of getting their share in these always crowded show-houses, the natural thing was to sing. Somebody would start, and off they would go. Far and away the most frequently sung of all the American tunes, a song that hypnotized the American doughboy in his leisure moments, was that languorous ditty:

> *I'm sorry, dear—so sorry, dear—*
> *I'm sorry I made you cry!—*
> *Won't you forget, won't you forgive?*
> *Don't let us say goodbye!*
> *One little word—one little smile—*
> *One little kiss—won't you try?*
> *It breaks my heart to hear you sigh—*
> *I'm sorry I made you cry!*

An entertainer who could start this song was as sure of her house in the rain-soaked, primitive conditions of wartime France, as was George Cohan in a patriotic flag-waving on Broadway. They would go on to "Poor Butterfly," "The Broken Doll," "Ireland Must Be Heaven" and "Oh, You Beautiful Doll."

Then there was that other splendid group of songs, the home sentiment songs: "There's a Long Long Trail Awinding"—it lifted the soldiers' hearts as clearly as the inspiration of any victory. "Hark! Hear the Soldiers Singing," "The Rose of No Man's Land," "My Belgian Rose," "Lorraine," "Keep the Home Fires Burning," "The Little Gray Home in the West," and "The End of a Perfect Day"—what visions arose before their eyes, what irresistible repose and confidence the music brought!

And how these memories in melody started the hearts of thousands of boys beating—how the eyes moistened as they fell into the melody of

> *It's a long way to dear old Broadway—*
> *But we're coming back to you!*

How the feet began to beat time with the heart, and bodies swung into the rhythm of "I Want to Go Back to Michigan—I Want to Go Back to the Farm," or "Back Home in Tennessee," "My Old Kentucky Home," "Carry Me Back to Old Virginny." But how those voices rose and the starlit skies of France threw back the echoes when they sang

> *I wish I was in de land of cotton.*

> *Old times dar will never be forgotten,*
> *Look-a-way! Look-a-way! Look-a-way! Dixie Land! . . .*
> *Den I wish I was in Dixie, Hoo-ray! Hoo-ray!*
> *In Dixie Land I'll take my stand*
> *To lib and die in Dixie—*
> *Away, away, away down South in Dixie—*
> *Away, away, away down South in Dixie!*

In all this spontaneous singing the entertainers, especially the trained professional singers, who "put over" songs with the zest and in the atmosphere that one gets only through a lifetime of practice, should be given their tribute. Elsie Janis's singing of "Over Here," and "When Yankee Doodle Learns to *Parlez-Vous Francais*," a song that was tremblingly laid before her by a doughboy with the faint hope that she might "give it a try," went like wildfire throughout the Army. The records will never tell how many a little entertainer came to be known among their chosen units as the "Smiles" girl just because she popularized and connected unforgettably with her own personal charm that lilting ditty, "Pack up Your Troubles in Your Old Kit Bag and Smile, Smile, Smile!"

There were others who created a saucy atmosphere with "N' Everything," or built up a fine heroic mood around a song which Margaret Wilson did most to popularize, "The Americans Have Come." Irving Berlin covered himself with glory by launching upon the world, "Oh, How I Hate to Get Up in the Morning," and "How You Going to Keep Them Down on the Farm?"

But the doughboys' greatest joy was to sing those spontaneous authorless songs that rose in the unique atmosphere of the A. E. F. itself. Most famous of all these was that classic which served through the War and is still going strong wherever A. E. F. men get together, "*Hinky Dinky Parlez-Vous*." It had an infinite number of verses, but it always started out with this one, which gives the full flavour of a real doughboy ditty:

> *The General got the croix de guerre, parlez-vous.*
> *The General got the croix de guerre, parlez vous.*
> *The General got the croix de guerre,*
> *But the son of a gun, he was never there,*
> *Hinky, Dinky, Parlez-Vous.*

Then there was that self-indulgent privates' *chanson* entitled "I

Know Where They Are," which, after describing in various *stanzas* that the officers were "down in Rosie's bar;" the sergeants were "eating the soldiers' grub;" the corporals were "mending the old barbed wire;" ended with this glorious tribute to the privates, with all voices at top pitch:

If you want to know where the privates are,
I know where they are,
I know where they are, I know where they are,
If you want to know where the privates are,
I know where they are—
Up to their necks in mud, I saw them, I saw them,
Up to their necks in mud, I saw them,
Up to their necks in mud.

Of course, the characteristic quality of these songs is absent unless you were there to hear the spanking music that linked up with the words and made them the most tuneful marching songs that ever were sung.

The army was just as rich in parodies. Of these, "Do We Go Home or Do We Hesitate?" probably evoked the most hearty and general approval of all. The most ironic lines of this song ran.

Twenty years from now General Pershing, he'll say, 'Gee!
I forgot about those boys in Germanee,'
Do We Go Home— Or Do We Hesitate?

The Alabama boys, who provided the wildest contingent of the Forty-Second Division, just naturally had a song all their own, the full effect of which unfortunately cannot be given here, but which struck a touching ironic note at the end of each *stanza*, "Oh, This Beautiful War!" This song, like many others of the great popular songs of the War, never has been and probably never will be committed to paper. In fact, many of the best known doughboy songs cannot be bought and perhaps have not been seen in their written form by most of those who know them and sing them on every provocation at their reunions. Anyhow, this is as good a time as any to include the words, to the tune of "The Ole Gray Mare," of the best known parody of them all, "Goodbye Kaiser Bill." They went:

Uncle Sammy he's got the infantry.
He's got the cavalry,
He's got the artillery.

And so by gosh we'll all go to Germany
Goodbye Kaiser Bill.

Goodbye Kaiser Bill, goodbye, Kaiser Bill,
For Uncle Sammy, he's got the infantry,
He's got the cavalry.
He's got the artillery.
And so by gosh we'll all go to Germany,
And goodbye Kaiser Bill.

For over a year in America Marshall Bartholomew had charge of the Music Department. He went to Paris about the middle of January, 1919, but it was necessary for him to leave for America early in March, 1919, as there were problems to be solved in the cantonments at home. It was at Mr. Bartholomew's request that Ernest B. Chamberlain wan urged to return to France. He was previously an instructor in music at the University of Wisconsin. On February 1, 1919, the Song Leaders' Bureau of the Entertainment Department A. E. F.-Y.M.C.A. was formally inaugurated by Mr. Chamberlain as director.

Louis N. Cushman appeared in the Le Mans Area in the latter part of February, 1919, to do sing-song work as a song leader in the camps. There he organised teams, with a song leader and accompanist. One team went into Tonnerre, where it spent a month with the Thirty-Sixth Division. Mr. Cushman had the hearty support of Colonel James, through whose interest singing classes were arranged among the soldiers. Men were chosen from the army and sent to the classes one hour a day for eight days. The Lawrence Course for Song Leaders used at Columbia was curtailed to meet the necessity for a short course. These soldier song leaders of chosen ability took a deep interest in the work.

Nightly a song leader would go out to different towns in the surrounding territory, accompanied by a folding organ to work the singing up to its proper pitch. At La Suze, Mr. Cushman recalls one evening when he managed to coax eight or nine men about him to sing songs of a popular style. It was not long before this small group grew to about 800 soldiers, and sprinkled among them were French children and civilians. He asked the French to sing "*Madelon*" and then the "*Marseillaise*." When they had finished the soldiers cheered. The soldiers were eager to return the compliment and sang a number of American popular songs. The French applauded them in their usual manner. In this way, through sing-songs, the *Entente Cordiale* was promoted and it had a great deal to do in strengthening the relations among the American soldiers and the French people.

One interesting experience is that of a song leader on a motor truck, accompanied by a rolling canteen in the Twenty-Ninth Division at Le Mans. Pauline Hayes was assigned to begin at Tours, where she reported to Mr. Hazenburg, song leader. Together they had sing-songs until the army division moved from Jussy to Le Mans concentration camp on March 26, 1919. Here it was that Miss Hayes had her happy thought. She asked permission to have a piano placed on an army motor truck. A canteen worker was asked to join them, a rolling canteen was enlisted, and these combined forces went out into the camps. There they served lemonade and cookies—and started the whole camp on an orgy of song.

The song leaders began to invade all sectors of the army. There was Fred H. Balmond at Le Mans; Frances Blackney, who was at Semur as assistant song leader; Louise Robins Curry, who went from Semur to St. Gervais; Charles M. Clear who was sent to Coblenz, and later on to Biarritz and Luchon Cauterets; Leo Charles Demack, choir leader at St. Peter's Church, Beverly, Mass., who was with the Third Army at Coblenz and then went to Bordeaux; Florence Eis at Semur; C. C. Gleason at Le Mans; Robert Good; Ira M. Grey, song leader with the Religious Work Department; C. F. Lamb, an entertainment secretary in the Eighth Region, at Dijon, who later joined Mr. Thrush at Coblenz; Edward Havens at Mentone; Milford Witts, entertainment director at Dijon; J. L. Newhall at St. Nazaire, one of the great successes as a song leader; W. Stanley Hawkins who after January 1, 1919, was sent to Coblenz to take charge of the Music Department in the Third Army; Eugene Foulke; Arthur K. Wyatt of the Kirk Entertainment Unit; A. W. Ely at St. Nazaire; and G. J. Edwards, who was sent to the Leave Areas. These are but a few of the song leaders in the field.

The experience of Hope G. Carrell is typical of the service. Transferred from the Women's Bureau she became a lecturer, soloist, and violinist. She interspersed the entertainment program with sing-songs, leading the audience of soldiers by starting the song. She started the work around Bordeaux, where she was assigned for two weeks and then went to Le Mans. Here the soldiers were usually encamped in their tents in the large fields. On a motor truck or a Ford, equipped with a folding organ, she led the sing-songs right there in the field.

In view of the rapid movement of the American troops for home, the assignment of song leaders to the field was discontinued at the end of May, 1919. The singing of these songs will continue at camp fires and reunions for fifty years to come, and some of the songs will remain when the Great War has become a part of America's tradition of humour and buoyancy under danger and difficulty.

CHAPTER 25

Enlisting Eminent Lecturers

Charm ache with air and agony with words
Much Ado about Nothing.

Not only did the actors and song leaders follow the armies—there were still others. Famous American authors, travellers, jurists, psychologists, clergymen, historians, journalists, lawyers, publicists, educators, playwrights—more than 500 of them, 200 of whom were in regular service—became lecturers to the American soldier. They, too, were equipped with gas masks and the paraphernalia of campaigning along the lines behind the front. It was their duty to instruct the doughboys in the principles for which they were fighting; to keep them posted on affairs "back home"; and to take advantage of this opportunity to instil the value of knowledge and self-development into the youth of the nation. Their first duty, however, was to entertain; and it is from this viewpoint that their service is here recorded.

American celebrities of the platform and pulpit were not the only ones offered to the American doughboy. There were famous men of letters and science from England, who crossed the Channel to speak; a few from France, whose mastery of English was sufficient to carry the interest of an American boy through an evening; and such personages as might possibly be recruited from other countries, such as Dr. Wellington Koo, Minister from China to the United States, head of the Chinese delegation at the Peace Conference, himself a Columbia graduate.

Early in December, 1917, Mr. Carter had proposed a plan to General Pershing to exchange the best American speakers with the British, in order to strengthen the mutual interests of the two countries. The suggestion won immediate approval and in this way the United States troops gained the opportunity of listening to some of the foremost figures in Great Britain's public life. There were Lord Bryce, Former British Ambassador at Washington, Viscount Northcliffe, Sir Walter Raleigh, Sir Johnston Forbes Robertson and Lady Robertson, H. G. Wells of "Mr. Britling" fame, Ian Hay (Major Beith), author of *The First Hundred Thousand*, John Masefield, the poet, Rev. Sidney Berry, Rev. B. T. Butcher, Professor C. S. Terry, Professor F. Morse Simpson, Professor H. F. Stewart, Ben Greet, Louis Casson, Sylvia Thorndike, Professor W. P. Paterson of Edinburgh University, Dr. MacMillan, Glasgow's noted Presbyterian divine, and Rev. Mr. Ferguson, one of the greatest lecturers on political subjects in the British Empire. Rudyard Kipling addressed American troops at Winchester and in other British camps.

In exchange for this galaxy of stars some of the American speakers sent into the British lines were Samuel Gompers, president of the American Federation of Labour, Edward Bok, for many years editor of the *Ladies' Home Journal*, Dr. Albert Shaw, long noted as the editor of the *American Review of Reviews*, Professor J. A. Field of the University of Chicago faculty, and Ernest Hamilton Abbott, correspondent for *The Outlook*.

This service was first instituted by Arthur Gleason, the magazine writer, early in September, 1917. The first American lecturer to appear in France—three days after the arrival of General Pershing—was Norman Hapgood, later sent by President Wilson as Minister to Denmark. He lectured in Paris as early as July 7, 1917, before the lecture service was organised. James Hazen Hyde, long an American resident of France, was another of the early speakers, addressing about 300 American soldiers stationed in Paris in July, 1917, on "Franco-American Relations Since 1776."

From the arrival of the first American troops on foreign soil the demand for lecturers was continuous. Due to the dearth of American speakers in France at that date, it was necessary for a while to utilize soldier talent. Many a soldier was an accomplished orator and entertained his comrades in the huts with convincing speeches on the superior merits of his home city or his home state, rising to glowing eulogies of the greatness of America. This was the kind of spirit which laid the germ that created the lecture service. It became so popular with the boys that it was found necessary to place it in a department of its own. Already Mr. Gleason was burdened with so many duties that he found it difficult to devote the time required by the increasing needs of this newer field. This important service was committed to the guidance of Dr. John Gaylord Coulter, a Chicago editor and lecturer.

The cry for facts about the war—the all-absorbing topic of the moment—its underlying causes, its political effect upon the future, was so great among the American soldiers arriving on the scene of conflict that when Dr. Coulter became Director of the Department of Entertainment and Lectures, he set about at once to recruit speakers who could talk convincingly on these matters. Thus began the long "line" of celebrities in American public life which stretched out into various divisions of the army to imbed deeply in the minds of the soldiers all the things for which they had gone to war, and to promote the American point of view and the fighting spirit of the men.

Dr. Coulter scoured the city of Paris for Americans of note, engaged in some other form of war service, who might be willing to address the soldiers. He was fortunate in finding a number who proved of inestimable value during those early days. Dr. Paul van Dyke, professor of English Literature at Princeton, was in Paris as head of the Princeton Division of the American University Union. George Henry Nettleton, professor of English at Yale, was presiding as chairman of the University Union's executive board. Charles W. Veditz, the economist and sociologist, was *attaché* of the Department of Commerce at the American Embassy. These and many others willingly contributed their time and talent to the cause, speaking whenever called upon.

A trio of French notables in the persons of the Comtesse de St. Maurice, Mme. Gilles Darmyl, the writer, and Hughes le Roux, all with a perfect command of English, joined the lecture forces. The *comtesse* related the experiences of the French during the German invasion of 1914. Dr. Woods Hutchinson, the American medical authority, extended advice to the soldiers. Other able American speakers in this original volunteer group were Will Irwin, the writer, Professor Mark Baldwin, Professor John Hunter Sedgwick, and Charles A. Prince, a conspicuous member of the Boston bar. Mr. Prince's lecture on "What the Boche Really Is," was very effective during the dark days of 1917 and 1918.

Dr. Coulter soon was able to add other speakers arriving from America. Among them were Professor Arthur H. Norton, Vice-President of Elmira Collie; Dr. Wilson S. Naylor of the Lawrence University faculty at Appleton, Wisconsin; George Palmer of Superior, Wisconsin; Harry C. Evans, a Des Moines editor and Chautauqua lecturer; and Robert P. Shepherd of Grand Rapids, well known to the Chautauquas.

The cordial reception accorded to all these early speakers by the soldiers wherever a lecture was given proved how hungry the American fighting force was for knowledge of European affairs and the background of the struggle. Winthrop Ames had noted this, too, on his tour of inspection among the camps and reported it to Paris. Dr. Coulter requested the headquarters officials to assign him every arriving secretary who could address an audience, whether professional lecturer, pulpit orator, educator, psychologist, scientist, statesman, politician, historian, dramatist, or actor—all who were accustomed to appearing in public and addressing audiences. Men who had been college presidents, clergymen, editors, authors, judges, platform orators went out into the camps, dotted like points on a spider's web, appearing before their soldier audiences unheralded, with no reference whatever to their positions in life—each delivering a vigorous message of patriotism and purpose.

As soon as it was learned that Anson Phelps Stokes of Yale had arrived in Paris, early in January, 1918, with a view to drafting an educational program for the Y.M.C.A., Dr. Coulter pressed him into service in the lecture department. Choosing the subject of "America and France," he probably was the first speaker to give an illustrated lecture along the American front. A tour was arranged for Paris, Chaumont, Langres, Bourmont, Neufchateau, Chalons, and Gondrecourt.

Dr. Coulter himself was a speaker of ability, and his powers of entertainment were proved on frequent occasions when substituting for others who at the last minute could not appear. Moreover, he was anxious to get out into the field where he felt a more intimate association with the soldiers awaited him. Mr. Carter accordingly released him to serve in his desired field. To fill his place was a perplexing problem. Happily, however, he remembered reading the reports of some clever impromptu entertainments which had been staged out at Beaumont, a battered French village standing right on the edge of No Man's Land. He felt that the man who was capable of arranging such good programs under those trying conditions ought to make the new department "go." So he sent for him—Charles Steele, who achieved the notable success related in a preceding chapter. Mr. Steele was a true American; he was willing to serve his country in any capacity, so he left the field where it was all excitement, and came into Paris, where for a year he ran the entertainment service.

It was not long before Mr. Steele had a line of lecturers moving regularly about his war camp Chatauqua circuit. There were Harry

Emerson Fosdick the author-clergyman. President William H. Crawford of Allegheny Collie, Rheta Childs Dorr the author, Judge John Garland Pollard of Richmond, Bishop Rogers Israel of Erie, Rev. Chester Emerson of Detroit, Judge Tod B. Galloway of Columbus, President Carl G. Doney of Willamette University, former Senator Le Roy Percy of Mississippi, Dan Poling, Robert George Paterson, Captain Beekman, Chaplain Monod, Eunice Tietjens, and Burges Johnson, professor of English at Vassar Collie, who gave his lecture "American as It Is Spoken in Forty-Two Different States." Each one met with overwhelming success, proving the truth of Winthrop Ames's statement that the men were hungry for serious and educational talks.

Great crowds gathered nightly to hear these speakers at such large troop centres as Rimaucourt, St. Blin, Tréveray, Givrauval, Boucq, Minil-le-Tour—the last place on the Toul front where one could go without a gas mask—and at Colombey-les-Belles. Here the boys were so hungry for an American speaker that when Mr. Paterson appeared there on the night the big offensive began he was greeted by an enormous audience which packed the place, standing and squatting in the aisles, and was introduced by Major Frank Copeland Page, son of Walter Hines Page, late ambassador to Great Britain.

Later, on the night of April 10, 1918, Mr. Paterson was in a gas attack at Beaumont, beyond Dead Man's Curve, and could lecture but little in France after that. Dr. Crawford followed into this region and met with overwhelming success. Rheta Childs Dorr, on her way back to the United States from Russia, spoke in many huts in French Lorraine, venturing as far toward the firing line as a woman was permitted. Bishop Israel did most effective work along the Toul front in the early spring of 1918, when the Germans were making their terrific drives. Dr. Doney, of Oregon, offered his audiences a variety of good subjects: "German *Kultur vs.* Civilisation," "What We Shall Get out of the War," and "The French and Anglo-Saxon Mind." Senator Percy, a member of the special Harbison Commission investigating the Y.M.C.A. in France, was always called upon in the huts visited by Mr. Harbison and his other associates.

Ella Wheeler Wilcox went to France in the spring of 1918, to work in the canteens and render what assistance she could. Immediately she was pressed into lecture service and consented to read her own poems to the soldiers in the base hospitals, who received her with great enthusiasm. As was revealed by her untimely death not long after, her health broke down in the service and compelled her return to America long before she could make the rounds of the camps that were clamouring for her appearance.

John Kendrick Bangs and Irvin Cobb were two big drawing cards for the lecture bureau. Both kept their audiences convulsed. Unfortunately Mr. Cobb's time was too limited to spare many days to the lecture department, though he devoted every evening possible to some soldier audience in Paris. Mr. Bangs always was ready whenever he was called upon, taking several extensive trips to the front. (*The Collected Supernatural and Weird Fiction of John Kendrick Bangs* is published in 3 volumes by Leonaur.)

Mr. Bangs commented on his return from his first lecture trip to the front:

> I spoke in many 'Y' huts and once in a barn. I had spoken to the boys of the motor transport service before and that little cheering did them a great deal of good. So I went out there again with only the starlight to illuminate the roads ahead. I spoke to the soldiers with the cannon roaring steadily a few miles away and with shells passing overhead. I told them funny stories and then gave them a serious talk about what America was doing to win the war. While at another place I reached the ruins of what had been a village. There in a tent, on the edge of No Man's Land, I found Norton, Vice-President of Elmira College, who was devoting his vacation to serving the soldiers in France.

William Arnold Shanklin, President of Wesleyan University at Middletown, Connecticut, was one of the most interesting speakers in France. The reputation of his talks on everyday problems travelled before him and he was greeted by crowds. One of the features of his lectures was the open forum he conducted afterward in which the soldiers participated, not only questioning the speaker but addressing the audience themselves. These discussions grew immensely popular.

Captain George C. Pidgeon was recruited from the Canadian Army, speaking on "The North American Spirit." Professor John Erskine of Columbia, later head of the educational department, lectured at the base ports on "Our Neighbours the French." Dr. John Deans, a well-known lecturer from Brooklyn, capitalized his first six months' experience as a hut secretary at the front and addressed the incoming soldiers at the base ports during the summer of 1918 on "My Experi-

---
1.

ences with the French People."

By the spring of 1918, Messrs. Steele and Johnson were sending out into the field a list of celebrities that would have been the envy of the American lecture bureaus. This included Lorado Taft, the American sculptor, who drew crowds at the Palais de Glace; Mme. Emma Nevada, the celebrated American *diva* who delighted Metropolitan audiences two decades ago; Ray Stannard Baker, American author and journalist; Edward A. Filene, the Boston merchant, active in The League to Enforce Peace; Henry Morgenthau, former Ambassador to Turkey; General W. W. Hard of the A. E. F.; and Reginald Wright Kaufmann, the writer. Mrs. Richard Mansfield lectured on *The Merchant of Venic*e, Euphemia Bakewell of Pittsburg gave talks on "Joan of Arc" and the "The Streets of Paris" with illustrated slides, and Mrs. August Belmont entertained with brilliant readings and talks.

Then there was a group of eminent American divines: Bishop Brent, before he became Senior Chaplain of the A. E. F., Bishop Luther B. Wilson, Rev. Robert Freeman of Los Angeles, Rev. Floyd Irving Beckwith of Chicago, Rev. E. B. Edworthy of Montana, John F. Babb of Haverhill, Mass., George Wood Anderson, the evangelist from Bellefontaine, Ohio, President Henry Churchill King of Oberlin College, Joseph E. Appley of Hancock, N. Y., Rev. August E. Barnett of Millbrook, N. Y., Rev. William E. Ice of Versailles, Ohio, Rev. James W. Smith of Manchester, N. H., and Rev. William Dent Atkinson of Grove City, Ohio, were conspicuous figures in this list. All these pulpit orators crowded the huts and tents wherever they appeared.

When the actors began to crowd into Paris, the duties of Messrs. Steele and Johnson reached such proportions that it became necessary to transfer the lecture forces, with the latest recruits—including Dr. Raymond Knox of Columbia, Professor Frank C. Lockwood, Dean of Literature of the University of Arizona, and others—to the educational department, Dr. Lockwood taking charge, although in Mr. Steele's own province he continued to send lecturers out into the field to talk on historical, industrial, and social subjects of general interest.

After Mr. Steele's return to America following the Armistice he was succeeded by Mr. Johnson, who had contributed so much towards the general success of the whole undertaking. Along in April, 1919, when the entertainment field grew out of all bounds, it was decided to place the lecture service in the hands of a professional Chautauqua manager, recruited especially for the purpose from the United States in the person of the late Chauncey D. Brooks. Mr. Brooks began auspiciously with a corps of helpers, rendering an excellent service during the time he was permitted to give it supervision. Lamentably this was not for long, for his life was cut short on June 14, 1919, when he passed away after a brief illness, and his department reverted to the management of Mr. Johnson and later of A. M. Beatty, where it remained until the close of the overseas work.

Among the lecturers secured by Mr. Brooks were Major René Martial, the distinguished French medical authority, publicist, and author, to whom Premier Clemenceau gave permission to address the Americans. Major M. Chadbourne was another speaker of the Peace Conference days, taking for his topic "The League of Nations—Will It Work?" Others were Firman Roz of the French War Office, Baron de Detrich, a prominent Alsatian, and Captain S. N. Dancy, a Canadian.

And there were many others—some 500 in all—ministers, editors, educators who helped out over France wherever they happened to be serving. The demand for hut secretaries exceeded everything else, so only a comparative few could be spared for assignment to this special work.

The lecturers did a big work; they deserve great credit. They kept the boys inspired from start to finish. After an invigorating address the soldiers felt like going out into the front line and whipping the whole German army singlehanded. As one lecturer was told by an earnest American lad after he had concluded at Givrauval and received three lusty cheers from his vast soldier audience: 'That talk was worth a dozen bayonet drills." As they are instructors of the public in secular life, so were the lecturers the instructors of the American Expeditionary Forces. They kept the army informed on topics of general interest both at home and abroad, they helped to entertain them during the restless days when every unit was anxious to set sail for the good old U. S. A., and thus they did their part.

Chapter 26

"Movies Tonight!"

> *A kind of excellent dumb discourse.*
> The Tempest.

One day at the front when Elsie Janis was having one of her unusually buoyant fits of optimism, she slung her fountain pen under the impulse of an uncontrollable idea, and started to compute just how long it would take to play to every doughboy in the A. E. F. After covering about six sheets of writing paper with estimates computed at her present rate of speed, she sighed and leaned back in the deepest despair. "Holy Shrapnel," she exclaimed, "who'd have thought it would have taken *five years!* Gee, I guess I'll leave it to the movies."

The good old movies! Every entertainer in France thanked his lucky star hundreds of times that they were there to fill in when mere flesh and blood actors could go no farther. From the trenches to the base ports, in every hut or shack big enough to have entertainment activities, there might or might not be entertainers, but there were movies. The movie screen, in the doughboys' mind and in the mind of those who "put over" the entertainment program, was the dependable, unfailing amusement for the American Army. From the unforgettable series of pictures, which hundreds of community agencies in America had cooperated in sending to their home divisions, wherein home faces and home sights flickered on the screen, the news digests and topical reviews, and the educational and travel pictures, to the Homeric antics of Charlie and Doug—the movie was an immense success.

Immediately on our entrance into the war, the Community Motion Picture Bureau offered its services to the Y.M.C.A.. This bureau had been organised in 1911 by Warren Dunham Foster, one of the first to grasp the value of the moving picture as an instrument in social welfare and higher citizenship. In the six years of its existence up to the time when America entered the war, it had put on a nation-wide basis the idea of choosing and exhibiting motion pictures for community education and civic value.

It thus precisely fitted the need of a clearing house for the Y.M.C.A. and other welfare organisations in putting movies on the huge scale desired before the soldiers of the American Army. It was in touch with the film producers and had at its command men and women trained in the complicated motion picture business. Its services to the soldiers were offered without profit and were at once accepted for the work rapidly opening in the home camps. The first agreement between the National War Work Council and the Community Bureau dates from May 15, 1917, although the latter had functioned informally even before that date.

The Community Bureau took over the responsibility for showing moving pictures at the student camps at Plattsburg and elsewhere. By July this service was well organised, with ninety machines in operation and nearly 2,000,000 feet of film running weekly. By the end of the year it was showing at practically every camp and cantonment, and by February, 1918, when the great movement of troops to France was ready to get under way, the soldier audiences were numbering almost 1,000,000 men a week, and from 6,000,000 to 8,000,000 feet of film a week had been fitted into programs and was in constant circuit throughout the camps.

The arrangement of the bureau with the War Work Council and with the other welfare agencies on this side was, to quote Dr. Mott, "*unselfish, if not sacrificial.*" The bureau was determined that the soldiers should have plenty of pictures and to their taste. The president, Mr. Foster, himself made a round of the camps, watching the audiences to get an idea of the type of pictures that were most popular. He came back to tell his editorial board to omit sentimental pictures of mother and home and of heroic soldier lads. Romances, however, and real war pictures and farces—these were popular all over the land. In order to test their programs more thoroughly, the bureau also used reaction coupons which brought reports from a million audiences.

The task of the editorial committee was heavy. Their business was to see all films and find enough that were healthful and vigorous in tone. They could never lose sight of the fact that the soldier was entitled to simple, unvarnished fun, and to plenty of comedy, even of the most violent slap-stick variety. That they succeeded in their task may be guessed on the one hand by the satisfaction of the men, and on the other by the fact that in their two years' service only three people characterized as objectionable any of the films that were sent out.

General Pershing in the summer of 1917 authorized the Y.M.C.A. to take charge of the entire moving picture service for the A. E. F. Seventy-five machines were sent in the late summer of 1917, twenty-four hours after the receipt of this order. The Cinema Department in Paris was in one matter even more handicapped than other bureaus in that first difficult six months of finding themselves in France. The moving picture business is technical and complicated always, and it needed then, more than ever, those trained to the business.

The first films sent over had one virtue. They were as poor in material as in matter, and, used by amateurs and under the worst conditions, they were nearly at the end of their careers when the work of the department was put into the hands of the Community Motion Picture Bureau in April, 1918. These, with what films it had been possible to buy in France, were all the army had seen up to Mr. Foster's arrival in February. Mr. Foster's comment, after looking over the field and considering the enormous problems of transportation and equipment, must have heartened the secretaries who had struggled against overwhelming odds to get pictures into the field. "I am more and more filled with admiration," he said, "at what our predecessors have accomplished in spite of their many handicaps."

Up to the middle of March, 1918, with the tonnage shortage and the torpedo that sunk the largest shipment, only 372 showings had been given. Two weeks later, when the Community Motion Picture Bureau had become the Motion Picture Department of the "Y," 700 showings were made each week and twenty-one portable machines were with the troops on the inarch, giving a hundred shows a week, often on the roadsides at the nightly bivouacs. The colonel of a regiment that had seen as hard fighting as any of our forces was asked what he most wanted for his men after they entered the French sector. He said, "Three things: Motion pictures; more motion pictures; still more motion pictures."

April saw the beginnings of what was to be a colossal cinema enterprise. A force was building of chauffeurs, mechanics, operators, photographers, editors, and supervisors, and branch offices within the year were to cover the ground from Brest to Coblenz, and from Brussels to Nice. In the spring of 1918 there were seven Americans and twenty French on the staff. A year later, the force numbered 115 Americans directly under the Motion Picture Department, and more than 1,400 soldier details, French aids, and secretaries working under its supervisors.

In the meantime, the first group of motion picture specialists had been seized on the way through England, where American camps were clamouring for movies. The outfit in England at that time consisted of eight films. Since half of the A. E. F. was to pass through England, and men of the Navy and the Merchant Marine were crowding the ports, something must be done and done quickly. One man was left in England. In two months he had managed to get equipment, films, and helpers enough to show what might be done, and his office was asked to supply films for the British Association, for the prisoners of war, and for the Colonials.

London being one of the greatest film markets of the world, time and money were saved by forming there a second editorial and purchasing bureau. Meantime to the "Y" headquarters in Paris came demands for help from Italy, and arrangements were also made to serve through the Association the Foyers, the Chinese Labour Camps, and other welfare organisation work with the A. E. F. in France, and the internment camps m Switzerland.

This enormous business, carried on under the constant difficulties of war time, gave rise to all sorts of odd developments. In England a school was opened to train disabled British soldiers as operators. In France it was necessary to open classes for training the amateur caretakers of the precious Delco machines, on which not only the movies but the lighting of most of the huts depended, for in the path of the motion picture camera there followed a lighting system which meant a cheery well-lit hut where candles and smoking lamps had cast gloom before.

The transportation problem was for the cinema, as for everything else, the toughest problem. The express service of France had entirely broken down. The only way to get the films out was to carry them out by train with special messenger, by motor, or by motorcycle. The moving picture men solved this difficulty in a unique way which, originally designed by Mr. Foster and his very able successor in charge of the work in France, Elmo Lowe, met all the difficulties of what looked at first to be an impossible situation. There was never enough gasoline, to say nothing of Ford trucks, to carry a regular supply of films around to the five thousand odd showing points from which the moving pictures radiated throughout the American Army.

So early in the game the department organised a little army of its own of French civilians, ineligible for army service, to act as special couriers carrying American films throughout France. The idea worked out remarkably, and not only was every feeding point which itself might be a centre for transporting machines through an entire area supplied for the omnivorous doughboy, but the courier service itself was used by army officers and by certain sections of the "Y" as the most trustworthy and regular transport service that could be found. These French civilians travelled by the railways, armed with a formidable array of passes and special permits, and although at first, among the sections of the French Army that did not like to see civilians abroad on any mission whatsoever, they travelled from guardhouse to guardhouse, eventually all these difficulties were ironed out and American movies circulated throughout the army with a speed which even staff couriers envied.

The routing of the programs was most carefully planned, in order that all points should be served and no films left idle. Each program was to be used four times a week, and in the height of the service nearly 5,000 points were to be supplied, so that a failure in delivery at one point might break up the plans of a circuit for a week, and error in any one of the seventeen operations necessary to each program meant that the soldiers were disappointed. This was no small matter if men had tramped kilometres through the mud for the promised pictures, or were setting forth to the Argonne at daylight, or had just had word of another delay in their transport. The men and women on this part of the task took it much in the spirit of that famous rider who "brought the good news from Ghent to Aix."

One woman writes:

> I had promised Verneuil, 130 kilometres from Bourges, that I would take them three films on a certain Friday. I left Bourges in the flivver at 1:15 and twelve miles out the car refused to go. I walked on to St. Just where I phoned to the Motor Transport Department, but the French central cut us off, and it took two hours and a half to get the call through the second time. By this time only a motorcycle could possibly get the films to Verneuil in time for the boys.

Absolute precision throughout the whole organisation was the ideal. If this were not humanly possible under the circumstances, yet the Motion Picture Department did so well that even early in its service Mr. Ewing, Chief Y.M.C.A. Secretary for Great Britain, said, "It is the best organised institution in the war zone."

From the commencement of active operations in France the motion picture played a dominating part in the soldiers' life. When the Second Division went into its first action near Mondidier in May, sixty motion picture outfits were operating with them on full time, with the cordial approval of General Bundy. One of the screens, which was set up in an old quarry, is still preserved, riddled with German shrapnel, as a mute testimony to how far up to the front these operators carried their work. When the Germans came over the top unexpectedly, one of the things they were likely to capture was a motion picture outfit. At Soissons, during the bitter fighting in May, one set of films changed hands three times and was a prize exhibit throughout the fighting divisions during the summer.

The movie man and his battered Ford followed the troops wherever they went and gave shows in ruined churches, in gullies and old quarries, in mills and abandoned *châteaux*, in the underground chambers of artillery positions, and on the whitewashed walls fronting the village square. Often these movie shows were given before groups of men lying on the ground just out of action and too tired even to stand up. The operators of the Third Division went with these troops in their weary march to the Rhine, setting up their screen each night.

By the time the leave areas were in full operation, and the Le Mans forwarding camp and the embarkation ports, it was comparatively easy to supply these regions and the cities, though it still meant working into the night, and called for endless persistency and ingenuity. When the Le Mans Area was at its height there were about thirty shows a day, with eighteen trucks busy delivering reels and caring for machines, and a force working from ten in the morning around the clock till three, and one of the office women always ready to take a car for an absent driver. It was in this region that a driver came late into the town where he was to give a show.

The officers were away, a sergeant in command, and the men had turned in. Nothing daunted, the secretary asked if they could not be "turned out," which they promptly were. The machine was set up in the street, a screen rigged on a side of a barn, and "those crazy Americans" poured out of their billets for a performance. The comment of the officers on this remarkable proceeding was permission to the secretary to do it as often as he wished.

In the French villages the movie machine was often set up in the market place, with the side of a building for a screen, and the entire population gathered with the soldiers. This outdoor cinema was indeed necessary in the villages, for many of the French country folk had never before seen a movie. They crowded the small huts to bursting, leaving little room for soldiers, yet when one saw the pleasure this gave to the war-harried people one could not turn them away. The Third Division went with these troops in their weary march to the Rhine, setting up their screen each night.

Outdoor screens were not the only makeshifts. For instance, with the Salvage Department at Bordeaux the only chance for movies was when some portion of a warehouse could be cleaned out. Whenever such a moment arrived the garage men, whose work went on day and night, turned in to prepare the place. Wherever, as with the coloured battalions at Le Rochelle, work went on throughout the night, movies were given in the afternoon. As to hours, the one unvarying rule that the department followed was to tuck in a movie wherever men had time for it. When the Twenty-Eighth Division was entraining at Columbey-les-Belles, it was learned that most of the men would probably have to wait hours in the middle of the night at the station. Travelling in France was hard enough at best for soldiers, and the enterprising secretaries who appeared on the scene at eleven o'clock at night, with a moving picture machine competent to run until five in the morning, had a warm welcome.

Perhaps nowhere did the cinema do better than at Romagne, where the coloured troops were working in one of our great cemeteries. There in the great hangar, where both white and coloured men gathered to forget the terrible tasks of the day, something was doing every night. Entertainers came twice a week, perhaps, but if there were nothing else, there were movies always. At Dom-sur-Meuse, the American films packed with khaki the theatre the Germans had built for their own enjoyment. At the Marseilles delousing station, where the boys were held a week away from their comrades, pictures were given nightly.

When the weather permitted, these were out of doors with the boys perched in trees and on the barrack roofs. In some of the hospitals and in the sick bays of the transports the pictures were thrown on the ceiling for the men in the beds, while, of course, they were everywhere supplied in connection with the Red Cross for patients who could be moved out into the recreation rooms. The movies on the transports alone deserve a whole chapter to themselves. On some ships they began at six in the morning and ran steadily until three and four the next morning, so that all shifts and ratings could see them. Due to this intensive program, there were actually more separate showings on shipboard than in France itself.

A curiously varied service was at Mirimas, where the "Y" supplied a British detachment, some British Indians, a French foyer, a foyer for the Algerians, a Chinese labour hut, and our own Knights of Columbus. The Chinese were especially interested in industrial pictures and comedies, and as they could not read the legends on the pictures, the screen was hung in the centre of the hall and space saved by seating the audience on either side.

With the Italian Army the travelling cinema camion service was most effective, carrying entertainment out into the devastated regions where no other diversion was possible, and where the officers were as keenly eager as the men. The Polish Legion in France had had movies along with all the other units, and when in March they arranged that the Y.M.C.A. secretaries go with them to Poland, they saw to it that a full cinema equipment and men to operate it were included. Films were, of course, being supplied for the work with the A. E. F. in Siberia, and men and pictures sent to aid the Americans and British in that dreariest adventure of the whole war, that in Northern Russia.

Here the machines were taken on sledges across long wastes and welcomed at isolated posts with an appreciation beyond words. The effect on the Russians who saw them was so marked that one of the secretaries wrote asking for captions in Russian, as an incentive to illiterates to learn to read. He said:

> In my opinion this would do more to assist the rising generation of this unfortunate country than any other work undertaken up to the present by any association whatsoever.

The department was early in the business of producing films in France itself. In May it had two French photographers at the front. In October it was asked by the army to aid the Aviation School Office in the taking of pictures of aeroplanes to be used for instruction in firing. Its aid had been asked also in making the whole army better acquainted with the work of the S. O. S. Out of this request from Headquarters grew one of the most interesting of the movie activities, *The Overseas Weekly*, a film prepared especially with the idea of keeping the soldiers in touch with events in the war. These pictures were for the most part taken by the Signal Corps, and the representative of the department worked in that office, choosing films and making the programs, directly under the officer in charge. These were sent out each week with a similar film on current events in the United States, *The World Today*.

First of all in popularity and morale-stiffening quality, however, were the wonderful "home folks" pictures, organised during the summer of 1918 through the initiative of the Community Bureau and with the cooperation back in America of the Committee on Public Information and scores of newspapers and community agencies throughout the country. To a soldier in France the most thrilling picture he could fancy would be a scene in his own town. So imagine his feelings when the dream really came true and he could sit in a hut in France and see a procession of the mothers and sisters of the doughboys in his own home town pass across the screen, and yell his head off as his mother or his girl waved a hand of greeting at him right on Main Street opposite Jones's drug store.

A picture that showed the ferry-boats plying about New York harbour with the old Statue of Liberty rising in the middle distance, or one of the shop girls coining out of the Chicago department stores in the evening, or a view of the Golden Gate or Mobile Bay, or the squat old State House rising on Beacon Hill, Boston—these had more thrills to the foot than all the desperate adventures of William S. Hart in the celluloid Wild West. These home pictures circulated among the Twenty-Sixth Division, for instance, which probably had the world's record for homesickness, until they were literally worn out.

Next in appeal came the great Charlie Chaplin. Every division had to have Charlie just so often, usually at intervals of about two weeks, and in size of audience, noisy approval, and number of showings throughout France, it must be conceded that he beat all records.

German propaganda films, which began to be captured by the score when the summer drive got under way, constituted another prime attraction. One of the greatest of these was a picture designed to prove to the German Army the results of unrestricted submarine warfare, but which proved nightly to thousands of American soldiers, as they saw one good ship after another blown to a terrible death by the undersea wolves of German piracy, the urgent need of going in next day and killing more Germans.

One of the movie producers made it especially her business to search out "unadvertised heroes," that is, units of which no one knew, and army work yet unheralded. In her wanderings she came across a row of "75's" on which were the words painted in red, white, and blue, "America's first shot."

"What does this mean?" she asked.

"This is C Battery, 6th F. A.," replied a soldier, "and those are the guns with which we fired America's first shot."

"How many hundred times have you been photographed for the movies?"

"Well, Miss, if you photograph us, it will make our grand total one time. We've never even looked at a movie camera."

America's first shot was fired at 6: 05 a. m., October 23, 1917, at Luneville. These were indeed the very guns, and no picture had ever been taken of them.

A fine example of the many educational films which were prepared is that on Paris, arranged, as the producer said, so that when the soldier came to the great city, "he should be prepared to find in it the beautiful and not the ugly."

From the point of view of the staff, surely there were no welfare workers with the army better paid for strenuous days and often strenuous nights than those of the movie staff. They worked at top speed. They were also under pressure, but there was always waiting for them an eager welcome, while never were there more amusing audiences for which to labour. Before the entertainers soldier frankness was kept a bit in check by some holdover of conventionality, but before the movies, khaki could say what it pleased—and it did.

Joy was uproarious when suddenly some recognised scene flashed on the screen; cheers welcomed an animal in a circus parade; sobs were likely to assist an over-sentimental romance; and no one forgets such evenings as that where the advertised villain of the play chanced to be the machine operator. His every appearance on the screen was greeted with reproof, execration, jeers, admonitions, and fatherly advice, that made an evening funnier than any ever caused by Charlie Chaplin.

The value of the wartime motion picture service is, like all else in the war, impossible to compute. Owing to the technical training of this personnel, and to its connections, it was able to get films at a tremendous saving. Film producers were, for the most part, generous in their arrangements, foregoing their film rights and taking payment only for the use of the films themselves. It was estimated that this meant a saving of $1,000,000. Because the bureau was doing the work without profit, it was able to rent films at from ten to fifty *per cent* below the commercial rates.

Out of the A. E. F. in France alone there were more than 94,000,000 men in movie audiences. Counting in the shows given in the United States, the gross attendance reached more than 210,000,000. If, as under ordinary conditions, the soldier had paid a minimum admission fee, say of fifteen cents a show, this single item in his entertainment would have cost him the trifle of $32,000,000. As a matter of fact, the Motion Picture Department of the "Y" actually succeeded in giving this program at a cost of something around two cents per show per man—and this in spite of the fact that it was administering during the war a moving picture business forty times larger than it or any other organisation had ever undertaken in the history of the cinema profession.

The value of the service, however, lay not in the amount received for the money, though that under the conditions is extraordinary; it lay in the fact that the movies were on the spot, whether that spot were a San Francisco navy yard, a Scotch lumber camp, or a French village. It lay yet more, as the experience of the first months in France showed, in the work of the Editorial Department in the choice of films, and in the prevention, by its satisfactory service, of the entrance into the camps of the purely commercial movie theatres. Without such professional service as was made available, this could hardly have been prevented.

Today, (as at time of first publication), in Germany the bureau is still with the "Y," giving a thousand shows a month in the Rhineland to the Army of Occupation in Germany; it has its place in every army camp in America and wherever American soldiers are. In other words, the wartime movie service is going on. It is one of the enduring features of the entertainment experience of the Great War.

Curtain

Americans have grown more used to being entertained; and less used to entertaining themselves than any other people. Take five million young men away from home and community restraints and, no matter how they are; drilled and hedged about with rules and regulations, the time will come when all but a few of the most exceptional individuals will seek diversion. The history of war is that the forms of diversion which have followed armies did more to destroy the armies than did the actual fighting. From the days of the Civil War and the Sanitary Commission those interested in the welfare of our army have been feeling their way toward some solution of the problem of keeping the fighting man normal under abnormal conditions.

In the opinion of some old-time officers and of some individuals uninformed on all the conditions of the soldier's life, the work of the welfare organisations was uncalled for and tended to coddle those who should be above such softening influences. That the real military leaders, men like Generals March, Pershing, and Wood, were not of this opinion is proved by repeated orders and promulgations urging the proper entertainment of soldiers. They recognized that soldiers were not super-men, no matter how well drilled and equipped, but were, because of the deadly monotony of drills and the nerve-racking of active service, in greater need of entertainment than the amusement-loving public at home.

When an army was created out of the boys of our own firesides, the folks at home, the welfare organisations, and the generals realised that our soldiers were men with the same needs, the same wishes, the same tastes as ourselves, but that there would be none of the old ways of using leisure and that many of them would be thousands of miles from home under new conditions in strange lands. It was certain that these millions of American youths, whether in the army or out, would get amusement. They were accustomed to games, sports, movies, theatres, music, athletics, and all forms of recreation. Our business, then, was to see that the amusements accessible in home camps and overseas were healthful and decent as well as entertaining.

The American people were willing that their boys should face hardship and danger, but determined that they should have the best and be returned sound in body and mind. It was this resolution which put public opinion back of the draft and made it a democratic and successful undertaking. Experiments had been begun in connection with the British and French Armies, and it had already been proved that healthful recreation increased men's fighting power and willingness to carry on. The testimony of all who worked with the soldiers, and of their officers, as well as the condition in which our troops came back, proves the correctness of this theory and the success with which it was carried out.

The most striking example of the effect of plenty of the right sort of fun is shown in the story of the leave areas. At the time of the Armistice we had overseas 2,000,000 men. The greater part of these were still fresh from civilian life, utterly unused either to army discipline or to travel. They were left suddenly without any object for their labour. Their task was done. All they wanted was to go home. True to human nature, their enthusiasm for their hosts, the French, and for the country in which they were forced to wait, cooled. The French, with nerves tense after four years such as our men, even those who had been in the fighting lines, could not conceive of, were tired of strangers in their streets. They wanted to see the last of British, Chinamen, Indians, Russians, Portuguese, and Italians, but most of all, they wanted to see the last of Americans.

Here were two states of mind that bade fair to make a fine international situation. The army officers asked, not for stricter discipline, but for movies, athletics, dances, entertainments, sight-seeing trips. That those dangerous months of waiting passed off safely is more due to the fact that the monotony was broken, and the leisure filled by all sorts of entertainment, than to any other one agency. We all know how our boys came home and are proud of their condition and the way they readjusted themselves to civilian life. Officers from other lands watching this undertaking had no doubt of its effect. They certainly had no sentimental attitude toward their men.

Yet the Y.M.C.A. was asked to introduce or to continue and develop its work in the armies of Poland, Portugal, Roumania, Czechoslovakia, and Greece. This would not be the case were not the military and civilian authorities of these countries convinced that such entertainment as the welfare organisations provided for the soldiers in France made better fighting men and better citizens. And our own army officers are of the same belief. The case has been proved under actual conditions. Whether it is carried on by welfare organisations or the army itself, there will always be entertainment for our army because of the success of the entertainment campaign in the Great War.

Appendix

HEADQUARTERS STAFF—NEW YORK
Overseas Entertainment
Thomas S. McLane, Chairman

Eunice A. Rogers
Ruth Buchenholz
Helen James
Helen Pratt

Fanny Baldwin
Mary Reiter
Emily O. Nelson
Madeline B. Campbell

America's Over There Theatre League

James Forbes
Johnson Briscoe

Virginia Chauvenet
Rose Schiff

HEADQUARTERS STAFF—PARIS

Dr. J. G. Coulter
Charles Moore Steele
Walter H. Johnson, Jr.
Gerald Reynolds
A. M. Beatty
Joseph Lindon Smith
John W. Beattie
Oswald Yorke
Carl J. Balliett
Wm. H. Duff, 2nd.
James W. Evans
George W. Doyle
C. A. Braider
W. H. Caldwell
C. A. Mayne
A. M. Richards
S. H. Crawford
R. N. Henry
J. I. Bond
H. M. Collins
James Forbes
T. F. Winters

Jack Gallagher
Harold Ross
Marion N. T. Carter
Marian M. Haley
Olive Johnson
Jane M. Thomas
Edith G. Walker
Linnie Nuckolls
Maude Utter
Florence Goodell
Enid Watkins
Louise Overacker
Sara Furman
Mme. Vignon
Mlle. Marcelle
Elizabeth Hugus
Helen Lucas
Iva Rider
Josie Ricks
Myrtle Ash
Emita Jewell
Marion Morse

Gladys Ross

OVERSEAS PERSONNEL
COACHES AND PRODUCERS

Abbott, Eleanor
Acton, Howard L.
Allen, Mary
Anderson, E. L.
Anthony, Charles P.
Armitage, Laura E.
Armstrong, Frank

Bakewell, Euphenia
Ballam, Frank
Balliett, Carl J.
Barkley, J. R.
Beatty, A. M.
Berkey, Hilda G.
Berry, Walter M.
Black, Gladys
Blandick, Clara
Blue, John D.
Bressak, Harry
Brocklebank, Blanche
Buck, J.
Buxton, Ethel

Cameron, E. Malcolm
Chamberlain, Alice
Chapman, C. J.
Chesmond, Dorothy
Corey, Madison
Cushing, C. C. S.

Darrah, Chas. B.
Davis, F. M.
Donnelly, Dorothy
Duskkin, Samuel

Edwards, G. J.
Evans, James W.

Farquhar, Marion
Forbes, James

Gates, Perle E.
Geoghegan, Harold
Glass, Rose

Goss, Aletta
Grimball, Elizabeth

Hall, Eugene J.
Hathaway, Louis E.
Henry, Grace
Hickox, Laura C.
Hicks, Lavelle
Holmes, Lucy T.
Howry, Elizabeth
Hudson, Ava B.

Jack, Edwin Booth
Jennings, W. L.
Johnson, Burgess
Johnson, Walter H., Jr.

Keith, Edna G.
Kennedy, Isabel Parker
Kennedy, Katherine F.
Kimball, Frederick

Lamb, Frances
Leopold, Fred

McDonald, Dinnie
Mays, Ora Lea
Moore, Elbert
Moore, Olive

Nash, John W.

Pabst, Norman
Porter, Chas. R.
Purnell, Anna

Quinn, Esther

Rawlinson, H. E.
Rochford, W. H.

Sage, Helen Amelia
Scherer, Maud
Schuler, Mabel R.

COACHES AND PRODUCERS—Continued

Schumaker, Edwin Bolden
Sedgwick, Mary L.
Sherry, Laura
Shipp, Clark
Smith, Jos. Lindon
Smithfield, Geo. F.
Steele, John Moore
Stevens, Thos. Wood
Stillman, Lila B.
Stubblefield, Henry T.
Swinburne, L. T.

Tappen, C. S.
Tichenor, Juanita
Truax, Harry A.
Twyman, James
Tyler, Dallas

Velsey, Graham

Walters, Sara
Wand, Clarence Cary
Waters, Wilford
Weadon, Frank P.
Werner, Blanche H.
White, Jessie
White, W. A.
Wilkes, Willamene
Willard, Alceth
Williams, Florence
Williams, Orlin M.
Williams, W. E.
Wilson, Hugh
Witte, Parvin
Witts, Milford
Woolston, F. Pate

Young, Jane H. G.

LYCEUM

Adams, Guila
Adams, Lucille
Alexander, Enid
Allen, Martha Marie
Allen, Maud
Anderson, Harry N.
Arnold, Beattie D.
Arnold, Pauline
Atlee, Carolyn
Aves, Ethelreda
Avirett, Donnell

Bailey, Marguerite
Barber, Jane
Bargeldt, Evelyn
Barnhard, Agnes
Bartlett, Hazel
Bassett, Ella May
Beatty, Earl
Beatty, Roberta
Beattys, Adele M.
Beaudry, Maud
Beckwith, Florence
Benjamin, Wm. A.

Bennett, Eva L.
Bennett, Helen F.
Bertram, Helen
Besler, Helen
Betz, Joseph
Bewley, Irene
Bingham, May
Blackney, Frances
Blake, Wm. H.
Bloomquist, Myrtle
Boardman, Wm. J.
Bohannon, Jean
Bohannon, Ord
Bolander, Alice
Bolander, Elise
Bolander, Mabel
Bolander, Pearl
Booth, Maud Ballington
Bourne, Olive E.
Bowcock, Evie Lee
Bowman, Billie Miss
Boyd, Hilda
Bradley, Frank
Bradley, Lucie

LYCEUM—Continued

Brown, Dorothy Spencer
Buchbinder, Lucy
Bulley, Carolyn
Bumstead, Gladys P.
Burr, Borden
Bush, Charlotte

Call, Dora
Call, Lucy Lee
Call, Zela
Cameron, Mary
Capelle, Angie
Carpenter, Elizabeth
Carpenter, Laura
Carr, Joe
Carroll, Elsa
Carstensen, Amelia
Carter, Annie Louise
Carter, Maybelle
Case, Chas.
Chester, Randolph
Chester, Lillian
Chisolm, Jessie
Chivvis, Ruth
Christie, Joe
Churchill, Estelle
Clark, Marguerite
Clinton, Margery H.
Coates, Helen J.
Cobb, Fredericka
Cogswell, Mynn
Cole, Alonzo D.
Coleman, Margaret
Colet, Madeline
Collette, Lucille
Combs, A. B.
Collins, Ernest C.
Condit, Albert Rae
Cookingham, Edna
Corey, Gladys M.
Cowperthwaite, Alfred
Cox, Edw. Eugene
Cox, Maybelle
Cox, Mary
Crabb, Addison W.

Craig, Jeannie
Critcherson, Samuel
Crofoot, Beulah
Crosby, Anna Gertrude
Crosby, C. Zelia
Culbertson, Sascha

Dalgren, Ada
Damon, Vera
Dana, Marion
Daniel, E. P.
Davis, Eliz. G.
Davis, Maida
Davies, Jos.
Dealy, Creswell
Dean, Lulu Richardson
Dilling, Mildred
Dillon, Jane
Draper, Ruth
Dudley, Ruth
Dunham, Herbert
Duval, Marguerite

Earle, Hetty
Easton, Elsie
Edgar, Elizabeth W.
Edgar, Geraldine
Eichorn, Anna
Emmerson, Mary
Emery, J. C.
Euwer, Anthony
Evans, Carmon
Evans, Mildred
Everett, Geo. I.

Farley, Gilbert C.
Farnsworth, Jessie
Faulkner, Georgene
Fay, J. W.
Field, Josephine
Fisher, Ethel
Flesh, Chas. E.
Ford, Gene
Foster, Bertha
Foster, Frohman

LYCEUM—Continued

Fox, Lois
Frost, Alfred

Gailey, Mary
Gale, Albert
Galloway, Judge Tod B.
Gardner, Stephen
Garton, S. B.
Gasaway, Adelaide
Gates, Harriet May
Geffen, Yetta
Gemmill, Chas. Walker
Gemmill, Paul
Gill, Ruth Dudley
Gilliam, Florence
Ginn, Clara T.
Girton, Eleanor M.
Godfrey, Mildred
Gold, Pauline
Goodrich, Gertrude D.
Goodsell, Virginia
Gordon, Mary Belle
Gorrell, Edith Tilton
Grey, Clara
Griffin, Elizabeth
Gross, Estelle

Haggerty, Elizabeth
Hall, Jeanne
Hall, Opal
Harbeson, Lindamira
Hardy, Lois
Harney, Eleanor
Harrison, Fred W.
Harrison, Inez
Hartman, June
Harvey, Maleva
Hass, E. M.
Hatch, Dorothy
Hausman, S. A.
Hays, Estelle B.
Hedges, Freddie
Hemmick, Marie
Hiltebrandt, Elsa
Hinton, Ethel

Hosteon, Jack
Hoes, Adele
Holtzschue, Mabel
Hope, Barbara
Howard, Clarence H.
Howe, Chas. E.
Howe, Chas. M.
Howe, R. T.
Howe, Warren T.
Hoyt, Frances
Hoyt, Grace
Hubbard, Chas.
Hughes, Anna
Hulbert, Winifred
Hull, Margaret
Humphrey, Cora
Huntington, Blanche
Huntington, Catherine S.
Hutchinson, Elizabeth P.
Hutton, Hugh

Irvin, Frances
Irwin, Chas. Jasper
Irwin, Robert

Jack, Julia
Jackson, Lillian
Jackson, Mary
Janauschek, Wm.
Jerge, J.
Johnson, Burgess
Jones, Mrs. Paul
Jones, Wm. S.
Jordan, Elizabeth

Kasner, Diana
Kendall, Marie
Keniston, Wilhemena
Kennedy, Pearl M.
Kennedy, Will J.
Keppie, Elizabeth
Kerns, Grace
Kilbourn, Henry J.
Kimmel, Frank S.
Knapp, Harold

242

LYCEUM—Continued

Knight, Robert F.
Konecny, Josef
Kova, Garda

Landon, Cornelia
Lanham, Cora Belle
Lawry, Justin
Lawry, Winifred
LeRoy, Merritt
Lewis, Chas. Allen
Lewis, Julia B.
Lewis, Lottie
Lineback, C. A.
Littlefield, Edith Gould
Loar, Lloyd A.
Lord, Marguerite
Lord, Marion
Lorraine, Joe
Lucas, Charlotte
Lyon, Roger

McAdams, Ivy
McCain, Leoda
McCartney, Eliz
McClure, Emily
MacCue, Beatrice
McDermott, Mary
McGehee, Ethel
McGreal, Roberta
Mack, Archie Roy
McKay, Mary Elizabeth
McLinn, Ruby
McKnight, Alex G.
McSweeney, Margaret
Maddox, Betty
Mathews, Muriel
Maydwell, Mary Alice
Mayer, Viola
Merritt, J. A.
Miller, Jeanne
Monaghan, Robert
Montgomery, Mina Belle
Moore, Earle A.
Morris, Kathleen
Morris, Mildred

Morrison, Margery
Munson, Margaret
Murray, Bonnie

Nattkemper, Leonard G.
Nelson, Florence
Newell, Fenwick
Newell, Mary J.
Neumam, Herman
Niedringhaus, Wallace C.

Odell, Cornelia
Olp, Lou S.
Owens, Hughetta

Palmer, George
Parker, Harry E.
Parker, Salem
Parkhurst, Anita
Parmalee, Cleo
Parmenter, Edward C.
Parnell, Charles T.
Paine, Cordelia Ayer
Payne, Howard M.
Payne, John Howard
Payne, Sally Landis
Pierik, Marie
Pike, Carolyn
Pearce, Corinne
Pease, Edward
Pease, Zuelettia
Peckham, Charlotte
Perkins, Lois
Peters, A. N.
Pettit, Gladys
Powell, Rosa C.
Pratt, Charles F.
Price, Katherine G.
Price, John W.
Provan, John S.

Quay, Gertrude
Quincy, Samuel

Rachford, Hugh K.
Ramsey, Lillian

LYCEUM—Continued

Raymond, Harold A.
Raymond, Katherine
Reynolds, Sarame
Redell, Harry
Redfield, Florence A.
Rees, May E.
Reiner, May Louden
Revare, Edna
Rich, Gladys
Richards, Helen
Richards, Irene
Richardson, C. O.
Ricker, Bessie B.
Robertson, Alice
Robertson, Genevieve
Robertson, Olive F.
Robertson, Robert
Rogers, Calista
Rogers, Faith Helen
Rogers, Francis
Rogers, Cornelia B.
Rogers, Mabel
Rogh, Charles
Romans, Beth
Rose, Jonsa Jonga
Ross, Roxana
Rossuck, Ruth
Rubel, Edith
Rundquist, Ethel
Rutherford, Althea J.
Rutherford, Forrest S.
Ryan, Ruth

Saleeman, T. J.
Satterfield, Alyce Lee
Scales, Cannon
Scandrett, Rebecca
Schochm, Arminta
Schwinn, Rose N.
Scott, Edith H.
Scotty, Jack
Scudder, Janet
Sears, Aline
Seiler, Mary
Selby, Ida M.

Selby, L. J.
Selby, Pearl
Shafer, Claude
Shanklin, Malvena
Shields, Milan
Shirey, R. W.
Shirley, Frances
Shoemaker, Frances
Shurtleff, Oliver
Smart, Henry C.
Smith, Dorothy
Smith, Elma
Smith, Em. E.
Smith, Helen E.
Smith, Marie
Smith, Norma L.
Smith, William P.
Smythe, A. H.
Soares, Geraldine
Southall, Patty
Souvaine, Henry
Spaulding, Art
Spear, Helen M.
Spencer, Laura Zoe
Stanley, James
Stanley, Eleanor
Stark, Robert
Steel, John W.
Stelzel, Charles F.
Stephenson, Elsie
Stevenson, I. C.
Stirling, Robert
Strong, Theo.
Strong, Walter W.
Struble, Marion
Struder, Mabel

Tabor, Robert
Taale, Agnes R.
Thayer, Maud
Thomas, Sara
Thompson, Alex.
Thompson, R. R.
Thorp, Evelyn L.
Threadgill, Lois

Thrower, Theresa
Tibbitts, Beatrice
Todd, Nellie
Torrence, Marie
Towne, Charles W.
Townsend, Betty
Townsend, Ellen
Trevett, Frances L.
Tromley, E. L.
Truitt, Beulah
Tuttle, Ada
Tuttle, Nina

Waddell, Elizabeth
Wakeman, Alice
Walker, Clifford
Walker, Corinne
Walker, Lucille
Wallace, Martha
Wallace, Wm. G.
Walter, R. B.
Ward, Elizabeth
Washburn, Carolyn
Washburn, Eleanor

Waters, Crystal
Watkins, Katryn
Webster, Harold
Weller, Beatrice
White, Harry C.
White, Mary
White, Winifred
Whittemore, Eleanor
Williamson, Mary Ruth
Willmer, Sarah M.
Wilson, Inez
Wilson, M. J.
Woblert, Louise D.
Wolcott, Helen L.
Wood, Elizabeth
Wood, Ellerbe
Woodberry, Frances
Woodfin, Alice
Woodward, Roy
Woolley, Robert
Wyatt, Arthur K.

Yeager, Edith

Musical

Adkins, Morton
Adler, David
Armand, Alfred

Benton, Ruth
Brice, Elizabeth

Coburn, Vera Ross
Coffey, Louise
Colley, Helen
Condon, Kate

Dallas, Gertrude
Davis, Helen

Elbert, Tracey
Ewell, Lois

Frease-Green, Rachel

Gold, Belle
Golden, Frances

Hand, Hinda
Hoban, Stella
Humphreys, Neida
Hunt, Ida Brook

Janis, Elsie
Jarman, Margaret

Lane, Camille Seygard
Larkin, Carolyn
Lyon, Wanda

McGibney, Mignon
May, Ida

Perry, Fayette

MUSICAL—Continued

Reed, Elsa
Rogers, Eleanore

Schaeffer, Marion

Sweyd, Lester

Temple, Paula

White, Tommy

DRAMATIC

Allen, Edward
Aug, Edna

Barnicoat, Betty
Barry, Tom
Baxter, Alice
Boland, Mary
Bourne, Olive
Brown, Marlyn
Burke, Fan

Carrington, Phyllis
Chobb, Bronwen
Clear, Charles M.
Clifton, Ethel
Craig, John
Craig, Mary Young
Crane, Hal
Curley, Leo

Dale, Theresa Malloy
Dale, Walter
Davis, Maida
Diffendel, John
Dodge, Jeanne
Dupree, Minnie

Emmons, Gladys
Esmelton, Frederick

Falls, Marie
Fisher, Grace
Fitts, Harriett
Fleming, Charles
Florence, Katherine
Fuller, Rosalind
Fullum, Dewey

Garland, Ruth
Goff, Helen

Grant, Jeannette
Grigg, Harold
Guthrie, Alicia
Guy, Eula

Henley, Rosina
Harris, Sidney A.
Haslett, Doris
Hamilton, Louise
Hampton, Mary
Hawthorne, Milton

Ives, Judith

Jones, Nancy Gordon

Kennedy, H. Bratton
Kimball, Florence P.

Lawton, Mary
Leake, Doris
Linwell, Delia

McComas, Carol
McIntosh, Burr
Mackey, Ralph
McMein, Neysa
McMillan, Lida
Martin, Alice
Martin, Ethel
Mates, Harry J.
Mayo, Margaret
Meredith, Lois
Miles, Homer
Milliken, Ralph
Mitchell, Mabel Ruth
Montgomery, Victoria
Mullican, Charles M.
Mulligan, William F.

DRAMATIC—Continued

O'Connor, Patricia

Paige, Elizabeth
Paterson, Agnes
Perry, Albert
Powell, Charles F.

Raymond, Jack
Read, Charlotte L.
Roach, John F.
Rocap, Read
Rochester, Mary Louise
Rowe, John

Schenck, Katherine
Scott, Helen
Seymour, Blanche
Shields, Sidney
Sitgreaves, Beverly
Smith, George Porter
Smith, Rita
Sothern, E. H.
Sothern, Julia Marlowe
Sterling, Harriet

Storey, Jack
Sullivan, Gerald
Sumner, Margaret

Tannerhill, Muriel
Tanner, Marion
Taylor, Ethel
Timmons, Irene
Troutman, Ivy
Truesdale, Fred C.
Tyler, Annette
Tyler, Dallas
Wallace, Hugh E.
West, Madge
Whitson, Pauline
Williams, Fritz
Williams, Margot
Wilson, Mary Lena
Wyatt, Alice Bertha

York, Oswald
Young, Walter
Young, Winifred

CONCERT

Adams, Edgell
Aehle, Elsie
Albert, Minerva
Aldridge, Rachel
Ayres, Paula

Babcock, Lucie
Baird, Martha
Baldwin, Marie
Barr, Winifred
Barstow, Vera
Benham, Emily
Bierly, Neva
Bolton, Mary
Botsford, George
Brazeau, Marie
Brazeau, Henrietta
Brockway, Helen

Brown, Pauline
Browne, Kathryn
Bush, Ruth

Cannell, Frank
Carey, Florence
Carkeek, M. T.
Case, E. Romayne
Chesley, A. M.
Corbin, LeRoy
Coulter, Joe
Craig, Mary Adeline
Cushing, C. C. S.

Damrosch, Walter
David, Ross
David, Mrs. Ross
Davies, Jos.

CONCERT—Continued

Devereaux, Marie
DeVore, Jessie
Dickinson, Ruth
Dismukes, Cornelia
Dixon, Jessica
Dodge, Beulah Chase
Donn, Betty
Dowdy, Leta Clark
Duddy, Frank

Everett, George I.
Everts, E. B.
Ewing, Grace

Farrar, Amperito
Farrar, Guadalupa
Ferguson, Helen
Ferguson, Israel Harry
Ferguson, Sara
Flood, Paul T.
Frost, Avon

Gamble, Ernest
Gideon, Constance
Gideon, Henry
Gluck, Margel
Glynn, Madeline

Harris, Floyd
Hartwell, Josephine
Harvey, Harold
Hasbrouch, Elsie
Haynes, Dorothe
Hearons, Anna
Hearons, Winifred
Hibbard, Susan
Hibbard, William
Hixon, Blanche
Hoople, William
Horisberg, Kate R.
Hunter, Ruth

Irving, Lydia Isabel

Jacobs, Irene

Jarett, Daniel
Jones, Edward C.

Karla, Constance
Kessel, Helen
Klein, Nell J.
Kuhn, Aline
Kurtz, Ada

Laughlin, Flora
Lee, Jack
Los Kamp, Virginia
Lippi, Edward
Luckey, Ann

McLinn, Ruth
Mackey, Ethel
Marple, Harriett
Mead, Frank L.
Meek, Edith
Meek, Edward
Moore, Jason
Mullen, Mary White
Myers, Edith Luckstone

Noar, Adeline Patti

Oglesby, Frank
Oliver, William M.
Ormsby, Ethel

Packard, Adeline
Paulsen, Hortense
Planel, M.
Plasschaert, Camille
Porter, Marguerite
Poston, C. E.
Potter, Florence
Present, Rata
Prosser, Eunice

Rabinowitz, Clara
Randolph, Muriel
Rea, Ethel
Rosser, Catherine

CONCERT—Continued

Schupac, Marcia
Scott, Grace L.
Sellers, Samuel Nelson
Smith, Jack
Stanley, James
Stanley, Eleanor
Starkey, Julia Meade
Stevens, Nella
Stucki, Emma
Sybert, Marie

Thomas, Edna
Tilson, George

Tris, Mary Adelaide
Tsianina, Princess
Tuttle, Jane

Walsh, Marie
Watkins, Enid
Watson, Edward
Weston, Isabel
Weston, Mary
Whitehead, Frank
Wiederhold, Albert
Wilson, Margaret

VAUDEVILLE

Abbott, Annie
Adams, Mabelle
Adams, Rex
Adams, Berta Bell
Addison, Mae
Adler, Harry
Anderson, Christopher
Arica
Arnold, Hazel
Arnold, Pauline
Aubrey, Helen
Aubrey, Jane
Austin, Tossing

Bailey, Bill
Baker, Patricia
Baldwin, John
Bannister, Joe
Barber, Jane
Bartell, Harry
Bell, Arthur
Bell, Leah
Black, Edward B. Flester
Blondell, Libby Arnold
Bloom, Irving
Bluefeather, Princess
Bordeau, Sim
Boston, Billy
Bradbrook, Geo. E.

Broad, Billy
Brown, Dixie
Brown, Himmie
Buford, Blanche
Buford, Ina
Burke, Eddie
Burns, Billy
Burns, Eleanor

Campbell, John
Cantwell, John
Carlton, Louise
Carlyle, Louise
Carman, F. Barrett
Carrette, Bessie
Carter, Jack
Caveny, J. Franklin
Caveny, Marie
Chalbert the Great
Chalfonte, Lola
Chaplin, Arthur
Chase, Frank
Childs, Emily
Churcher, Anita
Claire, Josephine
Clark, Solomon H.
Clifford, George
Clyde, Ora
Coe, Edward

VAUDEVILLE—Continued

Coe, Lillian
Collins, Howard T.
Corbin, Gilmore
Coulter, Theo.
Cowley, Frederick K.
Cressy, Will
Cristle, Joe
Cudlipp, Chandler
Cunningham, Elizabeth

Dacey, Billy
Daly, Mary
Darcy, Harry
Dayne, Blanche
Dell-a-Phone
Delroy, J. B.
De Mar, May
De Mont, Frank
De Mont, Gracia
Denish, Paul
Dermotti, Thos.
Deumm, Hettie
Deyo, Howard N.
Deyo, Jeane
Dietrich, Rene
Doherty, Leo. Jos.
Doherty, Mrs. Viola
Donnelly, Leo
Downing, Arthur

Edwards, Jack
Egan, Joe
Elliott, Agnes
Elliott, Del
Elliott, Edna
Elwood, Robert J.
Erickson, Knute
Evans, Jean

Fein, Laurence
Findlay, Al
Fischer, Arthur
Fivey, Robert W.
Florence, Katherine
Frances, Corinne

Franklin, Irene
Fredriks, Eddie
Freeman, Allyne N.

Gardner, A. F.
Gardner, Dave
Gibson, Gertrude
Gilmour, Boyd J.
Golden, Mabel
Goode, Nat.
Gray, Thos. J.
Green, Burt
Gregory, Gilbert
Guder, Carl

Haber, Eleanor
Haley, Harry
Hall, Jack
Hanson, Jack
Harrington, Jean
Haslam, Hazel
Hawley, Walter
Hayes, Pauline
Hazelton, Faynetta
Herbert, Roy
Hoier, Thos.
Horton, Amy
Howard, Clara
Hubbard, Nona
Hunting, Tony
Hutchinson, Mary L.
Hutton, Forrest

Irwin, James
Israel, Harry

Jackson, Jerome
James, Ada G.
Johnson, Dave

Kayne, Agnes
Kellogg, Mary H.
Kelly, James F.
Kennedy, John J.
Kessler, Mae

VAUDEVILLE—Continued

Kinsley, Frederick
Kouns, Nellie
Kouns, Sara

La Tour, Catherine
Laurence, George
Laurence, Jack
Laurence, Thelma
La Violete, Victor
Lazell, Milly
Lea, Will
Leonard, Bessie
Leonard, Mike
Lerner, David
Lewis, Andru
Lile
Link, Pauline
Lombard, John
Lombard, Richard

McCrea, Lottie
McCullough, Wm. T.
McDonald, Madeline
McFarland, Marie
McFarland, Mary
McIntosh, John
McIver, Daniel C.
Mack, Joseph P.
Mackay, J. Wallace
Maine, Lucy
Maillard, Chas.
Maillard, Fred
Manley, Walter
Marshall, Edward
Mills, Phil
Mills, Volney Ladd
Mohonga, Sergeant
Montgomery, James S.
Moore, George A.
Moran, Hazel
Morris, Bertha
Morris, Billy
Morrison, Maurie
Morrissey, Will
Moulton, Bessie

Murley, Josephine

Neumann, John
Nicola, The Great
Northland, Edna
Northlane, Ollie
Norton, Helen

O'Brien, James E.
O'Clare, Wm.
O'Clare, Madeline S.
O'Zav, Annie
O'Zav, William

Paley, Herman
Palmer, Olive
Paul, Eddy
Perry, Harry
Pierson, Hal
Pollack, Emma
Porray, Edmund
Pryor, Ethel
Pryor, Wm.
Primrose, Helen
Primrose, Louise

Ramsey, Lillian
Raymond, Catherine
Rhodes, Russell M.
Riano, Jack
Rice, Lew
Ride, Wille E.
Roberts, Annie N. M.
Rochester, Claire
Rogers, Jonathan
Roger, Charles
Ronca, Dora
Root, Esther

Sanders, Edith
Sanford, Jerry
Saltonstall, Rose
Sargent, Mamie
Savoie, Blanche
Sears, Gladys

VAUDEVILLE—Continued

Sherman, Paula
Skeel, Ruth
Snow, Bert
Spink, George
Stanford, Max
Stead, Sue
Storm, Joan
Storts, Grace
Storts, Harvey D.
Sturtevant, Adele

Tabor, Stuart
Tan (May E. Flester)
Tanean, Harry
Tate, Helen
Teed, James W.
Temple, Irene
Thomas, Vera
Townley, Phillip

Underwood, Will Lea

Van Tine, Ida
Vaughn, Minnie

Verdon, Frank
Verdon, Vera

Waldo, R. L.
Waldron, Joe
Walker, Reta
Walker, Raymond
Walter, Annie
Walton, Beûlah
Warwick, George H.
Wheelock, Esther
Whitell, Ermine
Wilber, Jack
Willard, Clarence E.
Williams, Dorothy
Woillard, Hazel
Woodbridge, Margaret H.
Woodelton, Jane
Wrenn, Helen
Wright, Horace

Yvette

Zenita

LECTURERS

Anderson, John F.
Appley, Jose E.
Atkinson, William Dent

Babb, J. Franklin
Bakewell, Euphemia
Barnett, Augustus Edw.
Beckwith, Floyd J.
Beene, Dow Bunyon
Billingsley, Dr. James J.
Bingham, Guy M.
Boyer, Edw. E.
Brown, Frank E.

Cambridge, Dr. Arthur A.
Candler, Walter E.
Carman, J. Ernest
Cave, Robert Lord

Cochran, Fred
Cochran, I. M.
Cockrell, Ewing
Cook, J. Hunt
Curry, Elvin J.

Dancey, Capt. S. H.
Deans, Dr. John
Dixon, Royal
Downs, Geo. W.

Eason, Isaac W.
Eason, Samuel R.
Eliot, Willard Ayres
Estabrook, Nina

Gale, Albert A.
Gibson, Lemuel E.

LECTURERS—Continued

Grant, Myran Louise
Grimes, Frederic
Grose, Arthur W.

Halsey, Don Peters
Hamilton, Frank M.
Hildreth, Melvin D.
Hulbert, Homer B.
Hussey, Dr. John M.

Ice, William Edward

Kelley, Frank B.
Kilbourne, Henry J.
Kline, A. D.
Kuonen, E. M.

La Follette, William

MacNeil, Alan B.
Mansfield, Beatrice
Mathed, E. T.

Oldys, Henry

Palmer, Asher F.

Perry, Edw. Russell

Risner, Henry Clay

Snudden, Benj. D.
Spencer, E. W.
Spencer, Wm. S.

Taft, Lorado
Taylor, Gordon J.

Victor, Rae

Ward, John Albert

Directing Staff
C. D. Brooks
W. Bedford Moore
W. C. McCroskey
Julia E. Ashburn
Helen B. Yenney
A. E. Whitney
Wells, Smith
E. A. Brown
Elisabeth C. Hamilton

LECTURERS—LES FOYERS DU SOLDAT

Horatio E. Smith—Director

Borgerhof, J. L.
Blanpied, D. R.
Brandon, E. E.

Cole, R. J.
Coleman, A.

Granberry, J. C.

Greene, N. L.

Hart, C. R.

Lingle, T. W.

Merrill, T. C.
Muyskens, J. H.

Williams, H. C.

SONG LEADERS

Anderson, Lawrence R.
Armstrong, Orland K.

Balmond, Charles
Burnham, Charles

Carroll, Hope
Clarke, Kenneth
Cushman, Lewis N.

DeMach, L. C.

Song Leaders—Continued

Echols, H. O.
Eis, Florence

Foulke, Eugene H.

Gleason, C. G.
Good, Robert
Grey, Ira M.

Hall, Orrington C.
Havens, Edward
Hawkins, Stanley
Hunn, Jessie M.
Hedger, J. A.

Jones, W. H.

Keller, Herman
Kinney, Miller E.
Kirck, C. M.

Lamb, C. F.
Lewton, J. E.
Likes, P. H.

McMichael, J. W.
Maier, Guy S.

Naftzger, Earle
Nelson, John L.
Newhall, J. L.

Strong, Jervis A.

Thayer, W. A.

Vincent, Wallace D.

Watson, Ed. A.
Winslow, H. E.

Recruited Soldiers

Addleman, Raymond W.
Allen, James E.
Angelotta, Albert
Atchley, Hooper

Bigelow, Bryant
Bitzer, Thos. F.
Budd, Wm. H.
Bull, Walter

Coe, Sterling
Collins, Monte
Crider, John
Currier, Harold

Dakin, Edwin F.
Dottore, Chas. A.
Demming, Robert

East, Edwin S.

Gallagher, Jack
Glover, Wendall

Goff, Guy B.
Gott, Thos.
Grupey, Paul

Hall, George
Hall, Howard R.
Hammersla, W. S.
Hamp, Chas. W.
Hauslieb, W. R.
Hicks, LaVelle E.
Hicks, Ray
Horn, Sylvester

Kilpatrick, Elmer
Knoff, Aubrey
Knoff, Harry

Ladd, Schuyler
Lane-Hefferman, Jack
Leary, Nolan
LeClerq, J. C.
Levy, Russell

RECRUITED SOLDIERS—Continued

Mitchell, Albert
McCusker, Stanley

Nushaw, A. K.

Orr, Victor M.
Oswald, John G.

Parmelee, Fred M.
Paulsen, Arvid
Peters, Newton

Reed, Carl

Russell, Samuel

Scotty, Jack
Silvernail, Clark
Sorg, Paul
Swain, W. C.

Turnbull, H. B.

Ward, Jack
Wysong, H. R.

Zapp, Albert

STOCK COMPANIES

Beune Stock Company
Bourges Stock Company
Brest Stock Company
Golden Players
James Forbes Stock Company
Le Mans Stock Company
Little Theatre Players (Gievres)
Little Theatre Stock Company (Coblenz)
Lone Star Stock Company
Silvernail Company
Tours Stock Company

UNITS

A Little Cheer from Home
All American Four
American Players
Bulley Party
Burnham Party
Caveny Company
Clipper, Comedy
Comedy Cut-Ups
Cressy and Dayne
Draper Party
Electric Sparks
Fifth Avenue Follies
Four in a Ford
Four Willing Warblers
Gloom Chasers
Gould Party
Hearon Sisters Concert Party
Hixon Party
Home Folks
Horisberg Party
Hunting and Frances
Jazzophiends
Just Girls
Khaki Trio
Kirk and Wyatt
Konecny Concert Party
Liberty Belles
Liberty Show
Little Bit of Everything
Live Wires
Luckey Trio
McFarland Sisters
Manhattan Four
Man Who Grows
Margaret Wilson Party
Mayo Shock Troupe

UNITS—Continued

Merry Mary Anns
Mills Party
Musical Foursome
Musical Maids
N'Everything
Playlet Players
Rainbow Quartette
Ramblers
Scrap Iron Jazz Band
Shamrock Five
Some Home Folks

Some Pep
Songs and Skits
Songs N'Everything
Souvaines Party
Strollers
Three M. Company
Those Three Girls
Uncle Sam Quintette
Vardon and Perry
Vaudeville Four
Warwick Unit
Y's Four

PROFESSIONAL ENTERTAINERS

The records of the New York office show that a total of 828 entertainers were sent overseas, divided as follows: Overseas Theatre League 180 men and 274 women, and as regular "Y" entertainers 87 men and 287 women. In comparing these figures with the list of names given, it must be borne in mind that the personnel in France was changed somewhat owing to recruiting from the Army and other branches of service. It is estimated that it would take one person 325 years to cover the same period of service as did those that went overseas.

Where the entertainers employ stage names, these have generally been used in the list.

The number of entertainers from the various states is as follows: Alabama 3, Arizona 2, Arkansas 4, California 31, Colorado 6, Connecticut 11, Delaware 2, Florida 2, Georgia 11, Idaho 0, Illinois 61, Indiana 16, Iowa 12, Kansas 16, Kentucky 14, Louisiana 4, Maine 7, Maryland 12, Massachusetts 56, Michigan 28, Minnesota 7, Mississippi 3, Missouri 23, Montana 1, Nebraska 6, Nevada 0, New Jersey 21, New Hampshire 3, New York 228, New Mexico 1, North Carolina 1, South Carolina 2, North Dakota 2, South Dakota 3, Ohio 45, Oklahoma 6, Oregon 8, Pennsylvania 63, Rhode Island 7, Tennessee 9, Texas 11, Utah 3,

Vermont 3, Virginia 2, Washington 5, West Virginia 1, Wisconsin 10, Wyoming 0, District of Columbia 6, and from outside the United States Norway 1, Italy 2, Ireland 2, Scotland 2, Russia 3, Panama 1, Canada 15, Roumania 2, Holland 2, France 1, England 10, Bavaria 1, China 1, Bohemia 1, Belgium 1, Switzerland 1, Russian Poland 1, Cuba 1, Sweden 1, Denmark 1.

This table indicates the division of talent as relates to their age:

Age	No.	Age	No.	Age	No.
18	1	34	24	50	10
19	3	35	30	51	6
20	5	36	29	52	6
21	1	37	37	53	3
22	5	38	30	54	7
23	23	39	35	55	4
24	26	40	22	56	5
25	75	41	13	57	1
26	44	42	14	65	1
27	49	43	10		
28	55	44	15		
29	39	45	23		
30	40	46	18		
31	28	47	9		
32	36	48	11		
33	30	49	2		

Trouping for the Troops

Contents

Part 1: On the Edge 265
Part 2: The Advanced Zone 288

To My Dear Little Mother

And to those who, like her, waited, watched and prayed against so many dangers that never came, I dedicate these pocket flashlights of the last three months of the war as seen by me and my fellow-players in an effort to carry to "the boys" a message of cheer that every sister, wife, and mother would gladly have brought in our place had she been permitted.

Part 1: On the Edge

Sunday, Sept. 8th, 1918
Somewhere in France.

It is just about one calendar month since we said goodbye to New York. "We" meaning a band of six players from the "Overseas Theatre League" who have come here to play under the "Y" in the American camps in France.

I understand now why those at home are so often disappointed in the lack of colour and human detail that they receive in the reports from the Americans over here. Things come too fast for us in this warriors' world and novelties have become commonplaces before we can find time to write home about them. Then, too, the lack of routine in one's daily life over here, the necessity for constant readjustment to new conditions, the desire to drink in new knowledge of a world about which all those who have come before are eager to report. All these things exhaust both time and vitality and when the "Good nights" are going round one is glad to draw the funny, fat, French feather bed over as much of one's anatomy as it will cover and console the conscience that is trying to get one to write with the old, familiar *manyana*." And by the way, I have discovered that the Spanish "*manyana*" and the French "*tout de suite*" arrive at about the same time.

On leaving "the other side" I didn't watch the Goddess of Liberty out of sight, nor even the New York dock and in this I am told I was not in the minority. In the first place, since all the friends and relatives of passengers had been forbidden to come within more than gunshot of the dock, a merciful provision for all concerned even in peace times, it was not necessary either for them or for us to stand first on one foot then on the other waving sickly farewells with smiles growing more and more forced. In the second place, there were three classes of persons on board, those eager to get away from conditions at home, those with splendid and difficult jobs to be tackled on "the other side," big humanitarian jobs, and those whose services the government had drafted. Any and all of these motives meant "eyes straight ahead" not backward.

A bored *ingénue* and ex-film actress who shared my stateroom with two other "Overseas" players, voiced her feelings about departure without much ceremony when she said:

"Why should I want to watch the darned Goddess out of sight?"

"I'm so sick of hearing what those pie-faced picture stars get, that I hope I'll never see the 'Land of Liberty' again."

I walked round the deck soon after this remark and most of the sallow faces and dull eyes staring out from the backs of steamer chairs were equally world weary. Of course there had been the long drawn fatigue of getting passports and standing in line for days in badly ventilated offices only to be told that whatever one had done or *wherever* one had come, preliminary to departure, one was all wrong and must start over again, and some of the lassitude that was on us now was from the relief of not having to make out any more "questionnaires."

About half way down the deck, there was one pair of eyes with a different light in them, a pure, holy, far-seeing light. They belonged to a woman who was crossing for the third time within a few months. Her name was Mrs. Ray Brown. I believe she was assisting in the extension and reorganisation of some of the hospital systems, though she never talked about herself, so I do not know. She, at least, knew *why* she was going and to what.

At the end of the deck I stopped to look over the rail. The deck below was swarming with red-coated Polish soldiers. There was a light in most of their faces, too, and a spirit of adventure quickened all their movements.

While I stood at the rail General du Pont, the powder king, joined me. He was in the uniform of the Y. M. C. A. and going over not only to study the activities of that organisation and the Red Cross in relation to the war, but also to "see the war" and to give service wherever the opportunity might offer. This is a sort of free lance soldiering permitted only to men of unusual power, influence and money and very much envied by the less fortunate who are restricted by a more limited field of action. The general was joined in turn by a rich young stock-broker who had been known around New York for years as a sort of harmless lounge lizard and indulgent "first nighter." His ambition at present was to get to the front and drive an ambulance for the

Red Cross. He had already acquired the uniform but I am told that he is now bewailing his fate in the warehouse of a dull French port where he has been set to "counting chemises." Upon hearing which, one of his friends remarked that his reputation on Broadway had no doubt preceded him.

The next person to join our group was the dark, snappy-eyed wife of a Spanish official who was greatly perturbed because America was not sending her most beautiful "*cocottes*" to the *cafés* of Spain to compete with the German *cocottes* who were there in great numbers heavily backed by their government to spread German propaganda amongst their table companions.

We were interrupted by an emissary to Belgium who pointed out to us the floating city that now surrounded us, merchantmen, sailing vessels, torpedo destroyers, battleships, transports, fruit ships, coalers, twenty-two in all moving forward in neighbourly proximity on a sea of gold, while airplanes and dirigibles floated like guardian angels above them. It reminded one of Venice in a late September sun with its canals and baby castles, and one felt almost as though it were possible to step about on this still sea of gold from ship to ship.

At noon of next day while most of us were at "*déjeuner*" our particular ship, the fastest of the convoy suddenly leapt ahead. The change in speed was so sudden and so apparent that some of the men went up on deck to inquire about it. They learned that a submarine had hit a provision ship just in our wake and our captain having women and children aboard, had, according to his orders, put on "full speed ahead." In an incredibly short time we were out in the now gray sea alone.

That night and every night no lights were permitted on deck, even the illuminated wristwatches which most of the passengers wore were ordered "turned in," meaning inside out on the wrist. The air was heavy and hot and the staterooms overcrowded and we were still in the danger zone so most of the passengers preferred to remain on deck and finally, when most of these dark mysterious figures had ceased bumping into each other and apologising for having got into the wrong chairs, arms, or laps, one of the American "entertainers"— Gray by name—woke many, and amused some of us, by marching along the deck with three attendants and calling out in a military manner "Cover up your wrist watches and your lieutenants."

When we looked round the deck in the approaching dawn we realised to how many couples this command might have applied and during the day the number of uniforms on deck seemed constantly to increase. We got the explanation of this at about the same time that it reached the Captain. Besides the officers who were booked on our deck there was a full company of our boys in the steerage and two hundred and fifty other boys who were trying to catch up with their commands, having taken too long on previous occasions to bid their sweethearts "goodbye."

Among the former was the son of a Milwaukee brewer who pays taxes on thirty million a year. When the pangs of hunger began to gnaw, our government having neglected to equip these boys with the bread baskets with which the average steerage passenger "pieces out," the son of our many times millionaire remembered a rich friend of his father's who was reported as being aboard ship. A message was manoeuvred to the said friend and a return message was accompanied by an official permit for young brewer to visit "father's friend" on deck. This was the beginning of a two days' successful foraging campaign from the steerage to the first class. Those below who had no friends above, got the word up on deck and were adopted. If they were not always permitted to visit their unseen protectors they could at least receive sweets and food from them and by noon of the second day every woman on board was surreptitiously dropping part of her meal into a paper in her lap and stealing out on deck with it to some waiting "prowler."

But on the morning of the third day when an overly hungry youth called at the stateroom of one of these ladies before she had had her bath and asked for the breakfast promised him, the stewardess who was in attendance thought the matter had gone far enough and evidently reported her observations to headquarters and by noon time the captain had issued orders that no more visits were to be permitted from the Netherlands.

There was a great deal of bemoaning about this and some depressing rumours came up from below. First of all one of the boys down there died of heart failure and was buried at sea, a second one engaged in a peppery bout with one of his fellows, was knocked off or fell overboard, a third jumped over and was drowned. Each of us tried to argue that a life more or less mattered little when so many were going to the sacrifice but each of us felt the double tragedy of these mere boys going under without the big chance of first "going over the top."

On the first Sunday morning of the voyage the sunlight returned to us and I ambled out on deck. I heard a monotonous mumbling. I followed the direction of the sound and soon looked down on hundreds of red coats on the backs of kneeling Polish soldiers. Against a background of ally flags a priest in white vestments officiated at an emergency altar made up of packing cases. A ray of sunlight fell aslant of his face as he turned with uplifted arms to pronounce the benediction.

The next night I stood at the door of the saloon after dinner with Parker Nevin, a typical New Yorker. The curtains were drawn to shut out the light from prowling submarines and the decks outside were pitch black, but inside, the atmosphere was quite as gay as in peace times and the lights quite as bright. Some Y. M. C. A. "Entertainers," two of them members of my unit, had just concluded a show that would not have bored a lover of the Ziegfeld Follies, and a dance was now starting in which there was no small sprinkling of "Y" and Red Cross uniforms. At the far end of the corridor through a cloud of smoke, one could see other members of these two organizations sipping light wines, smoking and playing bridge. It was all harmless enough but picturesque. I heard Parker Nevin's sigh. I turned to see him shaking his head sadly. I asked his trouble. He answered with a sad little smile that the world was all upside down, "The Y. M. C. A. dancing and the Red Cross drinking and the soldiers praying."

The short respite from danger zone to danger zone was soon over and new interest was provided when we failed to meet our convoy on the other side, at either of the spots designated. Using his own judgment our captain shot ahead full speed unconducted and a more decorous fellow ship just behind that waited for the convoy was torpedoed for its pains.

The moon burst forth on our last night aboard, round and red as harvest, and at midnight with the flood tide we made our way up the beautiful Gironde with "*La Belle France*" smiling from either shore. All the steamer chairs were occupied and many confidential promises were exchanged. Then again there were those who sat apart gazing silently out over the waters toward the soft, mysterious tree-fringed shores. Was this new phase of life going to fill the aching void or would it, too, disappoint them?

With the early morning came all the hustle and confusion of disembarking at Bordeaux. Officials demanding passports and health certificates and giving landing permits to some and subjecting others who were under suspicion to further examination, luggage to be weighed and checked, identification papers and photographs to be signed—Heaven knows what other details—and then all of us loaded into the toy French train bound for Paris. On our way to the station we passed our Polish friends, hundreds of them, in their red coats marching with a jaunty air and smiling faces. "*Bon chance!*" we called to them with lumps in our throats and they called back similar farewells to us.

Then hours of soul satisfying landscape each of us exclaiming at first at sight of a new *château*, picturesque courtyard or vineyard, then one by one subsiding under the calm of the beautiful well tilled fields, winding streams edged with poplars and the low lying hills over which creep the white ribbon roads that lose themselves in the pale blue horizon.

But we were barely under the spell of all this gentle domesticity when we were startled out of our reverie by suddenly whizzing through a dusty covered, training encampment of American soldiers and here we caught our first sight of German prisoners. They were laying American tracks under the direction of American engineers and a little further on we saw American locomotives and cars moving hundreds of American flying machines over American tracks already laid. From here on the landscape was repeatedly dotted by signs of the most stirring American activity. There was a certain pathos in the picture of a bent-backed old Frenchman bringing his one or two cows round his hay stack into his quiet little courtyard only to see them sent flying for their lives before a huge American motor truck that came rattling across his court yard almost upon his heels.

One began to speculate as to the permanent change that busy industrial America was going to effect in dreamy picturesque France.

It was night when we crept into Paris. No eager porters, "*facteurs*," to snatch our luggage from our hands, no one even to lift it from the railway carriages. We shoved, pulled, or pushed it onto the platform as best we could and struggled with it up an escalator that was not working. Outside in the semi-darkness a few army cars and trucks loaned to the Y. M. C. A. were waiting to take us to our various hotels and with hasty goodbyes to ship acquaintances scattering now to all parts of France, we rattled away over the cobblestones into the narrow winding byways, across the Seine that shone like a silver ribbon in the moonlight and into the lovely white, still gardens of the Tuileries.

We gasped at the beauty of it all. I had seen Paris many times in the full glare of its yellow night lights, its tawdry night prowlers exchanging cheap pleasantries, everything false, fakey and covered with tinsel to enslave and betray the senses of the already bewildered stranger, but I had never seen Paris robbed of cheap camouflage lit only by the moon and the starlight and a faint green ray that peeped from beneath the heads of the elevated street lamps; it was as though—someone of our party remarked—as though old Paris were dead and the soul of new Paris were arising out of the debris.

When we reached the hotel, the "Y" had seen to it that our rooms and a hot supper were waiting.

As I looked down the long supper table I knew for the first time just how many sorts and conditions of men and women had crossed under the auspices of the "Y" on our steamer. There were "spiritual advisers" as the boys call them, engineers for hut construction and road building, supply men to assist in the provisioning of these huts, athletic instructors, canteen workers, secretaries, stenographers, bankers, and other important American financiers and last, but not least popular, our own little band of American "entertainers" bound for we knew not what nor where. The interesting instruction given us before leaving America was so to arrange our programme that we would not be disconcerted if we found it necessary to cut our "show" in half and rush on to another camp where the boys were about to go into action and needed relief from their tense state of thought.

Upon talking to some of the generals since, I'm inclined to agree with them that it is the boys who have just come out of action, having been obliged to fight across the bodies of their fallen comrades, the boys who are trying to forget the sight of staring eyes in ghastly upturned faces, these are the boys who need to be wakened from their trance of horror and brought back to a realisation that the world still laughs and plays somewhere. These are the boys that we are hoping later to reach.

After supper we were informed that we were to report at a little chapel just back of the Madeleine at 9.30 the next morning for "conference." A murmur of rebellion was distinctly audible as we made our way to bed. Early morning conference about a lot of Y. M. C. A. dogma that could not possibly interest us when we were all dying to spend our first morning in Paris basking in the sunlight, gazing in shop windows, or sipping our coffee, French fashion, at the dirty little outdoor tables looking out on the busy boulevards,

The spirit of resentment was so strong in some of the travellers that they did not go near the chapel the next morning. Theirs was the loss for those of us who went to "scoff remained to pray."

We found not only a part of our ship's party there but hundreds of other recent arrivals under the "Y." Some had come by way of England, some on army transports, some on passenger ships.

The handful of men waiting to talk to us in an informal way was not made up of "preachers" as we had supposed it would be but of various workers—representing the more important branches of the " Y," activities, workers who had been at their jobs for many months, who had served not only in Paris and in the advanced zones of war but some of them up to the front line trenches.

They were not there to make us feel their superiority or offer advice; they were there to hold out their hands and help us across the stepping stones on which their poor feet and hearts had too often been bruised. They were there to beg that we, fresh from an unridden country with strong nerves and brave hearts, remember always the shattered condition of the nerves of our French allies ridden by four years of war, privation and discouragement. They asked the question, how many out of the hundreds of us assembled there were now living in the houses in which we were born; three persons raised hands. They asked how many of us were living in houses in which we had been for more than ten years.

A few more persons raised hands. Then they asked us to remember that the average Frenchman was accustomed to live not only in the house of his birth but in the house in which his grandfather and his great-grandfather had lived and that when this home was invaded, or threatened by invasion, he was like a lost child crying out in the wilderness and yet each one of the men and women amongst whom we were to take up our duties had lived in constant dread of losing the little left to them and there was not one among them who had not lost at least one person out of their lives whose coming had once quickened their pulses.

The speakers also reminded us that there were many tired, overworked, disappointed Americans who also deserved our patience and our admiration, men and women who had volunteered at the very outset of the struggle who had given up good lucrative positions at home, some of them big executive positions, and who for the good of the cause had forced themselves to fit into dull obscure niches over here and work for eighteen hours a day at secretarial jobs which they had outgrown at home in their youth. Some of the jobs were in out of the way ports far from Paris or the battle line, or from anything to stimulate interest in their performance and yet because some one must do this dull work these men and women had consented to be the martyrs.

It takes seven men behind the line to keep one man in the line so the experts have figured out and the man to be pitied is the man who has come to France with high hopes of picturesque service only to find himself the seventh behind the gun, relegated to counting packing cases in some out of the way port.

After our approaching relations with the French had been touched upon, the engineer at the head of the hut construction told us how: his men were managing to complete one hut a day at an average cost of from fifteen to twenty thousand dollars. He told us something of the difficulty of procuring the materials for these huts and how diplomatic bodies both in France and America had to pass upon a request for even a few pounds of nails. Next followed a report from one of the supply agents who explained that by command of General Pershing the "Y." had taken over the grocery department in addition to its canteen business. We learned that bacon was worth so much in Spain, chocolate so much here, sweet crackers so much there, etc., and to our amazement we learned that the Y. M. C. A. in France alone was handling in its construction and provision department more than one hundred million dollars a year.

Next came a report from one of the athletic directors and from him we learned that General Pershing had just directed the "Y." to teach baseball to both the American and French troops. He explained the inclination of the naturally polite Frenchman to sacrifice a home run while he apologised to his opponent for having seemed rude to him, he said too that the Frenchmen were often more anxious to acquire our slang than our strokes. Every good play with a Frenchman was a "*peepin.*"

One of the most important banking men in America who had enlisted in the service of the "Y" spoke of what he hoped to accomplish in the way of better exchange and somewhere far down the line some of the veteran "spiritual advisers" were permitted a word. They were each of them men, every inch, sunny, brave, and with faces radiating healthy humour and fine understanding.

Their warning to the new arrivals was not to take advantage of a world crisis to thrust their personal creeds or propaganda down the throats of the defenceless but rather to avoid reference to any creed and to post in the huts an announcement of a Jewish ceremony as quickly as the announcement of a Presbyterian one. They were urged to allow their lives and their deeds rather than their words to indicate their motives and one so-called "preacher" gave the following rule of living as sufficient creed for any man:

"Keep yourself persistently at your best;

"Keep yourself persistently in the presence of the best;

"Be your best and share your best."

On my way home to luncheon I kept repeating the words of this last speaker and I applied his rule mentally to the whole art of living, the aesthetic side, the business side, the physical and the spiritual side. It seemed equally sound in control of either.

When I got back to the hotel I found a "Y" secretary who had the Paris division of camp entertainment in charge, waiting to ask if our Unit of six would play in the Tuileries Gardens on Sunday afternoon to an audience of twenty-five thousand soldiers. There was to be a sort of continuous performance, the first of its kind ever given, it was to run from two until seven and three regimental bands and three singers from the Opera Comique were to fill a large part of the programme. Being a fatalist, I accepted though it seemed to me that our few small personalities and our limited bag of tricks could not go far in the open, scattered amongst twenty-five thousand men of dissimilar tastes and tongues.

It was a golden afternoon when we made our way up the high platform in the centre of the gardens. A backing of lattice and a roof of overhanging boughs was our only enclosure, yet, strangely enough almost every line that we spoke or sang got a hearty and almost universal response. After the performance which was hailed as a great success we were photographed and pampered and sent back to our hotel in one of the army cars. Frenchmen doffed their caps to us as we passed and Americans cheered us. It was all very exciting and much too pleasant to seem like war work. I remembered the rather stinging remark of a general in whose company I had dined the night before, as guest of the paymaster of Marines.

The general had been in an important command at Belleau Woods a few weeks before when the Marines prevented the Boche from entering Paris. He had acquitted himself so well that he was to receive the Legion of Honour on the morning following our dinner party. He was not a sentimentalist and he said that if the overseas entertainers were serious in wishing to accomplish real good they would devote very little time to the camps around Paris but get as quickly as possible to the boys fresh from action and scenes of horror. I was glad to have played in the Tuileries but eager to press on toward the front.

The next day, our last in Paris for a long while to come, we lunched at the Ritz, or at least most of us did so, some of us as the guests of General du Pont who had crossed with us on the steamer and who was now bidding us Godspeed and I as the guest of Mary Young and John Craig, who were in town for a few days to get supplies and who were eager to tell me of the splendid success they were having in the camps with *Baby Mine*. They had asked me for the use of the play when the first ship-load of our boys were sailing for France and while I had been proud of the opportunity to give it for such a cause, I had been sceptical about their being able to get any effect from it, played in tents or out-of-doors, with no scenery or properties.

They now told me laughingly how they carried three large bisque dolls under their arms to represent the babies and balanced a soap or cracker box on two chairs to suggest a cradle and tried, when possible, to seat the boys above them in a semicircle on the hillside and in this way they could play to thousands at one performance. Their eyes were dancing with the joy of the good they were doing and as I looked across the table at these two who had closed up their splendid house in Boston and turned their backs on the Stock Company it had taken them years to establish it seemed to me that Mary still looked only a child—and yet she and John had already given two boys to the army and one of them to the Field of Honour—and would continue to give of their best until the last big gun should be fired.

Just now, with characteristic generosity, it was their fixed purpose to make me feel that it was my play that had been responsible for their success and while I knew quite differently they did succeed in giving me a stouter heart for the bit that I was hoping to contribute to this "Man's War" and everything seemed to get very bright in the big restaurant and I noticed for the first time, that the sun had come out.

I looked round the Ritz and contrasted the present picture with that of the old days when Maxine Elliot used to sit at a certain round table in the corner in all her luscious beauty, bankers, leading-men, tennis and polo champions hanging over the back of her chair. I remembered a smaller table where Ethel Levy used to lunch during her great success in her first Parisienne review, and the chair on her left where her favourite poodle used to sit in state and a chair on her right usually occupied by the Younger Guitry.

The scene was much changed now. In the entire length of the dining-room and in the charming court outside, the only men to be seen out of uniform were the waiters and the few women present were also mostly in uniform, Red Cross or Y. M. C. A., and at a little table apart, wrapped in a long dark service cape, a veil bound round her now serious brow, sat the once gay and colourful Elsie de Wolfe. And on every side men in khaki, blue, or grey, but of all the uniforms present it seemed to me that the grey one with the black and white trimmings, that of the Italian flying corps, was the most interesting and the most distinguished.

In spite of changed accoutrements and conditions the same old gentle reassuring dignity hung over the Ritz guests, like a soft gauze canopy not to be pierced by harsh sounds. And the greetings and recognitions and goodbyes that would have been boisterous in the street outside sounded only like the humming of bees in June time. A Ritz is always a Ritz I thought as we passed out into the pebble pathed sunlit garden for our coffee.

At the far end of the garden, sipping his coffee and smoking a made-to-order cigarette, sat George Burr, in earnest conference with two officials of the Red Cross. He had abandoned the administration of large offices in every important city in America and crossed the ocean to offer his services to the Red Cross in any capacity in which they could use him—no matter how humble. He had no premonition that he was soon to become the beloved head of the whole organisation and be known by the fond title of "The Big Col."

He was joined by Gilbert White, America's most famous unpublished wit, now serving in the Signal Corps, and by Mrs. Florence Kendal. Gilbert had just drawn a cartoon of Mrs. Kendal, a charming young woman of fifty, leaving New York to establish an officer's convalescent home in France. On the curb, waving goodbye to his mother as she passed down Fifth Avenue, stood her popular son Messmore. He was saying ruefully to the bystanders—"I'm too old to fight but I'm sending mother."

We all had a good laugh at Gilbert's cartoon, then simultaneously, every one seemed to realise that "*dejune*"—the only enjoyable respite still permitted in wartime—was over and within a few minutes the garden and restaurant were silent and deserted.

That night another army car tore its way through the streets with us and out into the country to a little band of engineers stationed near some barge canal. When we arrived they were still busy with saw and hammer finishing a platform which they had erected hurriedly under a canvas covering. We were chilled to the bone and a little depressed by the dim light of two tottering torches but we gave what spirit we could to the show and left to their hurrahs, never having clearly understood to whom we had really played.

The next morning we left Paris amidst the customary confusion of mysterious servants arriving in the hotel lobby at the last moment and the laundry that always returns only in time to be carried under one's arm.

We had already begun the shedding process so familiar to even the most experienced travellers who come over in war time. Most of us had left our trunks containing quantities of soap and shoes and sugar in the keeping of our landlords, having cussed out the misinformants on the other side who had told us that these and many other things were not to be had in Paris.

Our first meal in the hotel had shown us that Paris was suffering from less food restriction than we were at home, and our first promenade up the Avenue de l'Opera had opened our eyes to the astonishing fact that, now as always, everything in the world was to be bought in Paris and many military things in much snappier more convenient design than at home. Even the woollens of which we had been warned there was such a scarcity, were displayed in every outfitter's window.

We had meant to write home about all these things for the sake of other benighted travellers who would no doubt follow us, and now we were leaving Paris without having found time for more than the conventional cable home "Well and happy."

At the station again confusion and distress, no porters, insufficient help for the weighing and checking of baggage, no compartments to be reserved, necessity for showing passports and getting movement orders stamped in order to "check out," train about to leave and only one or two bored officials to serve long lines of excited travellers, indifferent shrugging of shoulders on part of officials and yet some way or other when the toy train at last departed, amidst shrill boastful whistling, all those who had hoped to be aboard had managed to be there, hot, angry and perspiring to be sure, but present.

Some hours later our unit of six was clattering up the main street of Chaumont, one of the most picturesque, most historic villages in France. We were on our way to the principal hotel at G. H. Q.— meaning the General Headquarters of the American Army in France. If we had put on a wishing cap and succeeded in winning our wish we could scarcely have found ourselves in a more fortunate spot as a starting point for our campaign of the American camps.

Even before we reached our hotel we were receiving familiar hellos from every side and before we had had time to register and get to our rooms we had had to put our luggage down time and again to shake hands with old friends from England, America, anywhere and everywhere for to G. H. Q. sooner or later comes almost everyone engaged in the business of war. High officials, war correspondents, magazine writers, camera and "movie" men, Red Cross workers, canteen officers, American politicians and millionaires over draft age on their way to the front to catch a quick glimpse of the war, spies, staff officers, supply agents, all kinds, colours and conditions of men of all orders and ranks and degrees of preferment.

We got to our rooms as soon as we could for we were scheduled to give a performance that same night in one of the Y. M. C. A. huts on the edge of the town. When one of the young women of the company ventured a criticism of her room the tired proprietress explained in rapid-fire French that we were fortunate to get any rooms at all since no less a personage than a general had been obliged to sleep on a park bench the night before with his men around him on the ground.

My room was amusing in its outlook. From my window I looked down upon the back court of the hotel, with the old fashioned pump and stone laundry basins, plump-armed French maids preparing the vegetables for the evening meal, cats and mongrel dogs on the kitchen tables or under them, pigeons pecking at whatever they could find on the tables or under them, pigs grunting from a nearby pen, to remind the proprietor that it was also their supper time, guests calling in bad French from their windows to the servants in the courtyard below—in short, a typical French small town hotel, and back of this domestic scene of disorder and confusion a picturesque vine covered arch of heavy masonry through which one caught a *vista* of winding moss-grown steps and tangled garden that the greatest water colour artist of them all might have been delighted to paint. France! "*La belle France!*"

Before our hats were even off Isaac Marcosson burst into the room, fresh from the front and on his way up the street to the barracks now occupied by General Pershing and his staff and known by the boys as G. H. Q.

I had never before kissed Isaac Marcosson but in the excitement of the moment I did so now. I am inclined to think that Mary Young who was with me also kissed him. She had stopped off at G. H. Q. to see our performance before going on into Joan of Arc's country to resume the playing of *Baby Mine* while she rehearsed in the forthcoming pageant of "*Joan*" in which she was to play the maid herself.

In a few moments Mary, Isaac Marcosson and I were curled up on the foot of the high French bed, the only comfortable place in the room to sit, eating from a tin of chocolates that he had bought at a Northern canteen and reminiscing about our last meeting at Carnegie Hall in New York just after he had delivered his maiden lecture, and here we were such a short time afterward in such a strange place under such different conditions and he, in the meantime had seen three battle fronts. He touched upon a few of the high points and humorous incidents of his latest experiences with the rapidity of which he alone is master and went on his way with a promise to see us later that evening.

When we reached the hut where we were to play that night we found it so packed that we could scarcely force our way through to get back of the stage and the green Silesia curtains that had been provided for us. Bodies hung through the windows, heads protruded from the skylights and although we were early we were told that our audience had been in its seats, eager for good places, for as much as two hours before our arrival.

We gave our best and from the cheers that came back from the boys and the invitations to stay with them forever, they evidently found our best good enough for them. It was a wonderful night, or so it seemed to us. Generals, colonels, majors and lieutenants also thanked us and assured us that we had given them and their men the best show they had seen since they left America. The officers were not supposed to attend this performance as we were to give a special performance for them later in the week but several of them had "slipped in" as they put it, and some of them remained for a cup of chocolate and an American doughnut with us in the back office of the "Y" hut, where the hostess and the secretary of the hut had graciously prepared a little supper for us.

When we got back to the hotel who should emerge out of the darkness of the court but Arthur Ruhl who had been waiting for our return. He too was down from the Front, having just finished some new work for Colliers which he had managed to get "passed" by the censor that afternoon. The only thing that prevented him from being completely happy was the prospect of having to sleep in the hotel bath tub that night, a fate that frequently overtakes late arrivals. He was rescued later, however, by Charles Edward Kloeber, one of America's most picturesque war correspondents and general war time pet.

And so the hello's and goodbyes continued from early morning until late at night. The next day at luncheon I met a fashionable Westchester woman whose country place I had passed, near mine, for years. She was wearing a Red Cross uniform and her husband, one of the brainiest men in New York State, was serving on General Pershing's staff. She and I had never known each other at home but by the time we rose from the luncheon table we were fast friends.

The first few days at G. H. Q. will always seem like a glimpse of fairy land to me, the sunlit court of our funny hotel with excited French waitresses screaming at generals and privates alike, the gay little groups around the dirty, iron tables, war correspondents, staff officers, and all sorts of birds of passage, the quaint winding streets with huge dust-covered military trucks dashing through them, the guard mount, each morning; the wonderful marine band organised by Damrosch himself at the time of his last visit to see General Pershing, the hours I stole for dreaming in a still, secluded garden back of the old Bastille that looked down hundreds of feet upon a beautiful valley dotted with fields, homes, flower-strewn gardens and hemmed in on the other side by low-lying hills over which the broad white road made its way toward Paris.

A valley through which Caesar himself had fought, and on the other side of the town from a high bluff another view even more lovely of a lazy, poplar edged canal winding in and out through a still green meadow, a stream having broken from its banks and run wilfully away in an opposite direction, children of the peasants wading in the stream, cattle grazing by its side, a white road winding out of sight up the valley toward a famous old *château* where no less a personage than General Pershing himself was housed, and all this within ear-shot of the shrill whistle of French locomotives bearing troops back and forward from the front line trenches and not infrequently German prisoners. It was a rare sight to see a real troop train come home laden with all the paraphernalia of war, men lounging about in the flat cars or hanging their feet out of the open doorways while they played cards or checkers, horses and straw and fighting apparatus all piled in together and one day a curious sight came by—an entire train load of German prisoners guarded only by wounded French soldiers. These were glimpses one caught of what was going on further up the line, but the sunshine and the laughter seemed at first to make all the pain of it unreal.

Then, too, the first camps that we played differed so much in avocation and *personelle* that we were constantly excited by surprises. At the Gas School where deadly and important experiments are made we dined at the officers' mess which was served in what looked like an iron-lined hogshead. I pricked up my ears when I heard one of the men say he had to be up early in the morning to "shoot dogs." He explained to me later that it is necessary for them to shoot poisonous gases into the lungs of the dogs, rabbits and even snails to discover ways of combating their effect. He told me, too, of the experiments being made by injecting certain fluids or gelatines in the horses' hoofs and sealing them up there to protect the beasts from the poisoned earth where deadly gases have been used.

Dogs are procured from the neighbouring villages or shipped up from Paris by the car load. I began to wonder if the improved condition I had noticed amongst the Paris cab horses meant only that the fittest were spared from experimentation. "*C'est la guerre.*"

On our way out from the camp that night a soldier jumped on the running board of our car as we passed one of the sentry posts, refused to accept our countersign and ordered our chauffeur to take us to the guard-house. We were haled before a sleepy-looking officer who pronounced us suspicious characters, said he had heard of no entertainment being permitted that night in the camp and gave orders that we be locked up for trial in the morning. Tommy Gray, one of our players produced his false whiskers and other stage "props" in support of his contention that he was a mere actor, Will Morrisey offered to play his violin to prove that he was an "entertainer," Lois Meredith, our *ingénue* went into giggling hysterics to prove her right to the title, Elizabeth Brill our leading *chanteuse* became properly temperamental and I argued as calmly as my bad disposition would permit, but all to no avail, we were about to be led forth to a night of torture when a captain who had been chief host at the supper after the performance appeared in the doorway and "gave us the laugh" and we realised for the first time that we had been the victims of a clever practical joke. The story went the rounds of headquarters the next day and for some reason or other seemed to add to our popularity.

Of course it made confirmed sceptics of us and a few nights later when one of the boys brought in a small German balloon that had fallen near the tent in which we were playing we refused at first to even approach it for inspection for we thought they had concealed some explosive inside of it.

From the Gas Camp we were taken to the wood choppers' camp where hundreds of sturdy Americans, many of them engineers, were engaged night and day in cutting down and transporting to headquarters a forest in which Marie Antoinette had once played. (*Marie Antoinette and the Downfall of the French Monarchy* by Imbert de Saint-Amand is also published in the Women & Conflict Series by Leonaur.) Winter was coming on and it was necessary to work fast before the snows came, though even the snow would not stop them, so they said. To get to this camp we abandoned our big army Renault for the first time and took to Ford cars for the roads were thought difficult. They would not seem so to the average American. We were rather relieved to lose the Renault for with it we lost Conde, the speed fiend, who had been driving us up and down hill at sixty miles an hour and barely touching the earth, when we reached a level stretch of road. When we ventured a protest he reminded us that he had been the favourite driver of the late President of France and had also driven in the automobile races in New York. In his opinion this evidently made him immune from accident and criticism.

One night when we were irritated into being very sharp with him he admitted that he had been driving fast out of temper because three bees had "bited" him that day. Later on when I offered him ten *francs* to soothe his ruffled feelings he drew himself up proudly and reminded me that he was a soldier in the army. When I confessed my *faux pas* to a millionaire American that night he told me that he'd made a fool of himself by trying to tip a chauffeur that had been loaned to him from the Army Transportation Department and had discovered that the chauffeur was president of a company at home in which he merely owned stock and the chauffeur had twice as much money as he had.

Such awkward situations as these leave one entirely at the mercy of one's driver over here and when we got into the dark woods I was thankful that Conde was not at the wheel. Oh, those delicious woods, the smell of smoke from burning autumn leaves! We picked up a doctor, who was walking to a camp beyond ours to see some negro boys. He too was rejoicing in the clean fresh odour of the woods. What a relief after the smelly courtyards of the French hotels. He said France had knocked his germ theories all hollow for if there were anything in germs all France would have been dead long ago.

As usual we found our audience had been waiting for us long before the appointed time. They were a fine looking lot of young "huskies" and how they did laugh at the show and how they did cheer, lined up either side of the wood road, as we called our goodbyes to them and their camp fires.

The next night was "negro camp night" and I've never seen so many square feet of white teeth before nor since. The commander told me that he had four companies of these boys when he landed and he loved them. He'd lost a great many of them because they were unable to endure the damp and the cold and two of his companies had been detailed at Southern ports to work on the new American-made docks. We had seen one of these docks before landing at Bordeaux and the brave fearless way in which it juts out to meet incoming ships is guaranteed to thrill even the dullest edged American.

I could imagine these black good natured faces in front of me much more habitually gay down on the Southern docks than way up here in the north preparing to go "over the top" to what they call a "good mornin' Jesus." They had forgotten their troubles for the moment however, and so had General du Pont in the front row and Major Wills, the paymaster of the Marine Corps, and the Chief Censor of the War Correspondents and several other friends who had stopped in at our hotel to see us on their way down to Paris and decided to attach themselves to our party for the evening to "hear the coons laugh." And how those boys *did* laugh, and those teeth!

When our show was over the boys volunteered a return entertainment and with their commander's permission they hopped onto the stage and did some wonderful buck dancing and when we all piled into our cars and headed back for G. H. Q. our chief comedian again declared that it was the best war he had ever attended.

The next night we left our hotel early and drove, or rather flew, for Conde was with us again, over miles of beautiful rolling hills to the Ordnance Camp. We were to have mess with the officers and give a show for them afterward. This function seemed to take on more dignity than any of the others, perhaps because we were made serious before dinner by being shown through the laboratory and the class and experimental rooms where row upon row of hellish contrivances for killing were on exhibition, some of them of our own invention, some of them souvenirs from the enemy. It was the first time that I had known that powder comes in hard brittle sticks, some of it looks and feels almost exactly like uncooked spaghetti or macaroni. We were afterward told that the young captain who explained the mechanism of some of the more deadly bombs, was a very great genius and had just made a discovery of great importance. He had the clear blue, far-seeing eyes of a genius and looked like the sort of young man the world needs.

After the "show," as we call it, we found that some of the officers who were billeted in a town below, through which we must pass, had prepared a supper for us in the village tavern, and were determined to way-lay us. They did so and when I looked round the long, narrow, dingy walled room lit by a few sputtering candles and surveyed the picturesque, incongruous party at the long table, the blue of an occasional French uniform off-setting the khaki of our boys, a chaplain whom we had picked up on the way, the gay tinsel and chiffon of our gowns, and over it all the haze of cigarette smoke and through the hum of voices the popping of champagne corks from bottles of which the women did not partake, a little song, much laughter, it looked like a scene from François Villon, and I felt that life was being made much too easy and too picturesque for us, but the very next day we got our first introduction to the more serious side of it all. When we came down for breakfast in the court we found the place almost deserted, I looked at my watch thinking that I was later than usual. On the contrary I was earlier. I asked one of the *habitués* of the place what had become of everybody—meaning more especially the war correspondents, journalists, and staff officials.

He said that every one was up at G. H. Q. and I thought he looked rather sinister about it.

A little later I heard a young lieutenant at the next table say that thousands of troops had passed through the village during the night on their way to the front.

I went for a walk and was amazed to see how many grey camions had suddenly stolen into the streets as from nowhere.

At luncheon when the men returned from G. H. Q. there was a silent expectant something in the air and a constraint about discussing something that every one apparently felt rather than knew.

Later as we got more familiar with the traditions of war we came to know that this sudden suspension of social candour—this tightening of the moral fibre, always precedes the declaration of each big "offensive" and until the big guns are actually firing and the knowledge of the manoeuvre has become common property one has a feeling of being suspended in space awaiting some unavoidable cataclysm and not being permitted to discuss one's forebodings with one's neighbour.

So impossible is it to determine the extent of an "offensive" at its inception that it is only on looking back upon it that history is able to label it in relation to its most salient point. This movement was to be known in history as the "Saint Mihiel Drive."

We knew nothing of all this however when we were loaded into the car after luncheon, to "show" in our first hospital. It was a base hospital on the edge of the town. Even yet I don't feel like writing about it. I'll never get away from the consciousness of that side of war again no matter how funny the stories round the supper table. No matter how bright the morning sunshine, there will always be that dark, gaping, subterranean passage underneath all the flow of chatter and chaff and art. Of all the hungry disappointed eyes that looked out from those grey coverlets, eyes narrowed by pain, I think the childlike eyes of the dumb, puzzled negroes will haunt me longest. They made me think of wounded animals who had never harmed any one and who could only wonder at their fate.

On our way home we passed several lines of great dust-covered camions on their way toward "the front" and when we got back to the hotel we found what we called our "camp followers" waiting in the court for us, young lieutenants who had attached themselves to our party without consulting us, who insisted upon carrying our coats and usually ended by losing them, who frisked about like gay young puppies regardless of what mood one might be in. I was tired and longed to get to my room and I said irritably to one of our unit that I wished we could lose the infants for a while.

I had occasion to regret that remark the very next afternoon and I shall always remember it with shame. When we came out from luncheon there were our "Newfoundland pups" as usual in the court but their faces were grave and their smiles a little forced and their "roll-ups" were slung across their shoulders. They'd been suddenly called "to the front."

We knew what that meant. The white faces of those poor boys in the hospital yesterday rose between me and the red-cheeked youths who stood before us now. They held out their hands one by one, each with some message to the girl he had left behind in the States. And right here I want to make my first criticism of Uncle Sam even though I may be hanged for it. If he could know how his boys over here have lost confidence in both his conscience and his ability to deliver their messages to their loved ones at home he would be sorry.

"It's pretty tough," so one of them put it, "when you're 'going over the top' to feel you can't even get a last word back to your girl."

He showed me the picture of his girl, young brave, sweet and trusting. She was sitting outside a lonely looking shack in North Dakota. She seemed to be looking out over the plains for the return of "her boy."

The boy told me how he had written to her every single day since he left, nearly nine months ago, and how he had received a letter from her only yesterday saying that she had had only four letters from him since his departure. He had figured out that according to that average, it would mean that more than two hundred and fifty ships must have been sunk each bearing a letter from him. This of course was impossible, so what had they done with his letters? "Dumped them into the sea," was his conclusion, "It saves trouble." I'm sorry to say that is the cynical conclusion of many of the boys over here. I suggested to this chap that he might have written things that the censor couldn't pass.

"No chance," he answered. "The first thing a fellow gets in his head over here is that all he can write home is "well and love" and, then, half a dozen other guys have to read it before it gets a fair start, but some of us boys would like to get even that much back if we could, but I guess there's not much chance of my girl getting a last message from me unless one of you folks run across her."

I took her name and had another look at the dreamy face in the photograph, that sublime line of Masefield's came back to me,—"*Each man follows his Helen with her gift of grief.*" How many of these men would return to their Helens?

All the voices became blurred now in a general buzz of goodbyes, there was a genial reaching out of hands and meeting of eyes that said only too plainly that they knew it might be for the last time. I couldn't speak and I knew it would not be considered sporty of me to cry. I just held out my hand and nodded, and oh, the ache in my throat! It was my first necessity for keeping a stiff upper lip and I wondered how mothers and sisters and sweethearts live through such hours without breaking the courage of their men when I could suffer so about men who, a moment before, had been only a nuisance to me.

The mothers and sweethearts of these boys would have been proud if they could have seen them turning their faces to the front that day, each eager to "go over the top." They were a brave looking lot, God grant we may see them again in America as whole in mind and body as then.

At eight the next morning the speed maniac, Conde, was waiting in his big Renault to take us away from G. H. Q. to what and where? We had been told the name of our next headquarters but it meant little to us. We knew only that it was in the "advanced zone."

Part 2: The Advanced Zone

In the Argonne
Wednesday night,
11:15
Sept. 25, 1918.

Within a few miles of us the greatest battle in history is just starting. Big guns are thundering, the lights are flashing across No Man's Land, and air ships are buzzing overhead in the starlight and yet I am able to turn my back upon this and a golden moon and sit here in a tiny barracks room on the head of one of the three cots upon which I and two of the other players sleep, and write; for it is all so wonderful that one feels an impulse to share it with those who are not here, even while everything tempts one outside.

Day after day, night after night, camions have streamed along "The Sacred Road"—which is what the French call the broad white highway from Bar-le-duc to Verdun—infantry, cavalry, machine guns, tanks, one endless procession manned by Americans, French, Singalese, Amanites, Chinese, African negroes and American negroes—a line broken here and there by the pompous, cars of high officials, French or American, ministers of state, and generals. And back and forth on the newly laid American railroad tracks at the foot of the hill on which we are now billeted large American engines have been bearing hither and thither for days heavy artillery, gasoline, provisions and ammunition and sections of portable houses and long sections of empty Red Cross hospital cars.

Tomorrow these cars with the big red crosses painted on their sides will come back from the front but not empty. Many of them will bear back to the waiting nurses behind the lines some of the boys that we have seen staggering along "The Sacred Road" these past few nights, exhausted by long marches and the sixty pound packs on their backs—boys who were so weary that when the occasional order came to halt they would sink back in the roadway too tired to drag themselves to one side or to even remove their packs, and too numb to care for the huge camions that whizzed by so close to them that we, watching, feared for their lives. The surgeon who stood by my side explained to me that when one of these boys could no longer keep up with his comrades he was divested of his pack and considered good for six more miles.

If he could then stagger no further he was allowed to drop out until he was treated—his feet were bathed and protectors put over the blisters and then a man who would ordinarily be told to stay in bed for days—was shoved back into the march and told to catch up with his regiment—"and many of these chaps" he said "are college boys or mother's pets, tenderly reared." I looked at the ones who lay before me along the roadside—in the mud or on the wet earth. "That boy over there," I said to the doctor, "looks as though he were dead. Let's speak to him." The doctor shook his head. "He's still alive but he's too tired to answer," he said. "He wants only to be left alone—they all do."

We walked on up the road, past what seemed miles of these same mute listless figures. Sometimes the order would come to march and they would stagger to their feet and move on—still without even a murmur. "Boots! boots! boots!" Kipling knew.

The surgeon who walked by my side was a wealthy southerner who had been requested by the government to accept the direction of a large corps of surgeons and Red Cross workers. He had three homes in America, a devoted family and a large practice and yet he was glad to sacrifice all these, and more, to sleep on a hard cot in an advanced war zone, if he was fortunate enough to be spared for a few hours to sleep, and he pretended that he liked "corn willie."

His big, heavy voice grew very tender when he spoke of his doughboys and yet he told me quite calmly while we stood under a wayside cross, bearing the drooping figure of the Christ—a cross surrounded by pines and marking one of the bloodiest cross-ways in France, he told me that his first duty and *any* surgeon's first duty on the battlefield is to treat first the men who need treatment least, for these can be made to quickly fight again while the more fatally wounded are only a drag on the army and are to be treated only out of compassion after the more fortunate ones have been put on their feet. A few moments later this same big fellow gave to a tired doughboy his last cigarette— the cigarette he had been treasuring to smoke on his way home. "*C'est la guerre,*" he said when I smiled at his tender action so in contrast to the harsh principles of procedure that he had just outlined.

"*C'est la guerre—C'est la guerre!*" Everywhere from every one on every side one hears it. It comes rumbling back to me now from the first night when we pressed into the "advanced zone." But that night it was said merrily almost in a spirit of derision for we were dining in a famous old *château*—one in which General Joffre had lived during the Battle of the Marne and in which Napoleon was said to have taken refuge when he was trying to escape capture.

The wine which we were enjoying had been poured from bottles whose corks were mildewed from long storage in the vaults of the *château*—a late September sun was dancing in and out between the branches of the trees and the shadows lay gently on the long peaceful lawn and some of our players were dancing on the terrace to the strains of the band that had come to serenade us before assisting in the entertainment which we were about to give in the eleventh century stable which had been lighted by candles and decorated with flags for our performance.

Life seemed very idyllic and gay this night and death very far away, and yet the next morning these same officers would be leading their men in sham battle to prepare them for their part in the great death struggle that was bound to come soon to many of them. It came sooner than we expected and the next day we were ordered to "double up" on our performances and play our four days' schedule in that region in two days as the entire division of forty thousand or more was to move forward to relieve another division that was going immediately to the front. We watched many of them get under way—fine stalwart fellows, with the wild-cat insignia on the sleeves of their uniforms. I saw their handsome general later in Paris taking his first "permission" since the war and it was amusing to watch the admiring glances of the French girls change into slightly shocked expressions as they beheld the black cat on his sleeve which to them suggests a very questionable vocation.

While these forty thousand "Wild Cats" were moving forward we were called back to Paris to be fitted with gas masks, iron helmets, "roll ups," cots, and blankets before proceeding yet further into the advanced zone.

On our way to Paris we stopped for luncheon at Chaumont, G. H. Q, and here we found many old friends and got our first word of the American victory at St. Mihiel and two men who had been in the action the night before told us how the old men and women in the regained territory who had thought France lost to them forever had thrown their arms about the knees of the on-marching Americans and kissed their feet and wept. How also that not one woman in all that newly conquered area had been left undefiled by their late German conquerors and how all the young girls had been carried away by the now retreating Germans.

When we reached Paris that night it was in time to experience the first air raid that Paris had seen in a month and one of the heaviest raids it had ever seen—and as history has since proven, the *last*.

It came just as I had tucked myself in for the night. My first thought was that I was utterly alone and I was a little sorry for myself. I wished that I knew someone to whom I could go to get "snuggled up." Not knowing any such person and not even remembering on what floor to find any of the other members of the company I lay quite still and waited. There were occasional flashes of light from the barrage firing on the enemy planes and the changing direction of this firing caused the sound of it to die away and return like the rumble of thunder.

After a time I heard voices in the corridor. I slipped on my dressing gown and went out. Three men in white pyjamas were standing in the doorway next to mine. They asked me if I was nervous and whether I would not like to go down to the cellar. I replied that I was a fatalist and one of them laughed and called that a good idea. I went back to bed and with the barrage still thundering and dying away and returning, I finally went to sleep.

The next morning I learned that not one of our company had taken the precaution of going into the cellar while every French person in the hotel had done so. This was explained by an old American resident on the ground that the nerves of the French had been unsettled by a long succession of raids, while to us a raid was still in the nature of a novelty.

Armed with all sorts of military orders the next morning we set out on our quest for gas masks and helmets and had our first lesson in the use of the mask. It wasn't a very cheery business. The fat puffy lieutenant delegated to instruct us seemed very bored with us and we thought him in danger of apoplexy from having so often to blow up his cheeks and to hold the air in them while adjusting his experimental mask. To concentrate our attention on the business in hand, and on himself, he told us terrifying stories about what had happened to others before us who had been stupid or slow in adjusting their masks in battles and he repeated the old saying about there being only two kinds of men where gas attacks were concerned—the quick and the dead.

After more than an hour of this exhausting drill when he had alternately bullied and coaxed us to keep pace with his rapid counting—and when each woman in the party had been made to feel that her hair was a crime against nature because it would get entangled in the straps of her mask and when most of the men had decided that there was something defective in their teeth, nose, ears or lungs—after all this boredom the young instructor swooped down upon Elizabeth Brice and me with an accusing eye, thrust his fingers under the edges of our masks just beneath our chins and thundered at us that our faces were too small for our masks. We thought it would have been more gallant of him to have put it the other way round but we were too cowed and exhausted to protest and I personally felt that I would rather be gassed than go through this ordeal again and said so.

Again I was properly rebuked and informed that the army was not concerned with my preference in such matters and that we would not be allowed to enter the danger zone until our masks did fit properly.

Telephoning followed and it was ascertained that there was a carload of new masks—small sizes—on the way from Bordeaux but since this car was in charge of a "Frog"—as the lieutenant put it—there was no telling whether the masks would arrive during the present war. Anyway we could call the next morning and see.

This was rather a let down after our impatience to get off to "the front" and we were feeling a little depressed when we reached the hotel.

In front of the hotel we found Senator Hollis waiting with a friend from one of the Southern Encampments.

The senator suggested that we join them for dinner at Montmartre. We were tired and ready for our beds but we remembered that the senator had lost his only boy in the air service less than a week ago and we knew that we could help him by sharing the burden of entertaining his friend and also by trying to keep his mind off his loss.

How little I had known Montmartre in the old days—the days when I'd dashed up the hill in the wild hours of the night in a cab or taxi with a lot of laughing Americans whose only idea was to use Pigale's and the Moulin Rouge as a stopping place for another drink. There were no cabs nor taxis to draw us up the hill tonight. We took the "Metro" to the foot of the mountain, then climbed tier upon tier of steep stone steps—stopping at every landing to look down on Paris as we had never seen it before—Paris lit by the setting sun on the one side and the rising moon on the other—dim, mysterious, alluring Paris. I loved it for the first time in my life—and I knew for the first time the lure of Montmartre—how many lovers had climbed these steps in the moonlight and halted at each landing and looked down into the mist and then into each other's eyes. How little would the rich tourist ever know of the real Montmartre.

When we reached the top of the hill and made our way along the middle of the street on the rough cobble stones, we passed the Cuckoo and other famous little *cafés* made so by hectic writers and we stopped outside a semi-outdoor eating place from which we could look across the street at the Sacré Cœeur. The seats were all taken at the outdoor tables so we gave our dinner order and went on to the place of the Martyr to watch the afterglow of the sunset and wait our turn at table.

For the first time I saw the statue at the foot of the cathedral—the statue of the martyr that gave the mountain its name—the statue that has looked down so many years on gay, wicked, sorrowing Paris.

After dinner we wandered through the crooked narrow streets searching for the old Moulin Rouge. We were told it had been burned—probably by an exploding shell. A little further on we passed the Black Cat—it was too early to go home—we went inside. Here again was the real Montmartre. A funny, low ceiling vaultlike room with plaster walls daubed with cheap drawings, fine etchings, nude paintings, charcoal cartoons, black cats; bits of red and white plaid gingham, faded leaves, shelves containing pewter mugs, brass bowls and all sorts of discarded *bric-à-brac*, a platform at the far end of the room with a piano on it, a small picture screen behind it, a bar to the right of it and a stair to the left of it. Benches in the room and long tables and all of these occupied by all sorts and conditions of humans. Frenchmen, and French soldiers, American doughboys and officers, and here and there a cheap *cocotte*—and smoke! One could scarcely see the length of the room.

The entertainment was being given by French soloists and by naughty tales told in silhouette by paper figures on the "movie screen."

After an interval someone asked one of the Americans present to sing. He passed along the word that Miss Brice of our company could sing and in a jiffy she was forced on to the platform and Mr. Morrisey of our company was rattling off an accompaniment for her. The French and the Americans were wild with delight. She was given a "double *claque*" and made to sing until she was hoarse then we went out into the street again and glanced almost with envy at some of the gay little groups that we saw around some of the small bars, then we picked our way down the steep steps and farewell Montmartre.

The next morning our gas masks had not arrived but the young lieutenant having apparently had a good night's sleep decided that we could proceed with the large masks and use them as a camouflage if questioned *en route,* provided we would exchange them at one of the hospital bases further up where he had recently shipped some small masks for Red Cross nurses.

We went to another part of the town for our iron helmets and then returned to the "Y" armed with our new implements of war.

Here we accumulated our "roll-ups" blankets and cots, for we could be sure of no bedding accommodations in the region to which we were going. How we came to detest these blankets and cots during the following weeks when we staggered under them by day and tried to cling to them by night! And how we longed to throw away our gas masks and helmets and all the rest of our cursed paraphernalia and how weary we grew always having to go back for one or the other of these that some one in the party had always forgotten.

Our first irritation began at the Paris station when our trappings became entangled with those of other cross grained individuals also pushing and jostling to make the overcrowded train. But once we were on the edge of the country where real battles had been fought and looking out the car windows at shell holes, graves, grass-grown trenches and heaps of mortar and brick where villages had been, we forgot all our lesser trials and began to suspect something of the seriousness of the great tragedy that we were approaching.

A little further up we began to see on the white roadways, paralleling the track, long lines of grey camions moving north with men and supplies, then cavalry halted on the banks of the streams or canals for their noonday rest, then more shell holes—one with an impudent poppy nodding from its very brink, and hours and hours later, because the railways were congested with supply and hospital trains, we reached a town in the region of the Argonne, which we were to use as a central point for our scouting tours—a town that was to be for many months a point of contact between the Argonne trail and the more removed political and supply bases that fed one of the final battles of the war.

Day and night, day and night, so close that one could scarcely pick one's way across the road, the great grey camions rumbled through the streets of the little village on their way to "The Sacred Road" that would lead them later toward the encounter. Some of the camions were loaded with men packed so tight that they made one think only of the animals that one sees in cattle cars—animals being shipped to pens for slaughter. Other camions bore heavy fire arms and ammunition.

The streets of the village and the hotels were filled with wayfarers, some of importance, some who had failed to connect with their regiments, a few I have reason to believe who were trying to desert—young boys who had been detached intentionally or otherwise from their command and who feared to be caught by the local military police and thrown into jail.

One of these boys had been sent back down the line with a detail of sick horses, He had delivered his horses but had failed to catch up again with his regiment and was wandering about the streets, frightened and hungry when a kindly officer succeeded in getting his confidence and persuaded him to go to the police and tell his tale and escape capture and arrest.

Sometimes a whole company of lost men would drift into the village, hungry and footsore and with no place to sleep, some misunderstanding having left them without proper provision or command. In such a case the "Y" would allow them to sleep on the floor of the canteen and provide them, as far as possible, with chocolate.

We played two nights in this town in a theatre rented by the French to the "Y" for the price of the electricity. The show was a great success—it was the first that many of the hoys had seen since leaving America. Our audience was made up of cavalrymen, infantrymen, airmen, doughboys and officers, French and American, for every variety of soldier was either passing through the town or stationed near it. They all applauded and our own boys cheered and whistled. We were cold and hungry after our performance so the "Y" man led us back to the kitchen of the canteen where a tired soul was ladling out hot chocolate from huge caldrons on the range and by the time we left the kitchen the floor of the hall leading to it had become so occupied by exhausted soldiers that we had to fairly step over them to get back to the street.

There was no room for us in any of the hotels so we slept on our cots in a store room of the "Y" across the street—if one can ever be said to sleep the first night he rides a cot. I was wakened early the next morning to find a dignified old gentleman—a French official in silk hat and civilian clothes—waiting outside my door to apologise for what he considered the rude behaviour of the boys who had whistled at our show the night before. He said that he thought the performance most amusing and deserving of anything but derision, and it was only by the aid of one of his countrymen who was called in to interpret for us that I was able to make him understand that with the Americans whistling is a mark of approval, whereas in the French theatre it indicates the; reverse.

During the day we wandered about the streets and everywhere one turned there were opportunities for doing good. For instance some of those up here on the edge of the danger zone undergoing hardships were inclined to speak slightingly of those in Paris in executive positions who "had it easy," but when we pointed out to them that the chaps in Paris would give their eye teeth to be up near the firing line and that they were already dreading the day when they must go home and tell their sweethearts and families that they got only to Paris—then the chaps up nearer the front were happier again.

I climbed up to a magnificent view on a high mountain back of the hotel. Soldiers crowded every nook and cranny of the ruined cathedral on the mountain's crest. They also were on their way to the front. At the foot of the hill, tied to an iron ring in an old stone wall, stood a wreck of a horse with a festering shrapnel wound in his shoulder. The poor beast strained in vain toward a few spears of grass growing just outside his reach. I gathered the grass and gave it to him. I found a sympathetic French girl in a shack near by and she found some hay for the beast. I was so grateful that I cried. She brought me some water to wash the tears away and the sea that rolls between our two countries and the babble of tongues that confuse meant very little.

I couldn't leave the horse until some one had adopted him and at last an ambulance came and took him away, still munching the hay that we transferred to the ambulance.

Further down the street a French lad was carrying a fox terrier in his arms and crying over it—a passing camion had broken its leg. Again the tears came to my eyes and yet I looked down that same street at miles upon miles of human beings borne forward to slaughter in these same grey camions and I could not cry. It was all too horrible and too colossal—neither could I sleep that night for we were now in a hotel with rooms fronting on the street and the constant procession of hoofs and wheels on the cobble stones sounded to our tired nerves like the roar of the ocean.

As I came in that evening I had noticed through the open door of the room next to mine a bent old figure in black, sitting near the window, gazing into space. Near her on the bed sat a young girl so tragic and strained in her grief that I was sure she did not even know that the door stood ajar and I hurried into my own room feeling a little ashamed of having seen what was not meant for my eyes.

Later in the night, as I turned my pillow again and again trying to make it fit into the tired spot in the back of my neck, I heard the door of the next room thrown open and I could almost see the girl who fell sobbing with her arms round her mother. I've heard many women cry in my life and some men but I never knew until then what agony could come out of a human soul. And the mother spoke no word—it was no use. It was daylight when the sobs at last died into low infrequent moans and I learned that the girl had come from the death bed of her *fiancé* whom she and the poor old mother had travelled days and nights to find.

We played many nights in this town for the steady stream of troops continued to pass through it. We also played the engineering camps, supply camps and aviation camps thereabouts—there were sixteen of the last—and I shall never forget the first time that we drove up to one of the most important of these, the "First Pursuit Group." Everything as far as the eye could reach had been camouflaged, hangars, huts and trucks and the green and yellow new-art designs looked so fantastic and queer in the twilight.

"The Little Major," as he was fondly called by the men of his group, had arranged for us to dine before the show in the mess tent at the foot of the hill, below a newly ploughed field. By the time dinner was over the rain was coming down in torrents, the field was a lake of mud and it was impossible to move the automobile that had brought us.

We set out on foot toward the distant hangar where men from other aviation camps were also waiting for us. We were not supposed even to use our pocket flashes, for enemy observation planes might be far above us in the black sky. The women carried their evening slippers under their arms, meaning to put them on later when we reached the hangar and it was not until we were at the very entrance of it that one of the girls discovered that one of her slippers was missing. Such a to-do! It was not an easy matter to get satin slippers in this benighted corner of the earth and we were headed for even more benighted regions.

She was tired and depressed by the long pull through the mud and she fell onto a camp stool inside the big truck that had been rolled inside the hangar to serve as a dressing room and began to cry. Her street shoes were caked in mud to their tops and she refused to try to play in them.

Three aviators Immediately shot off into the darkness with one of our own men to search the muddy field for the missing slipper. They returned with it at last and by this time the audience which we had *heard* but not *seen* were booing, whistling and clapping with impatience. At last the missing slipper was recovered and on the lady's small foot. I was frightfully nervous as I pushed aside the green Silesia curtains that we always carried and cleared my throat to make the supposedly comic speech with which we always opened the show. I never could remember afterward just what I said, for of all the picturesque audiences that I had ever seen this was certainly the most fantastic.

There were twenty-five hundred men, so we were afterwards told, huddled together on the ground and above them imperilling their own lives and those of the men underneath, were hundreds of others intertwined in the huge steel framework supporting the largest hangar that I had ever seen. Some of the men seemed to be holding onto their perches like monkeys, their feet crossed round a bar of steel, others had made themselves comfortable on, wide beams and were lying with their hands crossed under their heads, and all through the performance I could scarcely keep my mind on the lines of the playlet for trying to locate various members of the audience and fearing that some of them would tumble off their perches when they released their hold to applaud—and how they did applaud and yell, and how wild and picturesque it all looked in the fog that had crept in through the cracks and made golden circles round the dim torch light. And then came the whir of an enemy observation plane overhead and a hush and nothing said and then on with the show.

The next day we were sent to a camp nearby where it was hoped that Miss Brice and I would at last find the small gas masks. There was nothing among the American masks that would do, so it was decided to give us the old style French masks for which we were devoutly grateful for they seemed far easier to adjust. It was pointed out to us that the oxygen in these would not last so many hours as in the American masks but we in turn pointed out that we couldn't run more than one hour at the most.

We had received our final equipment none too soon for the next morning with our blankets, folding cots, new masks and helmets we were loaded into an army car and taken yet further up the line to an engineering camp on the side of a hill on the edge of the Argonne forest.

It was explained that we could be billeted here in the engineers' barracks because there was a supply station nearby, from which provisions and ammunition were "shot" up to men in the front lines, just above, and we would also have thousands of troops to which to play, as the woods for miles around were sheltering troops that kept under cover by day and marched by night, so that the enemy's observation planes might not discover the full strength of the blow that we were preparing to deliver.

Some of the officers in the barracks were kind enough to give up one of their rooms to the three women of our company and our cots were tucked into this room so closely that we had to crawl over the foot of them to get into bed. The men of the company were put into an equally small room behind the kitchen of the officers' mess and Mr. Morrisey says that he will never forget the sound of the rats claws as they scratched their way up and over the slick surface of the tarpaulin under which it was necessary to sleep to keep out the dampness. He says he used to lie awake in the night and gamble with himself as to which of the rats would get "over the top" first.

At the foot of the hill below the main building was a black little "lean-to" called "The Greasy Spoon."

It was at the intersection of many lines of track that our American engineers had been laying for months—track connecting with our main bases of supplies hundreds of miles below, with the ships' docks still further below, and with intermediary hospitals and supply bases, and finally with the very outposts of what was to mark the starting point of the great and final offensive.

And over these tracks every twenty minutes American engines were passing with long trains of American cars—cars bearing food, guns, tanks, aeroplanes, Red Cross supplies, humans, live stock, portable houses, hospital tents and huge barrels of gasoline and oil. And wherever these latter were known to be sidetracked the Boche planes were quickly overhead to drop explosives in the hope of starting a general conflagration. The light from these explosives, sometimes near sometimes far, was almost the only light that we saw these nights, for the camp was obliged to keep itself in utter darkness lest even one tiny spark of light might serve as a target for the Boche planes constantly hovering overhead.

The hut in which we gave our first show was hermetically sealed and the entrance hung with double curtains so that no ray of light should escape, and not even a lighted cigarette was permitted to anyone departing from it and the same rules were applied to the mess room and sleeping quarters.

In fact divers tales were told of a whole company being wiped out near that very spot by an idiot who had lighted a cigarette just as a Boche bombing plane was passing overhead, though it was suspected by some that he was a spy and took this way of giving a signal.

In any case, the black surroundings did not prevent the thousands of boys hidden with their commands in the adjoining woods from finding their way to the hut for our first show and in spite of the fact that we gave two shows the same night hundreds had to be sent away with the promise of other shows the next night for those who had not been swept on toward "the front." It was late when we'd finished the second performance and as usual we were hungry, so one of the officers helped us to pick our way down the hill to "The Greasy Spoon" and here we met our first "Corned Willie" also some undecorated heroes.

A youth who had been on duty forty-eight hours, his face smeared with soot, his hands red and swollen, stood with his back to the glowing oven "slinging" corn willie, beans, and coffee across a counter of dry goods boxes to tired grimy trainmen who were averaging only three hours' sleep a night and were putting through a train every twenty minutes—an American train over American tracks laid by American engineers, manned by American soldiers, bearing American supplies, ammunition, and men. Just now they were rejoicing in having run a train for the first time over the last section of track laid to the very line of what was soon to become our fighting front—these last miles of track had been laid under shell fire but would save eight hours in the transportation of the wounded and that eight hours would mean life or death to hundreds.

It was in "The Greasy Spoon" that we first heard the doughboys' frank opinion of what they called "Sammie backers," meaning the fellows who stay at home and send them cigarettes and "good wishes."

In fact there were few things, persons, or institutions that did not come in for their fair share of criticism in the black little shanty with its long benches and tables lit only by flickering candles and the yellow light from the open oven. Generals, presidents and fickle sweethearts were introduced and retired with a phrase or a shrug and above the jangle of tin pans and forks one caught fragmentary reports of the night's happenings, trains overturned, gasoline cars shelled, tracks blown out, and trainmen killed.

I was inclined to wonder if these moody, overworked men and boys were colouring some of the details to entertain us "tenderfeet"—but next morning in the officers' mess where we were treated like members of the family, we could not escape hearing most of these reports repeated and we began to look with new admiration on the grim business like men who sat with us at table. They were not typical army men nor were all of them young enough to come within the draft age. Some of them were men not unlike others I mentioned earlier, rich, successful and at the height of their business careers. They had given up interesting occupations to assume duties they had left behind in their youth and had not seen their homes since the very start of the war. Who can say when the records of these years are printed that there is no idealism in the business world of today?

After breakfast, we walked to the little French Cemetery on the top of the hill, above the barracks, and here the American flags told the tale of many who would never see their homes again—not men who had been mentioned for brilliant service or had the thrill of going "over the top" but men who had died in obscurity providing ways and means for their more fortunate fellows to go "over the top."

The chaplain of the regiment joined us in our walk and asked if we'd like to take a look at a lost division that was making camp in the woods above. We asked what he meant by "lost." He told us how the commander of these twenty thousand men had received instructions to proceed to this point, where further orders were presumably to be waiting for him, but, finding no orders, he had no other course than to conceal his men in the woods and bide his time.

From where we stood there was no sign of life whatever, but we had not beat our way more than a hundred feet through the thick underbrush when we literally fell upon thousands of burrowing, slashing humans, hacking their way through the vines and bushes to make trails to central points of manoeuvre, and using the cut boughs to camouflage the tops of their "pup tents" and wagons, so that enemy observation planes could see only what was apparently a thick forest. These thousands of busy, bent figures made one think of ants taking possession of a new home.

So close and so well concealed were their "pup tents" that it took us some time to realise that we were in the midst of whole villages of them—canvas coops, so low and so small that the two men allotted to each have barely room enough to crawl in side by side and roll up in their blankets—the canvas is supposed to protect the men from the rain but it is taken as a matter of course that in case of hard rain the men wake up in puddles of water. One of our players remarked that these must be called "pup tents" because no dog would sleep in them. And speaking of dogs our doughboys have dubbed the identification tags which the army are compelled to wear on their wrists or necks "dog tags." This is typical of the matter-of-fact way in which our men regard the grim business of war. They have no false sentimentality to buoy them up, no love of adventure, no inborn lust of blood, nothing but a frank abhorrence for the wholesale butchery and brutality into which they find themselves plunged and a steady stoical determination to see the job through.

"Somebody has to do it," one of them said to me, "so we might as well get it over as soon as possible."

One doughboy, hacking at a tough root near a space being cleared for the cooking oven, expressed what most of them feel about France. He was hungry and tired and drenched to the skin and he didn't care who heard him. "The only thing that would serve the Germans right," he said, "would be to give them a damned good licking and then give them France." The officer who stood near me pretended not to hear, but I caught a sly smile lurking around his lips and I remarked that the French scenery didn't seem to impress the doughboys as much as it did the American tourists. He answered that it was not the scenery that got on their nerves but the lack of sanitary plumbing, and he admitted that it would be a pretty hard matter for travel pamphlets ever to "'sell" France to any of our doughboys.

"Come on, fellows," shouted this particular boy when he'd finally torn out the unruly root and given way to the mess sergeant who was waiting to lay his brick for the oven.

"I'm going down to the de-louser." The "de-louser" is the name the boys give to the public baths that assist them in separating themselves and their clothes from their cooties.

"Those boys are willing to miss their mess to get that bath," the officer said, "they're a damned clean lot," and so they were and soon a long line of them was filing down the hill, some toward the de-louser, some to carry up the water for the mess—and by the time we reached our barracks midway on the hill, some of them were already filing back again and once more I was reminded of ants—busy and steady, their minds thoroughly on the affair of the moment.

This "lodging for the night" we soon learned was typical of hundreds of others in the forest all round us. And each day our local "Y" guide would take us in a car to some thicket where within twenty minutes we would have such an audience as none of us shall probably ever see again. Sometimes we would mount a truck for our performance; for wagons, artillery, and horses were also concealed in these woods, but more often we would play on the ground, and the officer in command would give the order for the first few hundred boys to lie flat, those behind them were permitted to kneel, those at the back could stand and those who were "left over" would "shinny" up the trees like squirrels and drape themselves across the branches and hang suspended in strained attitudes during the entire show. If we happened to be playing in a young forest we were sometimes almost dizzy with the swaying of the slender saplings waving back and forth under the weight of human bodies.

Sometimes our performance would be cancelled or cut short by the men to whom we were playing being suddenly ordered forward. On one occasion when our "Y" conductor had happened to leave us to the colonel of the regiment who had volunteered to send us home in his car, the whole division was ordered forward in the midst of our performance. The colonel had no alternative but to move with them and we were obliged to walk to the nearest railway station and beat our way "home" huddled together on a meat chest in a box car. We arrived about midnight, hungry and chilled and as we picked our way through the mud and the darkness up the hill toward the barracks Ray Walker our musician drew his foot out of a hole and paused long enough to remark that he was sick of life and he didn't care whether his gas mask fitted or not.

But the next morning we were all going back down the hill in the sunlight with the despised gas masks and helmets, because the colonel of the regiment where we were billeted had decided that we had been working so hard that we deserved a little pleasure trip and had detailed one of his lieutenants to take us, in a limousine, to see the ruins of Verdun a few miles distant. Verdun! White dust-covered heaps of stone and bricks, crumbling mortar, silent streets paved with huge, shiny cobblestones, solemn faced gates that have withstood for ages the onslaughts of man and of nature, the sluggish Meuse winding stealthily round the base of the hill and, looking up from the Gateway, the walls of the magnificent cathedral still crowning the hill-top.

We halted the car at the foot of the hill and our lieutenant went in search of someone who would give us permission to enter the fortress underneath the mountain.

He was gone so long that our party disappeared, one by one, up the mountain side—each impatient to do his or her own exploring. I was last to leave the car and as I did so I noticed a small man in black coming toward me round the bend in the white roadway. With him walked a soldier in American uniform and several French officials. He made his way up the hill with them talking earnestly. It was Secretary Baker.

Out of the golden stillness came a "Hello"—our lieutenant was returning with a military guide to lead us through the fortress. We entered by way of a cold damp tunnel through which narrow gauge cars were being pushed—they were laden with provisions and presently we were in the midst of huge bakeries where miles of bread, flour and cereals were stored from there we passed to what looked like a wholesale grocery store and from there to a restaurant where thousands of men were having their mid-day meal, discussing the politics, feuds or amusements of their underground world with the same vehemence with which we discuss similar matters in our over-world.

With the artist's desire to show us a contrasting picture the guide now led us to a gay little chapel—still underground—where these same men were accustomed to worship. It was charming and reassuring in colour and detail but it always seems incongruous to think of men communing with God underground and later when we passed out into the sunlight I felt as though I had emerged from a strange world of gnomes.

On top of the hill, sublime in its isolation and with dignity wrapping it round and enfolding it in a soft mantle of haze, stood the great cathedral.

We climbed up to it—no tourists—no voice to break the silence save that of one lone watchman.

We gazed in awe at the high vaulted entrance that still remained intact, then stepped with reverence on the worn stones leading to the main body of the church—stones over which so many thousands of feet had so often borne aching or rejoicing hearts.

We were barely out of the shadow of the vestibule when a shaft of light made us turn our eyes upward and there before us stood the four great twisted columns of marble that had once supported the canopy of the high altar, now reaching their empty arms toward the sunlight pouring through the shell-torn roof and to the blue sky beyond.

And the altar itself—that fine slab of unadorned marble that seemed all the more imposing stripped of everything save its own enduring quality and symbolism! We edged nearer to it and lingered there, saying little. Its very presence gave one a confidence in the ultimate survival of the fine and the strong.

Next the guide led us to one of the smaller sanctuaries of the cathedral where a shell had just shattered the crucifix above the altar—fragments of blue glass still lay on the tiled floor where they had fallen from a broken vase. We turned our eyes again toward the high altar. Doves now flew in and out at random through the great shell hole in the vaulted ceiling, the altar was bathed in noon sunlight and through the shattered windows in the opposite wall unruly vines were beginning to creep from the garden of the Convent of Marguerite, nestling with such confidence under the eaves of its great protector. And everywhere there was majesty and calm dignity—damage, perhaps but not destruction. There was a spirit within those battered walls that seemed to defy destruction.

We were late reaching camp for our luncheon and I at first thought that the restrained air of the colonel and the heavy silence of his men was due to our tardiness. Then I remembered another and similar change in the social atmosphere weeks before at G. H. Q. just before the big drive on Saint Mihiel and I felt certain that the hour of attack was at hand. Week upon week of preparation had been under way and it had been remarked the past few days that the necessary apparatus for the placement of some of the large naval guns converted to land service was the only thing delaying the announcement of the "zero hour." And now no doubt the big guns were in place and one might expect to hear their thunder at any moment.

This conclusion was strengthened by the arrival of a courier before we had finished luncheon. He had come to tell us that the "matinee" we were to play that afternoon for his regiment in the woods nearby must be cancelled. The division was moving forward in response to a sudden order.

Being set free from all other engagements, there seemed no reason why we should not consider an invitation to a pleasure party to which "the Little Major" of the Aviation Camp, miles back down the line had been trying for days to entice us. He had 'phoned our colonel of

Engineers about it and even sent one of his flyers over our barracks to drop a note in our vicinity reminding us of it. And after a few hints on our part to our colonel, who was no doubt glad to be rid of our prattle at such a critical moment we were loaded into his car and sent down the line to the Aviation Camp—it being understood of course that we were to return to the barracks at a reasonable hour.

When we arrived at the Aviation Field we found that the "Little Major" and some of his officers had taken up their billet with a charming old French couple in the village nearby and it was here that a dinner and dance were awaiting us—the first real dance since we had left America. The lion of the occasion was to be Eddie Rickenbacker who had just brought down his eighth Boche plane and who was soon destined to win the title of "The American Ace" and to be told by the commander decorating him to increase his chest expansion to accommodate the many more decorations awaiting him.

The major's charming dining room with its polished walnut and candlelight and flowers looked strangely civilised after the rough surroundings to which we had become accustomed and he had managed to get together a stringed orchestra and it played between courses and we all danced and "The Little Major" seemed in fine spirits. One of his men confided to me that it was because he'd got a Boche that day. He said the men could always tell when they saw the major coming home whether he had got a Boche for if he'd had a good day he always did a flip-flap over the hangar. I expressed surprise that a commander of a wing should be permitted to fly. His *aide* replied that the major ought not to do it, but he did.

The major discovered by now that we were talking about him and he became self-conscious and blushed like a girl, so to change the subject, I asked the man on my right the customary bromidic question as to what had been his most thrilling experience in the service. He told me of having been ordered one night during his earlier term of service to proceed to a certain point, pick up a certain passenger to whom he t was not to speak, proceed with him across the German lines, drop him at a certain point, still without speaking, and leave him there. The man was, of course, one of our spies but my partner said that the most disagreeable moment of his whole life was when he was obliged to depart without even a word of farewell leaving his unknown passenger in that "black land of hell."

By the time he had reached his dramatic climax the others at table suddenly burst into boos and derisive cat-calls and declared that the party was becoming much too solemn, so the dinner table was pushed aside and we began dancing in real earnest and every one was feeling deliciously reckless and merry. Then suddenly "The Little Major" was called to the 'phone and again the old air of suppressed excitement about which no one speaks but every one feels, and later, without any one exactly saying so, it seemed to get round from guest to guest, that we would hear the big guns before morning.

When we reached the foot of the hill on which our barracks stood, it was later than we had meant it to be. The moon had escaped from the few shifting clouds and the whole valley was bathed in a soft hazy light. We were still in a very happy mood and we stopped half way up the hill to look down on the valley below us and at the dark line of the Argonne Forest beyond it, when suddenly out of the silvery distance at a quarter past eleven, came the boom of the first Great Gun of the last great battle of the World's Greatest Conflict—and in quick succession more guns—great naval monsters pressed into land service, far from their natural bases—then flashes of light in front and to each side of us until we stood in a wide horse-shoe of light. Oh, the thrill of it!

I sometimes think if I am ever to be born again I should like it to be as a war correspondent with just enough income to insure me against a poverty-stricken old age, and then I should like to stay always in sound of the guns. Great commanders must manipulate affairs from afar, their lives are too precious to be put in peril, doughboys are soon killed if they are given their chance at the front, but war correspondents are free agents—they can follow the sky rockets of war and dash from battle to battle wherever the fighting is thickest.

All night the heavy firing continued and when it died down the next morning, I was alarmed, lest something had given us a temporary set-back, but the seasoned campaigners assured me that the silence was a good sign for it meant that we had driven the enemy so far that we must cease firing until we could move our artillery forward to pursue them, and so it proved to be, and so it continued to be day after day and week after week.

And as our army advanced our little "Entertainment Unit" was also permitted to advance, and next time, after fond farewells to the Engineer group with whom we had been billeted so long and so well, we were loaded into a big brown touring car and carried up the "Great White Way" toward the direction in which the big guns had again resumed their booming. Now that the battle was on, the army no longer confined itself to moving troops and supplies by night and we had to pick our way in and out as best we could between the steady stream of heavily laden camions moving forward and the returning stream of empty camions moving back for fresh supplies. It was tedious business and we were sometimes blocked for hours and, at times like this we would amuse ourselves watching the strange assortment of men and things moving toward "the front."

Few regiments of men were without their animal mascots—sometimes it would be a huge shaggy dog balancing himself as well as he could on top of the rolling, rocking munitions, upon top of which he had been placed, sometimes it was a goat held in the arms of some youth staring into space with dreamy eyes, sometimes a rooster or a parrot. I even saw an eagle and a young pig with a ribbon round his neck. And they all moved forward together—infantry, cavalry, artillery—black, white and yellow—all toward a fate that promised them little hope of escape from mutilation.

When we finally reached our destination it proved to be a somewhat shell-torn town in the heart of which two important war arteries crossed and so great was the congestion that we could scarcely work our way to the entrance of the canteen above which our unit was billeted.

When we did finally get to the door and up the rickety stairs and look down upon the streets from the windows of the one, desolate room where the three women were to sleep, I fairly gasped at the colour and picturesqueness of the surging billowing sea of camions, men and animals all striving to fight their way through the congestion at the cross-roads and in spite of the waving arms and harsh commands of the American military police, the "Froggies" would get their camions out of line and the more excited they became by argument the further out of line they would get and general bedlam would prevail with everyone except the stoical round-faced Amanites who seemed to sit at the wheels of their huge motor trucks without speaking, smiling, or looking to the right or the left at the Red Cross wagons, the machine guns, the "baby tanks" or parent tanks, the French cavalry, the black or white infantry, or mules—all struggling to disentangle themselves from the constantly occurring "mix-ups."

When we had tired watching this "'midway *plaisance*" effect from our windows we closed the shutters and lit our candles—here again no ray of light was permitted without everything being hermetically sealed.

The sole furniture of our room consisted of the three cots which we had brought with us and on which the men had placed our blankets, one long rough board table with bench and one dry goods box on which was placed a small tin pan and near which stood a tin pail filled with water. This was all. The walls of the room were streaked with weather stains from the last rain and the cracks in the uncarpeted floor were filled with the dirt of ages.

The resident "Y" man had broken up some packing cases to make firewood for us and we started a little blaze and got out our towels and soap to make ready for dinner which we were told we were to eat at the sergeants' mess across the street and after which we were to give two performances in the town theatre—a little old glorified stable that had defied both shell fire and the ravages of time.

It did boast a stage, however, and tin reflectors for the footlights. The organ for this festive occasion, so the boys at the mess table told us, had been purloined from a distant "Y" hut and might be requisitioned at any moment.

We learned other things in this jolly little mess with its open fire and long benches and its tables covered with gay oilcloth and its kitchen with glowing range gaping through the open door and sunny faced good natured boys officiating at the range and smiling at the thought of the surprise that was going to "knock us cold" when they gave us pumpkin pie for our supper. We gathered from this fragmentary conversation that here, at last, we were to play to the men who so many of the commanders had said were in greatest need of us—the men who were just on the eve of "going over the top."

The boys of the mess were stationed in the village as were their whole division—a division that had been "stuck in the mud" up there for months holding the Argonne line which they and their dead comrades had helped to establish four years ago and it was only since "the big offensive" had begun to shove this line back that the currents of fresh war activities flowing toward the firing line had begun to vitalise the air of their torpid little village.

These currents were running flood tide now—sometimes the men passed through in whole divisions but more often in isolated hundreds or as individuals and those last were the ones who touched our hearts most, they were called "replacements." They had been detached from their own regiments or recruited from convalescent wards and shot forward into unknown terrors with no comrades by their sides, knowing only that on the morrow they must take the places of the fallen. And this village was their last stopping place on the night before going into action. And on and on they came in such numbers that it was impossible for the army, the "Y," or the residents to find shelter for them and they would curl up in doorways or in the thickets beyond the village, or in barns, or stretch themselves on the "Y" floor, if they were early enough in town to find space there, and draw their overcoats or their blanket over them—for by the time they had reached this place they had been stripped of most of their other equipment. It was impossible to march long, under the weight of a sixty pound pack and extra rounds of ammunition, and although the weather was beginning to be bitter cold, when asked to choose between extra ammunition and their blankets, I am told they invariably chose the extra ammunition.

Oh, the joy of being able to offer shelter for at least a few hours each night in the theatre to at least a part of these cold, lonely, friendless and to make them forget that they were only so much fodder to be fed on the morrow into the same relentless maw that had swallowed up their comrades before them.

An unfortunate thing happened one night, Miss Meredith, our *ingénue*, was ill and it had been decided that we had better not attempt more than one performance that night, for in addition to our night work we were playing the camps in the woods during the day and we feared that the young lady might lose her voice entirely.

The "Y" man failed, however, to post a notice of the second performance being cancelled and when I came out the back entrance of the theatre, with two others of the company, he rushed up to me to say that thousands of the boys, out in front, were clamouring for admittance, and that they had stood in line for three hours expecting a second show and were about to break in the door.

It was pitch black in the streets—no lights were permitted—not even a pocket flash—our company was stopping some distance from the theatre—and the others had gone home some time before us.

I suggested that they open the doors and let the boys in so that we could explain to them. The "Y" man said that once they were in, they would demand a performance and probably tear up the place if they didn't get it. He suggested that I go round to the front of the theatre and speak to them in the street. I picked my way through the dark alley as well as I could and found myself in the midst of thousands of them. When the "Y" man told them I was there—it was so dark they couldn't see me—they were quiet and attentive but when I explained that we could not give a second "show" they booed and protested.

I told them that if they would only come again the next night we would play all night for them if they wished it.

"We'll not be *here* tomorrow night," came a voice out of the darkness. "You needn't trouble. We'll be in the trenches tomorrow night," was another bitter answer, and I knew it was the truth.

By this time I was desperate. I resolved to rush back to the two members I had left at the stage entrance and see if we three could not give a show. When I got back through the crowd and the darkness they had gone. I stumbled up the dark street as best I could, the "Y" man also having become detached by now, and I burst into the room where Miss Meredith had made ready for her cot. She was in her dressing gown and very white but willing to make an attempt at another show if I could find the others.

I looked in the back part of the building where the men were quartered, not one of them there, and at last I fumbled my way back through the dark street to tell the boys waiting at the theatre that there was no hope of another show. But they had evidently divined this and had slipped away into the night, no doubt cursing us in their hearts. I went back to our desolate little room and sat by the few remaining embers with my head in my hands so tired and so depressed and so sorry for the bitter thoughts that those boys would carry away with them that I didn't care a whoop whether I lived or died.

One of the officers scolded me next day when I was still in the dumps and said I would never make a good soldier if I was going to have regrets, but I did have regrets and each day and night no matter to how many men we played I was always conscious that we would never again have the opportunity of playing to those men who had waited so long that night in the dark and the cold and who are now—God knows where. And so long as we stayed in that town—no matter how heavy our work during the day, nor how ill or tired we felt at night, we always gave our two shows, for here, if ever, they were needed, for day by day and night by night the steady stream of victims and war implements never ceased passing under our windows—feeding—feeding—feeding!

And soon came back the returning stream—the dead and the dying—and sometimes came with them long lines of German prisoners being marching to the barb wire pens already provided for them further down the line—and most of these looked young, well fed and content to be taken.

Soon the temporary hospitals in the barns and woods nearby began to fill and overflow with the maimed and gassed and what a pity that those at home could not have seen the unbelievable efficiency with which the great sanitary experts and surgeons of our country handled the hygiene and surgical necessities of situations, that men of less resource would have considered impossible.

The relay system, the tabulation system, the impromptu operating devices, sterilising devices, and heating apparatus, the specialisation for gas cases, psychopathic cases, surgical cases and medical cases, handled in tents, stables or sheds and the Herculean endurance of these men who kept their brains clear and their hands steady for seventy-two hours at a stretch. Oh, Humanity, be proud! You can never be proud enough of your best—never!

We tried sometimes to play to some of the men in the hospital tents who had not been too seriously gassed, for while our nights were still needed at the theatre our days were now comparatively free. We found, however, that as soon as the patients were sufficiently recovered to take notice of us, they were relayed to hospitals further down the line in order to make way for new cases, so we gave up these attempts and went back to our old scheme of hunting out the encampments in the woods or playing to troops halted along the roadside.

One Sunday we were sent forward to within three miles of the firing line, into woods that had been for the past four years in possession of the Boche. We were to play chiefly to a company of engineers who had not even seen a woman in eighteen months. They had belonged to one of the detachments that go in advance of the attacking forces to cut the barb wire or follow behind to clean up the wreckage left in the wake of victory. The roads through the deep rain-soaked wood were almost impassable and by the time we reached the place where we were to leave the car and proceed on foot we were already late. We came upon our audience still farther in the thicket sitting on the wet ground, or logs, round a stage that they had built and equipped from German loot which they had salvaged from the recent drive. It was screened from above by a thick canopy of leaves and boughs so as to escape detection by the enemy planes.

Four small German machine guns, also salvaged, served as chairs for us and the table made from beech wood was edged with German shells and adorned with German canteens filled with goldenrod—a flower that apparently blooms in every country. There was even a piano salvaged from a nearby dugout that had been occupied for four years by German officers. We inspected the dugout later and found that it was cement lined, calcimined and wired for electricity. The piano which had been originally captured by the Boche from the French was now to be played by an American musician.

Being Sunday the army chaplain opened the "show" with prayer; then standing we all repeated the oath of allegiance with the men and officers; then the regimental band that had marched from a camp some miles below played the National Anthem, and at intervals throughout it all came the steady boom of the big guns, slaughtering while we prayed.

On our way out of this section we passed through another part of the forest. There were a great many graves by the roadside made for the German dead during their four years' occupation. The Huns had stolen tombstones from the French cemeteries and painted German inscriptions over the carved inscriptions of the French.

When still further down the line in a desolate little village we were requested by a colonel's *aide* to give a performance to part of a division temporarily quartered there, we did so—on the steps of a shelled cathedral, the highest point of vantage in the town. The men stood on the side of the hill beneath us. We felt several times that we were losing their attention, even though their eyes were on us, and we heard the faint whirrings of machines evidently high in the clouds. One of the officers confided to us later that he had been obliged to have the order passed from man to man not to look up, for he knew from the peculiar throbbing of the engines that they belonged to the enemy and a sea of white faces turned upward is far easier to discern than the tops of heads—*bald* heads, of course, excepted.

We were growing quite accustomed to overhead enemies by now but we all looked up a few days later when we were giving a performance to what was left of an Oregon division and we counted 107 of our own planes flying past at sunset in perfect formation toward the front. We learned later that some of our friends of the first pursuit group were among them and that they formed part of one of the largest formations ever sent across the German lines. And *all* of them returned.

When we got back to our mess that night we were perfectly certain that some rumour was going the rounds in which we were not partners and the next morning Tommy Gray of our unit who had been sighing for a priest to confess him fell upon the information that had not yet reached even our camp officials.

After walking miles toward a camp where he arrived only to find the priest down with the "flu," a Jewish *rabbi* undertook to guide him to a camp of the Seventy-Seventh Division, further on, where he believed a priest was to be had and to their astonishment they found men loading an aeroplane with provisions and homing pigeons which it was hoped they could drop to a battalion of their men that had been cut off by the enemy—a battalion that has since covered itself in glory, and become one of the picturesque features of the war.

It was quite a feather in Tommy's cap to have found out something that none of the men in our division actually knew, and while he wasn't encouraged by the officers to talk about it we had become such close friends with the boys in the sergeants' mess that it somehow leaked out, and since it only confirmed rumours which they had already heard, it seemed rather stingy of us to be too reticent about it and each morning each asked his neighbour guardedly if he had "heard anything." But it was not until weeks later that we heard the details of the ultimate fate of the battalion and of the stout heart of commander Whittelsey who shaved each morning with death at his elbow just to keep up the morale of his men.

In the meantime our friendship with the boys in the mess grew warmer and we used to linger longer and longer over our hot cakes and molasses to hear the boys spin their yarns and chaff each other.

Rodeheaver of Billy Sunday fame "blew in" for coffee one morning and told us of the songs that he'd been singing in the mouths of the cannon and the boys responded with fifty-seven verses of a doughboy lay which seemed familiar to them but was quite new to me. It was something about a boy from Arkansas who couldn't bear to kill a fly and what happened to him at the front and the refrain was always the same—"Oh this bloody, Bloody War!"

Rodeheaver chuckled with delight and told us some funny stories and left us laughing when he said Goodbye and after he had disappeared down the alley the boys proceeded to dissect him and religionists in general and other celebrities of their country and of every other fellow's country and there was enough American humour forthcoming from that group to have kept George Ade chronicling for the rest of his natural life—tender college youths, wild western thoroughbreds, East Side gangsters and country yokels all equally dear to each other and all determined to have their little joke till the finish. One chubby faced youth with an interrupted college career put his chin in his hands and gazed at the fire and said dolefully: "To think that one so young as I should have been through two wars!" I asked what he meant and it seems he had been through both the Mexican Border flurry and this and he still looked too young to be out at night.

Only twice did I ever see their spirits even temporarily overcast. The first time was when two of the "casuals" from another division "helping out" in the kitchen were ordered back to the front. They, too, were infants, but they had already been "over the top" once and landed in hospitals from which they had beaten their way to this place and now they were off for their second chance with death. It touched one's heart to see the other chaps stuffing cigarettes and chocolate into their pockets and digging up mascots for them—and as the two infants swung out the alley and into the street they called back to us gaily, "Goodbye, fellows, see you in New York or hell."

The next morning at breakfast one of the boys brought in a letter on the envelope of which was scrawled in a fine, feeble hand the name of a youth whom they knew and in the corner of the envelope was this request from his mother: "Will someone please give this to my boy somewhere in France." The youth had been the chauffeur of the colonel in that regiment and he had been killed by an exploding shell only that morning. The letter had been wandering around France for five months and had missed him by only five hours. And again *"C'est la Guerre."* Some lines of Grantland Rice came back to me lines from a *Mother's Prayer.*

> *My baby's gone; gone is my little lad;*
> *And now a man stands in his place,*
> *Stands where I cannot be, or see or shield.*
> *God guard Thou him!*
> *When guns are still and strife is overpast.*
> *Whisper to him, where'er he lies this night,*
> *The words I fain would speak could I be near;*
> *For, though he is no more a child,*
> *I always am his Mother.*

There was a hush at the table after the directions on the envelope had been read aloud and we all hailed the first opportunity of interruption when one of the boys rushed in from the street and told us to "come and see the fun." It was pretty well over when we arrived but it had evidently had something to do with a goat that was travelling as a mascot on top of one of the big camions and who had taken advantage of the congestion of the traffic to start a little attack of his own on the unsuspecting driver whose back had been toward him.

In front of the goat's vehicle was something even more amusing—an American driver swearing at French mules in English and then trying to conciliate them with the few words of French that he knew.

I noticed that the mules had no gas masks tied under their chins while all the horses wore them and I was told that the mules were so "damned stubborn" that nobody could ever get the masks on them in time to save their fool lives, so the government had given up supplying them with them.

Our little street party was broken up by the news that a perfectly good German piano had just been captured and unloaded on one of the salvage dumps further up the line and, before we knew it, the mess sergeant and half a dozen of the boys had got a truck and were off to get that piano for us, to replace the poor one that we were in hourly fear of losing from the village "Show Shop."

The fact that the salvage dump was under shell fire only heightened their enthusiasm and some of the members of our unit decided to go with them. They didn't get the piano but they got sensations about which they are still strangely non-committal and the next day when I went over the same trail with one of the officers and saw the death and desolation that lay either side of it, I realised why those returning from it had had nothing to say. "*The Salvage Dump!*" What will all Europe be after this frightful struggle but one huge Salvage Dump? Odds and ends of wreckage, animate and inanimate, heaped together on the blood-soaked shores of the flood of war.

When we woke next morning we found a large car waiting outside our window to bear us back to Bar-le-duc, the headquarters of that particular region—and we were told that the Paris office had been wiring for us for days to proceed to the next "sector" where we were long overdue. It was not easy to say Goodbye to what had been our first real taste of battle and as our car edged its way back down the line against the steady stream of men and munitions still pouring toward the front and as the din of the big guns grew fainter and fainter our spirits sank lower and lower.

At Bar-le-duc, however, where we were to stay for the night, we were met by "Helios" from every side and in the main hotel we found war correspondents from New York, London, and Paris and many friends we'd not seen since the beginning of our tour at G. H. Q. It was by one of these that we were dubbed "The Mayo Shock Unit," we having been farther to the front, at that time, than any other "Players," and the title stuck to us for the remainder of our tour, much to the temporary distress of my mother who heard about it without knowing the compliment it implied. Bar-le-duc it seemed had become a non-official headquarters for all those who needed to keep in close touch with everything going on at the Argonne front—journalists, war lords, and war heroes, air conquerors and naval *attachés*.

In one corner of the *café* munching cheese and jam sat Will Irwin, George Barr Baker, Maximilian Foster, Bozeman Bulger, Arthur Ruhl, Cameron McKenzie and Charles Kloeber at the other side of the room with their rum and coffee were Damon Runyon, Claire Kenamore and Eddie Rickenbacker, now the American Ace. Further on were A. L. James, Douglas McArthur, the youngest general in the army, Allen of the London *Times* and a half dozen comrades. At the cashier's desk was Alexander Wolcott, Patron Saint of "the Stars and Stripes," threatening to report "the joint" and have it closed if the proprietor did not make good a five *francs* overcharge to one of the doughboys.

It seemed as if we were in the Knickerbocker Café and the Savoy Grille and the Crillon Restaurant all rolled into one, and then some one mentioned Don Martin and that only he out of that whole crowd was missing. There was a silence after this, then one of the boys suggested that we all walk round to the Press headquarters and find out what day had been fixed for his funeral in Paris. We stopped on the way to look from the bridge at the sluggish canal and at the gay coloured crockery that accidentally decorated some of the steps leading down to it. At the office there was apparently little news from the front and Will Irwin fell into a chair by the fire and began pounding his beloved typewriter. The rest of us had a look at the big map on the wall and felt vexed to see that the horrid little kink in the line, at the foot of the Argonne, was still unstraightened and so many lives had been given in the effort. Less stubborn strongholds were yielding, however, and the line was moving forward rapidly and as we returned down the street some one dared to prophecy that peace negotiations would be under way by Christmas.

This was considered by the others as being highly absurd and one chap, who insisted that he had come over with the first Napoleon, gave it as his opinion that the blooming war would never be over and became so depressed about it that it was decided to take him into a *café* nearby where *somebody* had a special "pull" and could get *everybody* a hot rum with spice which was thought most necessary by now to counteract the cold. And over the spiced rum the possible end of the war was again discussed and when obliged to face the thought of a world without a war they became more and more melancholy and some one decided that the least our government could do for us in such an emergency would be to rent a nice warm country like Spain and allow those who had no other occupation to start another war. One preferred Bulgaria for the cheese, another Palestine for the tangerines and someone else China because of no "grafters," and by the time the map of the world had been covered with imaginary battles it was decided that they now needed the cold to counteract the rum and again we ambled down the street.

At the French post one of the English boys left us to send a wire to his "little French girl." Another woman of my unit and I pretended that our vanity was hurt because he was so willing to abandon our company, upon which he remarked: "There is no satisfaction in you American women because your brains never cease to function."

When we got back to the "Y" we found our old chauffeur, "Conde—the speed maniac"—loading papers and cigarettes into a large army car in front of the door. He was blissfully happy, having received permission to make one trip each day to the very front line, if he could get there, to deliver those things to the boys. He had to drive all night to get back in time to make the next day's trip, but was perfectly satisfied with the three hours sleep that he got each morning. Upstairs other packages of papers and cigarettes were being prepared for some one who was to drop them over the fighting front from aeroplanes. One of the bystanders suggested that the secretary had better put some "Y" cards with the gifts or the boys would think that the "Knights of Columbus" had sent them. The busy little secretary answered that he didn't care if the boys thought they came from God so long as they got them and this is probably what the boys did think.

We went into the next room to inquire for our mail and I found a second and more insistent telegram from Paris saying that it was most important that we report back there at once. I couldn't imagine anything more important than the work we were leaving at the front but we, in our small way, were also soldiers and under orders and as soon as we could get the necessary travel papers we caught the night train for Paris. It was impossible to get sleepers or reserved seats, for every available comfort was retained for the wounded and all trains were running out of schedule to make way for the "*Blessés.*"

No lights were permitted in any of the compartments and at each station mobs of desperate travellers forced their way into our pitch black compartments, fell over our feet and our baggage, sat upon us and cursed us as we cursed them and the entire night's ride to Paris consisted of a series of pitched battles between those in the train and those, at way stations, attempting to *get* into it.

When we finally reached headquarters we found that we were to be sent next into the quarantined camps in the S. O. S. where the Spanish Grippe and the Flu had necessitated the men's being shut up for weeks with no diversion and where the inaction was making savages of them.

It was not an easy matter to leave the big guns so far behind but we were promised that if we would go into the S. O. S. for two weeks that we might return to the Front at the end of that time. I shook my head and answered that the fighting would be over before we ever got back to the front. The "Y" secretary said, we'd be lucky if the war was over in two years, but as it turned out I was right.

I find it as difficult to *write* of the S. O. S. as our men find it to *go* there, or to remain there, and yet many of our *true* heroes are there and have been there since the beginning of the war. There has been no pomp, glory nor excitement for them. They have had to play the unpicturesque role of *The Man Behind the Gun*—I dare say there are not ten amongst all those thousands that go to make up the great belly of the sea that sends its waves toward the front, who would not gladly have risked arms, legs, and life itself, any and every hour of the day in preference to the enforced safety of those who must prepare the ways and means for those who reap death and decoration.

Mothers and sweethearts and those at home take care that no shade of disappointment crosses your face when your returning man tells you that he did not get up to "the front." Remember that it takes seven men back of the line to keep one man in the line and that your government, not your son or sweetheart, has "the say" as to who the lucky seventh shall be who goes over the top, and remember, too, that it is the consensus of opinion of those who have dealt in this bloody business that "there are no cowards."

Then, too, you'll hear tales of misfits, men reduced in rank, or relieved of their command,—this does not prove cowardice, it means only that in the business of war as in the business of life some men, many men, through no fault of their own get shoved into the wrong cubby holes. These must be reclassified.

In one of the big re-classification centres in the S. O. S. I found the following lines by Robert Freeman printed on a little pamphlet in the hall of the "Y" Hut.:

> *I played with my blocks, I was but a child,*
> *Houses I builded, castles I piled;*
> *But they tottered and fell, all my labour was vain.*
> *Yet my father said kindly: "Well try it again!"*
>
> *I played with my days. What's time to a lad?*
> *Why pore over books? Play! Play, and be glad!*
> *Till my youth was all spent, like a sweet summer rain.*
> *Yet my father said kindly: "Well try it again!"*
>
> *I played with my chance. Such gifts as were mine*
> *To work with, to win with, to serve the divine,*
> *I seized for myself, for myself they have lain.*
> *Yet my father says kindly: "Well try it again!"*
>
> *I played with my soul, the soul that is I;*
> *The best that is in me, I smothered the cry,*
> *I lulled it, I dulled it—and now, oh, the pain!*
> *Yet my father says kindly : "Well try it again!"*

Our only glimpse of home life in the S. O. S. was provided by Mrs. Mallon, the matron of the "Y" hut at Saumur—only *this* time the "hut" Happened to be a handsome *château* converted into a social haven for the men and officers of the big artillery training camp. There were large cosy arm chairs in front of the open fire, and books to read and a piano and a writing room and a dainty tea table where chocolate and cakes were served each afternoon and on the mantel the photograph of Mrs. Mallon in the centre of a large family group.

She saw me glance at the photograph and the colour crept up to the edge of her lovely snowy hair. A little later she bent over me and whispered: "It's in awful taste for me to have that photograph there but it encourages the boys to tell me more about themselves when they realise that I am the mother of that family," and still later, by the fire that night, she told me how many boys out of a sense of chivalry and, not knowing the French customs, would find, after calling a few times on a French girl, that they were considered by the family to be engaged to her and rather than place her in an awkward position they would often place themselves in a very unhappy one and would be breaking their hearts in secret because of the girl at home whom they really loved.

She said she used to watch them day after day when they began to droop and lose and very often they would finally ask her about her boys and little by little they would confide in her and permit her to help them out of difficulties with which she with her worldly knowledge and experience knew how to cope.

Not all of the men in this town were there for reclassification. Many of them belonged to the light artillery that was fighting sham battles each day on the planes just back of the town and straining to get into "the real thing"—others were there for cavalry training and it was a wonderful sight to see them sitting their horses so splendidly and taking the jumps on a field where Napoleon himself had trained.

From the artillery, cavalry, and re-classification camps of the S. O. S. we passed into what is known as "The Forbidden City"—a name given to Tours by the men in the smaller towns near it, who are forbidden to enter it. Perhaps this is because America already has more men there than can be comfortably disciplined in one town—for grey-roofed, mud-ridden Tours is the very hub of the wheel of America's war industry in Europe—a wheel with spokes pointing toward Paris and the fighting from beyond it, toward Switzerland, Italy, the South of France—in any, and all directions, where we are obliged to deal in the ways and means of butchery and its after effects.

Outside the city walls were miles of tracks laid by our engineers, acres of railroad yards devoted to the loading and shipping of our war implements and food supplies, trucks, automobiles, aeroplanes and hospital equipment—and within the city walls the streets teeming with our army officials, engineers, carpenters, mechanicians, telephone girls and technical experts. For instance some of the finest watch makers are needed for the delicate adjustments of the aeroplane mechanism and I was told that the superintendent of the Waltham Watch works was putting in ten hours a day in Tours as one of Uncle Sam's dollar a day men—and that he was one of many rich volunteers from America's business world who were sacrificing fortune and family comfort without any hope of recognition for service beyond that given them by their own soul's approval.

Tours was a little world of itself, and with the military and the industrial factions running hand in hand or rather watching each other out of the corner of the eye one got that uncomfortable feeling of hidden treachery, secret rebellion, sullen fear and hate that I used to feel under the smiling surface of Germany's suavity or sometimes under the smooth waters at Salt Lake City.

It is a condition that arises out of the disciplining of the every detail and thought of lives that, robbed of their natural freedom, feel justified in cheating the oppressor who has robbed them, and then follows suspicion and hatred and intrigue and frantic striving for power lest one be destroyed lacking it, and the next evolution is called politics and out of that grows corruption, dishonesty and every other horror and the end of it all is open war. And in a small way the little Kingdom of Tours while loyal to the country of its birth and fervent toward the cause that it was pledged to serve, seemed to me to be going through all the internal agony of a militarised industrial centre and I knew once and for all that I should rather be dead than obliged to live long in any atmosphere where one must be eternally on the alert against the subtle tyrannies of a military government.

I was homesick for the big free spirit at the front where each man took it for granted that his fellow was more than equal to looking after his own job and I wished—as they wished—that each man in Tours could have a breath of "the air up there" even though it might eventually be charged with gas. Anything was better than this heaviness and dullness and drabness. I was thankful when our work here was done. In fact we played two performances here each night—and most days—not altogether out of kindness of heart—but in order to cover this area that much sooner and be on our way.

In the next town we arrived late, having been sent by motor and lost our way—not so late however as we should have been by train for the tracks were now so congested by "*blessé*" trains relaying the wounded to hospitals further down the line that all train schedules had been practically abandoned. We were hustled into another car with very little supper and were again driven miles through the cold to the outskirts of the town where we played to an audience of twenty-five hundred men who had been in quarantine for "ages" as they said and who were feeling perfectly desperate for a break in the monotony.

One of the "Y" women and a Red Cross nurse came back to the dressing room of the hut to tell me confidentially that the men had worked until seven that night decorating a new hall that they themselves had renovated and painted and that they had been scheming for days to "get up" a supper after the show and would be heart broken unless we came. We all looked at each other in despair for, in spite of having had better living accommodations in the S. O. S. than on any other part of the tour, the depressed state of the men to whom we played, or the great number of hospital shows, or the constant rain or something or other had pulled us down in a few days more than all the real hardships at the front and we were so tired, as one of the girls put it, that our very souls ached.

The men of our unit tried to explain this for us but the inevitable answer came back—"Just come for a few minutes. They haven't seen any girls for so long. It will do them so much good." We knew the speech by heart and we had often responded to it when we were longing and aching for our beds, and tonight on the way out we had pledged ourselves to each other not to give in to it again, and now we were all ashamed to refuse them and also ashamed to go back on our word to ourselves and to each other.

I looked at the weaker of the two girls and said : "Well, how about it?" She answered that she would do whatever the rest of us did.

The men of our unit argued, and truthfully, that it was the girls that the boys wanted to see and that they would never be missed and were going home.

When we saw how hard the boys must have worked to decorate the barracks and with what pleasure they watched each course of the supper come onto the long tables we were glad that we had not disappointed them but, Ye gods, there were hundreds of them and they had a band waiting to play dance music and there were only three of us.

I shall never forget that dance—it seemed to me I'd only been turned in one direction when someone from out the long lines of uniforms that penned us in would seize me and turn me round in another direction and someone else would snatch me from him and step on me, and then release me to another before he'd even consoled me and so on and so on for hours and here and there out of the corner of my eye I could catch fleeting glimpses of a pink dress and a tan coloured dress and I knew the same thing was happening to the other two girls.

Some time later on we leaned backed in the car too exhausted to speak. When we were about halfway home one of the girls said wearily—"Well, I've only *one* life to give for my country, thank God !"

And the next morning I thought my time had come to give mine. The expected had happened—after dancing with men just recovering from Flu and just taking it on—I'd got one of the "going or coming" germs and it was only by the aid of all my will power, Mr. Morrisey's rum, and Miss Brice's quinine, that I was able to keep going until we had played our last performance in the S. O. S.—temperature 104 and fallen exhausted into the first train that would get us back to Paris.

Three times we were booked out of Paris to return to the front and as many times were we stopped by delays in travelling permits, illness this, that or the other, and before we could make a fourth attempt came rumours of the approaching armistice and with the probability of a rapid shifting of troops it was decided to send no more entertainers north until something decisive could be learned so, as I had predicted, we never again reached "the Front." Instead, we played the remaining ten days of our signed service in and around Paris, at Long Champs once the fashionable racing course, now converted into an army transportation headquarters, at the Palais de Glace, once the old skating rink, now the "Y" Theatre, at the Soldiers and Sailors' Club, the Pavilion and other places, and while there was very little thrill in playing under such normal conditions there was at least the interest of daily and conflicting rumours from the front and one night on our way home from the Palais de Glace where we had played to twenty-five hundred cheering men and seen so many New Yorkers in the audience that we almost thought it a first night, we met the French people surging through the streets, their arms round each other—and we were told that the *Kaiser* had been dethroned and that Berlin was in the throes of revolution. There was an hour's pandemonium in the streets of Paris and every one devoutly hoped the Huns were wreaking upon the *Kaiser* some of the vengeance that we should have liked to wreak on him.

And then came the morning of November the 11th when all ears were open for the sound of the cannon that should proclaim the signing of the armistice. I myself heard nothing, but at noon boys began parading down the Avenue de l'Opera with flags—their hands on each other's shoulders. By two o'clock the streets were swarming with men, women and children, marching aimlessly back and forth, hugging and kissing each other and sometimes trying to sing the *Marseillaise*.

At three o'clock when I looked down on the Place de l'Opera from the top of the Equitable Building, where I had joined friends, the streets were a mosaic of black, blue and tan, the red caps of the French soldiers with their yellow cross bars standing out like sunflowers amongst the more sombre colours of the swaying masses of humans below us. Occasional vehicles overladen with shouting soldiers made their way here and there through the streets but these were few and far between and there were no bands or horns available to help out the voices that were trying to sing.

Across the street from us in front of the Rue de la Paix, it soon became the fashion for American and French soldiers, hands on shoulders, to form in long lines and march into the bar of the *café* for a drink.

We watched the crowds without finding much variety in their antics until the wonderful Paris twilight began to wrap the distant steeples and turrets in mist. Opposite us the victory group on top of the Paris Opera House was silhouetted sharply against the sky and just underneath it the siren that had sounded so many alarms to terrified Paris in the four dreadful years just passed, seemed to be brooding on its lost occupation and I wondered how many years it would be before all the "Cave de Secours" signs would have disappeared from over the cellarways that had so long offered sanctuary to the fleeing.

With friends of the Marine Corps I drove down to the Place de la Concorde out through the Champs Elysée and into the *bois*.

The guns from the submarine on the Seine were still booming their tidings of victory as we neared the Arc de Triomphe. A procession of French men and women bearing the flags and banners of the Allies swept through the splendid opening and on toward the *bois*, singing the *Marseillaise*.

As we passed further into the *bois* we saw no one save here and there a pair of strolling lovers, unmindful of any tumult, save that in their own hearts. And ephemeral things, such as war, and immortal things, such as love, seemed once again, after four years of nightmare, to slip into their rightful proportions to each other.

The haze grew more dense, little lakes here and there were barely discernible, the tall groups of poplars, in some of the more open spaces looked ghostlike and majestic against the poorly lighted sky. And nature, as though pitying the tired hearts and worn nerves of its war-weary victims, wrapped lovers and lone souls alike, in one of those soft enfolding nights that seem to bless and restore.

We returned by way of "The Dolphin," found ourselves the only guests there, drank our tea, port, or champagne-cocktails with what spirit of conquest we could muster, and reached the edge of the Bois just as a searchlight shot a long yellow stream of flame from the Eifel tower. It was the first time the tower had been lit since the war and it was the most lovely and most thrilling moment of the day's demonstration.

The crowds were becoming more subdued and less dense as we reached the hotel at the far end of the Tuileries Gardens.

I had barely time to dress before our final performance at the Pavilion and, in one way, all the unit were glad to be playing, for each one of them was too highly keyed by the day's events to want to stay in doors.

The performance seemed like an anti-climax after the one we had given the previous Saturday night at the Palais de Glace and both we and our audience were eager to get into the street again and be a part of the mob.

Both feigned enthusiasm, however, and at last we sang our final chorus, as a unit, having played to more than one hundred and twenty five thousand American men in France.

So ended our last three months, as an official unit, also the last three months of the war. In spite of all efforts to hasten our departure from America, Fate had timed our finish, to a day, to the finish of the fighting in France.

www.ingramcontent.com/pod-product-compliance
Lightning Source LLC
Chambersburg PA
CBHW030229170426
43201CB00006B/157